Shakespeare
on Management

$\mathfrak{S}$hakespeare on *Management*

Leadership Lessons for Today's Managers

Paul Corrigan

**KOGAN
PAGE**

First published 1999

Apart from any fair dealing for the purposes of research or private study, or criticism or review, as permitted under the Copyright, Designs and Patents Act 1988, this publication may only be reproduced, stored or transmitted, in any form or by any means, with the prior permission in writing of the publishers, or in the case of reprographic reproduction in accordance with the terms and licenses issued by the CLA. Enquiries concerning reproduction outside these terms should be sent to the publishers at the undermentioned addresses:

Kogan Page Limited
120 Pentonville Road
London
N1 9JN
UK

Kogan Page Limited
163 Central Avenue, Suite 4
Dover
NH 03820
USA

British Library Cataloguing in Publication Data

A CIP record for this book is available from the British Library.

ISBN 0 7494 2845 7

Picture research by Elaine Willis

Typeset by Saxon Graphics Ltd, Derby, UK
Printed and bound by Maple-Vail Book Manufacuring Group, Binghamton, NY.

To Hilary Armstrong

CONTENTS

INTRODUCTION

Perhaps, to some, the similarity between Shakespeare's stories and modern management issues will come as a surprise. But there are a number of strong bridges between his time and ours.

Whilst management may appear to be a part of modern society the experience of running organizations is actually an old one. Shakespeare was a part of an organization that produced plays. During his lifetime members of Elizabeth's court were setting up the first British secret service and it was her grandfather, Henry VII, who created the modern Civil Service. Her father Henry VIII created a new religion needing a new organization and a new rulebook. All these institutions needed management.

In Shakespeare's time the 'senior manager' was called a 'leader', whose job was to lead a nation, a clan or a county. Leaders were also called kings, queens, dukes or lords. Then, as now, organizations needed leaders; managers either led or failed; and leaders had to worry about managing with limited resources. Good leaders managed their staff well and bad ones badly or not at all. Good managers understood the vital need for information and bad ones ignored it, feeling that communication with subordinates was not necessary.

In the 16th century there was not an extensive management literature (although Machiavelli's *The Prince* was a best seller). There was however a fascination with good stories about leadership, and Shakespeare wrote very successful plays for that audience. Play after play had a central character whose rise and fall to and from a monarchy formed the core of the story. Play after play taught the audience lessons about how leaders organized their rise and how their failures precipitated their fall. It is not surprising that many of Shakespeare's plays are about politics, authority and power. Many more of his plays tell stories of leadership than of romantic love. Yet his plays very rarely dwell upon an abstract notion of sovereignty or authority. Instead he makes these concepts move through the individual characters of the people who have power.

All of us who like Shakespeare enjoy the way in which he develops the personality of his characters to make the story flow. He tells stories about power through the individuals who strive for it.

> Politics for him is not a search for solutions to social and economic problems, but a search for power and authority for politicians themselves. [This is because] he is a man of his time... At a time when the average citizen's ability to participate in public life was limited or non-existent, it was natural that instead of thinking about political structures and functions people would be more inclined to watch the pageantry of greatness, the rise and fall of the very few who had power.
>
> (Leggatt, 1988: 238)

In the Elizabethan age, power was personified – few people had it and their personalities mattered. It is important to remember that Shakespeare's age is not alone in this preoccupation with the personalities of politics; most modern interest in politics focuses on the people who wield power rather than the abstract notions behind that power. The eight years of President Clinton's two terms have had many more column inches written about his character than about any political policy he carried out.

So understanding power through the personalities who wield it is a modern preoccupation too. Shakespeare does not address our abstract interest in authority but rather helps us to recognize that his leaders were like us, individuals. Over any play Shakespeare builds the personality of his leaders to convince us how they strive for and carry out leadership not as abstractions, but as individuals. In this book I quote extensively from his plays – many extracts are from speeches written for his leaders. These quotations demonstrate that Shakespeare writes about the individual characters who lead, thus providing us with a view of how we, as individuals, might operate in both similar and different circumstances. His narratives address us as individuals and tell us stories about leaders who are also people.

Nearly everyone who has enjoyed a Shakespeare play will comment on how 'meaningful' the characters were. In every play the meaning of the story is told through the characters, not through abstractions. Their selves talk to our selves, and it is their selves we learn from. It is thus through the characters that Shakespeare provides us with lessons about leadership.

In Part 1 I extend the argument about this strong relationship between Shakespeare and management.

Part 2 explores the way in which Shakespeare creates individual leaders who fail because they believe that power and authority are wrapped up in them as people. This group of leaders, like many in contemporary managerial positions, believes that having the title gives you sufficient authority to manage. In three different plays Shakespeare shows how this assumption is wrong:

- For Shakespeare's Richard II simply being a king is enough. Having the title provides him with the expectation that everyone will obey him automatically.
- For his King Lear the enormous authority he had developed as king is assumed to continue even after he stupidly gives away the land from which he derives his power.
- Shakespeare's Antony believed that his power did not derive from Rome (as the state that gave it to him) but was enshrined in him as a person and could be used however he wanted.

All three are examples of those who believe that leadership can be personalized and abstracted from the organization. All three end not only in death but humiliation.

Part 3 covers three different leaders – Richard III, Macbeth and Coriolanus. They all believe that authority resides not from the way in which God anointed a given king, but in the ability to manipulate and gain power. All three then use fear to maintain this authority. In this sense these characters are more modern than the previous three. They recognize that a man can become a king if he works at it:

- From the very beginning Shakespeare's Richard III is ambitious to become king. He murders his way to the top. In so doing he creates a world where nobody trusts him and he becomes isolated from any allies.
- Shakespeare's Macbeth starts his play as a great and bloodthirsty warrior. His ambition drives him to murder the king to whom he was previously loyal. His life degenerates into murder after murder and ruin.
- Shakespeare's Coriolanus starts the play as a magnificent warrior-leader. He leads by example, but in so doing separates himself from his troops until he is alone. Cut off from his own feelings he is very vulnerable. In the end he is brought to earth by his emotion for his mother.

For much of the three plays the leaders' use of fear as one of the main tools of authority seems to work well. But Shakespeare demonstrates how this strategy is flawed. These three, too, fail and die in humiliation.

Most of Shakespeare's lessons about leadership concern failure, and not just small failures but gigantic, humiliating failure. This failure follows a period when it appears that the leader's tactics and strategies may succeed. With Shakespeare it is important always to check the ending of the play before learning the lesson.

In modern business life it is not hard to find parallels for these Shakespearean leaders – chief executives toppled because they became complacent about the power of their title, or who botched the succession in the family business, or metaphorically murdered their way to the top. Lee Iacocca, who became a highly successful head of Chrysler, the US motor manufacturer, thought he was doing well in his previous high management role at Ford – until Henry Ford II summoned him one day and fired him out of the blue with the immortal words: 'Sometimes you just don't like a guy.'

Sibling rivalry in the immensely wealthy Moores family that owns the Liverpool-based Littlewoods stores and mail-order business ensured in the end that neither Peter nor John Moores became chairman of the company.

'Chainsaw Al' Dunlap revelled in his fearsome reputation as a corporate axeman, laying off thousands and pointing to the improved balance sheet as justification. But in his success lay the seeds of his sudden downfall – a couple of poor results from Sunbeam Household Appliances Corporation and the board realized that the only thing this widely hated man had going for him was his ability to deliver the bottom line. Without that they saw no reason to keep him and sacked him, to the general delight of corporate America.

In Part 4 I explore the one heroic and successful leader Shakespeare created and wrote a play about – Prince Hal, who later becomes Henry V. As we shall see, Shakespeare's Henry succeeds because he is not a one-dimensional hero. He recognizes that to become a great king he has to learn how to do it. And in order to learn how to do it he needs to learn not from other kings but from his future subjects.

Jack Welch of General Electric (GE), probably the world's most admired business leader, had to learn that lesson the hard way. He began his restructuring of GE in the early 1980s the Chainsaw Al way, shutting plants and making thousands redundant. He became known as 'Neutron Jack', a label he felt was unfair. He began to listen to his 'subjects' and learn from the people who really knew GE's various businesses at their grass-roots. Now GE is known for its ways of harvesting good ideas from the workforce; productivity has leapt and Welch is seen as an icon of dynamic management.

Shakespeare's Henry succeeds and the chorus at the end of *Henry V* makes clear his success. In the Epilogue for Henry Shakespeare claims that he was 'Lord' of the 'world's best garden'.

> *Fortune made his sword;*
> *By which the world's best garden he achieved,*
> *And of it left his son imperial lord.*
> **Henry V**, Epilogue lines 6–8

Part 5 of the book demonstrates both in management and Shakespearean terms the importance of sub-plots. It shows how it is vital to understand the life of the post room as well as the board room. Both Shakespeare and modern management demonstrate how the two are interconnected, and a brilliant leader must never forget that. Building on the plays already covered, Chapter 10 explores two major

Shakespearean characters. In *King Lear* the Fool is also one of the king's closest companions, whose task it is to tell his king the truth. Over the two plays *Henry IV Parts 1* and *2* the role of Falstaff dominates the plots and the sub-plots. In both of these characters we see that strong personalities who provide messages contrary to the company line are very important to the generation of good leadership.

A handful of companies have learned this in the 1990s, giving some respected, independent-minded managers the brief to be anarchic, to say the unsayable to the chief executive officer (CEO). One even had the title 'Corporate Jester' printed on his business card.

One final point in this Introduction. The large number of excerpts from Shakespeare's plays will strike a chord concerning some of the management issues you face today. However, you will learn even more by reading the whole play or by watching it. It *is* possible to learn from small parts of the plays, but it is much better to experience the whole narrative. Please use this book as a sampler for Shakespeare's plays. Of one thing I am certain – his language is much richer than mine, and his plays read much better than this book.

Part I

*U*niversal
lessons

Laurence Olivier as Hamlet (source: Kobal Collection)

Chapter 1

From Shakespeare To Tom Peters

Management literature over the last 40 years has emphasized the importance of leadership. Book after book argues that without leadership managers and organizations will fail, and that it is this quality that is missing from the day-to-day work of real managers.

Yet leadership is not something that has only developed in the last 40 years. Shakespeare demonstrated 400 years ago the different roles a leader can take and the different skills those leaders need. His characters demonstrated very different ways in which leadership could be provided. Between them, his plays are a master class of what leaders should and should not do.

Shakespeare was writing these plays at a time of great historical change, changes that affected every aspect of society. They included shifts in the models of leadership that had dominated European society up until the end of the 16th century. Until then nearly everybody believed that great leaders were born, not made. They believed that individuals who were strong authority figures best carried out leadership. Leaders, born to rule, were born into very separate worlds from the people they expected to follow them. Once born into those separate stations of life there was little you could do but carry out your role, and followers had no alternative but to obey the direction in which leaders, from their separate world of authority, led them.

Shakespeare argued strongly against this view. Some of the leaders that he created fail precisely because they base their authority on the fact that they were born to rule. This book explores the congruence between Shakespeare's lessons on leadership with similar views of modern management theorists in the last few years of the 20th century. Both of these very different literatures argue in favour of certain leadership styles and against others. For example, the question of motivating staff is at the core of much modern management literature. How does a senior manager reach everyone in an organization with the message that links an employee's actions to the organization's vision? All managers, however large their staff group, have to struggle with the importance of communicating motivation. By now everyone recognizes this as an essential but difficult task.

Many managers see this task as a technical one. How do I ensure that every member of my staff reads the newsletter? How do I get them all to the staff meeting and to listen to the company's vision statement? But the issue of motivation goes way beyond these technicalities. For example, Tom Peters argues that leaders have to work very hard to provide meaning for their staff: 'The role of the leader is one of orchestrator and labeller; taking what can be gotten in the way of action and shaping it into a lasting commitment to a new strategic direction. In short to make meaning' (Peters and Waterman, 1982: 75). This demonstrates a much more powerful method of providing staff with motivation. To orchestrate the different ways in which staff think about their work is to provide meaning to their work. Without that meaning, work is just a set of day-to-day activities for which staff get paid. And they don't work very hard if there is no meaning to their work. So the point that Peters is making is that great leaders make meanings for their staff, and that meaning provides them with motivation to work harder.

To demonstrate the link between Shakespeare and the tasks of the modern manager, it is difficult to think of a better example of a leader making meaning for followers than Shakespeare's Henry V's speech during the battle of Harfleur. The battle has been going on for some time. Henry with his English troops is besieging this northern French town but they are facing strong French defensive opposition and Henry's troops are beginning to falter. He rallies them with a speech that represents one of the clearest examples of a leader providing – in Tom Peters' words – a 'lasting commitment to a new strategic direction':

Once more unto the breach, dear friends, once more;
Or close the wall up with our English dead…
                              On, on, you noblest English,
Whose blood is fet from fathers of war-proof!
Fathers that, like so many Alexanders,
Have in these parts from morn till even fought
And sheathed their swords for lack of argument:
Dishonour not your mothers; now attest
That those whom you call'd fathers did beget you…
For there is none of you so mean and base,
That hath not noble lustre in your eyes.
I see you stand like greyhounds in the slips,
Straining upon the start. The game's afoot:
Follow your spirit, and upon this charge
Cry, 'God for Harry, England, and Saint George!'
Henry V, Act 3 Scene 1 lines 1–2, 17–23 and 29–34

Why is it that nearly all the managers I know would like to deliver a speech like that to their staff? They want to make this speech, not because they want to be in a war, but because they would love to be as certain as Henry is that their people will follow them. Shakespeare's Henry leaves you in no doubt that, at the end of this speech, when he turns to charge *once more* into the battle, he is certain that his troops will follow him into danger. It is this certainty that, when asked, people will follow you, that we all want to create in our staff.

Such a relationship between leader and staff only happens when the leader has been successful in providing the staff's work with a wider meaning. The staff that Shakespeare's Henry needs to motivate are soldiers. For this wider meaning to provide the basis for motivation, it must first be understood by staff. This speech not only appeals to their skill, expertise and courage, but also imbues that courage with some very powerful meanings. Henry reminds them that, in that same area of northern France, other British soldiers have fought from 'morn to night' and only stopped fighting because of 'lack of argument'. These other soldiers were their own fathers, and Henry encourages his soldiers to demonstrate that they were their father's sons by fighting well. In this speech, Henry provides both personal and national meaning: on the personal level the soldier should fight as well as his forebears, and on a national level he should fight for his country.

As we shall see, Shakespeare demonstrates that the manager's ability to deliver such a speech springs from spending considerable time learning how to communicate and motivate staff. The ability of managers to communicate with their staff doesn't come out of thin air – it must be based upon a strong knowledge of the people with whom they are communicating. Before he became king Henry spent considerable time with young men in the bars of London, during which he found out what they were like through communicating with them. It was this communication that gave him an insight into how he could motivate them to go into a battle where they would be in great danger. If we want to be able to communicate with the strength of Shakespeare's Henry then we need to spend the time and effort understanding our staff in the way that he did.

Talk to any of Richard Branson's staff at Virgin Airways and you quickly realize how well he communicates, partly – in the early years at least – by helping cabin crew in the aircraft serve drinks and meals. This helped to build Virgin's special culture and spirit, which proved its mettle in the 'dirty tricks' allegations against its mighty competitor British Airways.

In this part of the book I underline the different reasons why Shakespeare's leaders can provide lessons for today's managers. It is important to see how Shakespeare's characters do what they do as *leaders*, since the issue of leadership is at the core of the concerns of most modern organizations. As we shall see, the level of uncertainty in the modern organization's environment puts a high premium on leadership, and if the organization is to chart a way through all of this uncertainty its managers have to lead. In the past you could keep a close watch on competitors with a few phone calls; now, in a global market, anything can be happening at any time and in any place. The pace of technological change may mean that an entire investment programme of millions of pounds is made redundant by a new industrial process.

Change dominates the life of a business and, however much managers want it to stop, it goes on getting faster and faster.

This pace of change creates an uncertain environment for managers and makes them anxious about leading. If so many things are going to change, and you don't know what they are, how can you lead your business into such an uncertain future? In these circumstances many leaders are paralysed by the uncertainty and become immobilized. Just when their organization needs leadership it becomes much more difficult for managers to lead.

I will go on to argue that managers can only manage at all if they are prepared to take responsibility for the work of their staff. This may seem obvious, but in many organizations individual managers expend a lot of effort trying to duck that responsibility. If they succeed, then the organization is not being managed. Throughout history there are examples of what happens when senior managers fail to take responsibility for their staff, who then act on their own, without any reference to their own management. One of the most dramatic recent examples was the financial trader Nick Leeson, who plunged his employer Barings, the Queen's 200-year-old bank, into losses of £869 million and brought it crashing to ruin. His managers in London were so pleased with the massive profits he was making in the Singapore markets that they failed to monitor how he was doing it. Consequently they missed the special account he set up to hide his losses when his luck ran out. Within Leeson's own morality, and left to his own devices, he saw himself as a brilliant operator and thought he could gamble his way out of trouble. The result of his lack of management responsibilty was catastrophic. The venerable bank went bust and the founding family was forced to sell it for a nominal £1 to a Dutch financial house.

However, as we shall see, the problem for managers is that they have to take responsibility for their part of the organization, but have to do so in a context that they can never completely control – a difficult experience. Of course, managers can attempt to get *more* control, but they cannot be sure of everything that affects their span of responsibility. For example, managers are responsible for ensuring that their staff come to work. A manager who fails to take this responsibility, and allows staff absenteeism to rise, will fail as a manager. So taking responsibility is vital. However, a manager cannot control all of the factors influencing staff absence. A blizzard leaving two metres of snow overnight will stop all transport, and few members of staff will get into work. The manager cannot control the weather, but is still responsible for the staff's attendance. A serious flu epidemic will also affect staff attendance – again outside the control of a manager, but still within his or her responsibility. This experience of responsibility without control is at the core of management.

Nor do Shakespeare's leaders control their world: the bad ones pretend that they can (or say that without control responsibility is impossible); the good ones tussle with the dilemma.

This book is different from most management texts in that it stresses that managers can only succeed if they recognize that if they are going to manage people successfully then they will have to engage with their emotions as managers. Given the importance of the motivation of staff in developing any organization, emotions are a vital component. As we shall see later in this chapter, I argue that emotions are as important a part of the process of management as the more rational and intellectual aspects of the work. Once we recognize how important our emotions are to management then it becomes more obvious that a playwright such as Shakespeare, who obviously works in the realm of emotions, can talk to us about management.

After dealing with the important absence of women from the contemporary productions of Shakespeare's plays and the lack of women leaders in his texts, I discuss the issue of gender in modern management. This introductory part of the book concludes with an analysis of how modern managers can learn from the different world that Shakespeare creates.

MANAGERS MUST BE LEADERS

Whatever managers *think* they are doing, the one thing they *have* to do is lead. At every moment staff watch how their managers cope with all aspects of management, from their ability to listen to staff to the way in which they make major decisions.

In modern management everyone wants managers who lead. Book after book explores this need.

A great, almost urgent renewal of interest in the subject of leadership has characterized the last two decades. Scholarly and popular books that identify strong leaders and attempt to analyse the nature of their success have found a wide and hungry audience. Organizations seeking to adapt to a level and pace of change that can seem frightening and that is unpredictable have funded countless forums and workshops to instil leadership skills.

(Helgein, 1996: 19)

In the last two decades of the 20th century it would appear that within the management of organizations there is a crisis of leadership. If they want to fill the leadership vacuum, organizations either have to attract leaders from outside or try and develop them inside through 'forums and workshops'. McDonald's, for example, has a strong policy of building its own leadership from within the organization. Recognizing the importance of the culture of the firm as one of the determinants of business success, it creates leadership from within, thereby ensuring that the culture of the firm does not have to be 'taught' to its leaders and that the firm is 'growing' leaders. General Electric is a prime example of a giant global corporation that consistently grows its own leaders through an efficient internal 'succession engine'. All its CEOs have come up that way, and there are always three possible successors' names in a legendary envelope should one be needed unexpectedly. Asea Brown Boveri, the Swedish-Swiss power engineering group, is another successful global group that constantly grooms and monitors its potential high-flyers.

Why has this need for organizational leadership become so significant? Helgein provides a clue by emphasizing the necessity of organizations adapting to the 'level and pace of change... that is unpredictable'. Organizations uncertain about their environment need much stronger guidance and leadership than those that operate in an atmosphere of certainty. If you know what is going to happen you don't need too much foresight and ability to run an organization. But if the organization also knows what is going to happen then it doesn't really need a leader. Leaders become necessary at precisely the time when it is difficult to 'see into the future' – and it is at that time that so many managers become immobilized by simply not knowing what is going on in their business environment.

Running your firm at a time of boom and a buoyant market makes little demand upon your ability to see into the future, and leadership is easy. But if the market conditions are uncertain, and it's not easy to know what will happen to your product, then that's the time when it is important to provide strong leadership. In the new millennium, following the globalization of the economy and with profound technological change, uncertainty will get greater and greater – placing a premium not only on leadership but on great leadership in difficult conditions.

The modern world is one of uncertainty, requiring managers to develop foresight and the ability to push their organizations in a certain direction. In this development leadership gives the organization a direction that the environment of change around the organization does not. The pace and level of change that takes place at the moment is such that organizations have become afraid of what is going to happen to them. Under these circumstances strong leadership within the organizations is the one thing that may help.

This is an important issue for this book. Whilst there is little in Shakespeare about accountancy and company law, he writes about leadership in nearly every play. His leaders do many things – they joke, they love – and they do them all as leaders. Nearly every play provides us with an insight into how managers can learn to lead – sometimes through failure and sometimes through success. If there is a growing recognition of the importance of leadership, then it makes sense to look closely at Shakespeare's plays on leadership, since they are relevant to the current crisis of leadership in management.

WHAT MANAGERS DO WHEN THEY MANAGE: THE ISSUE OF RESPONSIBILITY AT THE HEART OF THE MANAGEMENT EXPERIENCE

When people take up their first management post, what do they do in that work that is different from what they were doing in their job before? In essence they begin to *take responsibility*. Junior, middle and senior managers account for differences between their levels of management in terms of their 'spheres of responsibility'. Managers are responsible for the work of all of those people 'under them'. They are expected to take the responsibility for their actions. I am responsible for five staff and a budget of £200,000. Another manager may be responsible for 2,000 staff and a budget of £40 million. Usually the person with the greater span of responsibility is paid more and is felt to be on a higher level of management, with 'more to manage'.

Taking responsibility is also at the heart of one of the simplest definitions of management, that is that a manager is a member of staff who takes responsibility for the outcome of others. This differentiates a manager from any other member of staff, since if a staff member does badly, the manager is partly responsible.

The skills and tasks that make up management flow from this *engagement* with responsibility. For example, managers learn to deal with a budget because it is part of their job to be responsible for finance. They learn to gather and précis information because they are responsible for finding out how their service or product is doing. They worry about their staff sickness records because they are responsible for their staff turning up and working. They are restless in search of market information so that they can change their product to fit the marketplace. Without the recognition that this is their responsibility there is no point in having the skills necessary for these tasks.

This may appear obvious. Managers know they have to take responsibility for moving things forward, but there are many ways in which this may not happen. Over 40 years ago Peter Drucker outlined this issue of personal responsibility by discussing the difference between being satisfied with what you achieve and taking responsibility for it: 'Responsibility – not satisfaction – is the only thing that will serve. One can be satisfied with what somebody else is doing; but to perform one has to take responsibility for one's own actions and their impact. To perform one has, in fact, to be dissatisfied, to want to do better' (Drucker, 1954: 297). This is an important point. Managers must go beyond satisfaction. They must be dissatisfied with what is happening today and they must act upon that dissatisfaction. Satisfied or complacent managers will not make things happen for their organizations. Restlessness is at the core of management.

Shakespeare's plays contain some leaders who seem satisfied with their place in the world and many that do not. As we shall see, Richard II is pleased to be king. He believes that his position is securely founded on anointment from God, that his crown is literally God-given. This is why he is complacent about the rebellion against him. The Duke of Gloucester (who becomes Richard III), on the other hand, is powerfully ambitious and sets out to *make the world*, rather than be made by it. Macbeth persuades himself that in the end one assassination will be sufficient to change his world. For Henry V, the world is in constant need of development and change, and needs a great leader to understand and change it.

In most of his leaders Shakespeare demonstrates how leaders act upon their dissatisfaction and, sometimes for personal reasons and sometimes for reasons of state, change the world. They are very active and are antagonistic to the experience of the *status quo*. Change and the management of the change process are what most of Shakespeare's leadership stories are about. His plays about leadership concern the tactics and strategies of putting dissatisfaction with the *status quo* into effect. How can they change their position? How can they change the world? In this way Shakespeare's stories show us how individual managers, through their dissatisfaction, can change something.

Given the contemporary importance of the management of change this is an important theme for us to learn from. Peters (1989: 418) talks about this responsibility in moving language: 'It requires us, as managers, to persuade people quickly to have our sense of urgency about new priorities; to develop a personal, soul-deep animus towards things as they are; to get up the nerve and energy to take on the forces of inertia that work against any significant programme for change'.

It is worth looking at this on a number of levels. First, the language is moving. Managers need to have 'a personal, soul-deep animus towards things as they are'. It is not rationalist language but it is in its own way poetic. Good managers need souls that force them to be discontented with the *status quo*. The *status quo* in the software industry was something that Bill Gates disagreed with. He not only created new products but has re-engineered the entire industry through his actions. He took the responsibility by going out on his own to change this part of the world. His discontent was put into action.

Peters talks about this in unusual language. This language of the soul is startling for a management text, yet it is one that people who read and hear Tom Peters enjoy. Yet the language of the soul is much nearer to the language that Shakespeare uses about leadership than that usually found in textbooks about management, and comes from one of the most quoted management texts of the last decade of the 20th century.

Second, having an animus to the *status quo* seems much nearer a political, social or religious movement than the business of management. Indeed it is the sort of activity you would expect a revolutionary political movement to ask its members to sign up to. Managers have the image of being in favour of the *status quo*, but Peters correctly demonstrates that if they want to ensure their organization has a future, they need to have a passion for change.

This passion for change drives great business people. It moves them restlessly from industry to industry. Richard Branson of Virgin fame built his business on records. Having been successful there he moved aggressively into the business of airlines, and having been successful there into the market for condoms and then financial services. Each move is a recognition that he is dissatisfied with the way the world is. Each move is an attempt to change the way in which markets work.

Third, this quotation expects managers not only to have a soul-deep need to change the *status quo*, but to act upon it. To bring about change they need to take the responsibility for motivating others to share that need for change. They need to take on the 'forces of inertia' that favour the *status quo*. This is a considerable responsibility to take on – to change the world and to engage others to change it with you.

I will show how some of Shakespeare's leaders have a soul-deep animus to the *status quo* and how they motivate others to move against the existing order of things. Occasionally we will see his leaders, such as King Lear or Richard II, content with the *status quo*, defending their whole structure of authority based upon the past. In Shakespeare's plays of 400 years ago the leaders who try to protect themselves against change fail. Peters makes the point that they also fail in today's world. In Shakespeare's plays they die, in Tom Peters' world their firms just go bust.

In Britain in the 1960s and 1970s entire industries died because they tried to protect themselves against change. Britain used to be famous for making great motor bikes, machine tools and cars, but now the first two industries have been surrendered to the Japanese, while British car manufacture, except for niche companies such as Morgan and TVR, are run by US, Japanese and mainland European companies. The price of a failed belief that industries were in some way too important to ever be under threat, in the end left them completely at the mercy of change. Being content with the *status quo*, fatal for one of Shakespeare's leaders, is dangerous for modern managers.

Failing to see change coming, complacency with the *status quo*, can affect the most admired companies, notably Marks & Spencer and Sainsbury's. For decades their market share and stock price rose with reassuring consistency, but senior management at M&S failed to spot the coming competition of the younger fashion chains and at Sainsbury's they failed to see how Tesco was 'stealing their clothes' and going upmarket, as well as introducing innovations like loyalty cards. Mighty IBM set its market lead back years by failing to recognize the rising power of the personal computer; Howard Johnson, long a household-name hospitality chain in the United States, failed to see the threat of Marriotts' aggressive policy of continuous improvement. Britain's aristocratic Vestey family, for over a century owners of a great meat-packing and shipping business, failed to see its trading world changing around it and lost family control under pressure from 70 creditor banks.

Management achieves little without managers

Contained within the current crisis of leadership lies the significance of the manager as an individual. As individuals, managers act within this process of management – and if they don't very little happens. Some management books forget this and address the issues of management as if they were carried out by structures and not by individuals. Structures achieve nothing if individuals do not make them move. Therefore if there is a crisis of leadership within management it lies within the nature of the manager as an individual.

This is a vital point, both for this book and for any possible learning from Shakespeare. As many of you reading this will be managers, the book addresses the experience that you as a real person have in trying to make something work. As an individual you have emotions. Structures don't. As an individual you learn and change. Structures don't.

Shakespeare addresses real issues, problems that are faced by individual leaders and not by abstractions. He very rarely expresses any interest in authority in an abstract way, but recognizes that his leaders were like us, individuals. This is demonstrated throughout this book by the many quotations from Shakespeare's plays, all of which are written for individual characters whose leadership is expressed through their opinions and actions, thus providing us with a view of how we, as individuals, might operate in both similar and different circumstances. Shakespeare's narratives address us as individuals and tell us stories about leaders who are, like us, individuals.

This is mirrored in our interest in modern leaders. Bill Gates is interesting to us in a way that Microsoft is not. Richard Branson intrigues us, but his insurance company is really pretty boring. Clinton or Blair are interesting to most people, their policies to only a few.

The time has past when it was thought that the best managers were those who could follow abstract rules as automatons, when it was best for managers not to have any personality and humanity. Managers are now recognized to be people. They can learn, make decisions and bring about change. Since we are individuals we can clearly learn from Shakespeare's leaders as people.

THE IMPORTANCE OF EMOTION

Management texts often write about management as if it were a purely rational experience. If this were the case then a lyrical playwright such as Shakespeare, who works so strongly on our emotions, could have nothing to do with the (rational) world of management. But in the real world of management activity this is simply not true. Douglas McGregor pointed this out over 30 years ago:

> The tacit belief reflected in much managerial behaviour is that at least some can become, if they choose, rational logical decision making machines, with respect to business problems. Verbal persuasion is

usually applied to make men [*sic*] into this kind of manager: 'let's keep personalities out of this', 'let's deal with the facts', 'consider the problem coldly and objectively'.

(McGregor, 1966: 218)

These last phrases are ones that all managers have heard and most have said to others. We know what they mean. They are a plea for rationality and against the messiness of personality. However, it is a fact that the 'personality' of bosses is significant and cannot be kept out of the way in which they manage. Rupert Murdoch has created an enormous international media empire, and very few commentators fail to recognize the power of his personality in that process. His old opponent Robert Maxwell had a personality that built and lost whole industries, but again everyone who studied their rise and fall would comment on the importance of Maxwell's own personality rather than the existence of a cold accountant-manager. However hard we argue for rationality, it is never possible to exclude emotions from the people relations that are at the core of management. It may well be that it would be inappropriate to express many emotions at work, but that does not mean they are not a major part of the day-to-day experience of managing and being managed. For much of our time at work most of our anger, anxiety and pain has to be experienced internally, but denying its existence doesn't mean that it does not happen.

Peters sums up this whole process and underlines the positive nature of emotions and their relationship to management:

Managing at any time, but more than ever today, is a symbolic activity. It involves energising people, often large numbers of people, to do new things they previously had not thought important. Building a compelling case – to really deliver a quality product, to double investment in research and development, to step out and take risks each day... is an emotional process as much as it is a rational one.

(Peters, 1989: 418)

Getting large numbers of people to do new things they previously had not thought important needs managers to build that compelling case for action, which in turn needs to motivate staff. Without motivation in an organization managers achieve very little. Yet motivation, really moving people to do something, needs emotion. Without that component, motivation is only a short-term activity.

In Britain a company called Unipart has become famous for completely changing its relationship with its workforce. It recognized that in the modern world the motivation of staff was of crucial importance and set about achieving this through changing its relationship with its staff. The firm created an extensive training and educational scheme and has gone so far as to call it Unipart University. Here staff, who may have had few educational opportunities in the past, are encouraged to take not just work-related courses, but to develop a portfolio of educational qualifications that may in due course lead them to work elsewhere. Working for Unipart, however, they are motivated by a culture that cares.

Since we all now recognize that the mobilization of people to achieve the organization's goals is one of the main activities in which modern managers must succeed, it is inevitable that we recognize the importance of emotion for managers.

In the early 1980s much management literature recognized that there was a crisis in US private enterprise. To understand this crisis Peters and Waterman journeyed across the United States in search of excellent managers and organizations, returning with a range of different stories about success. The core of success could be found in those large companies that motivated their workforce in a wide variety of very traditional ways.

> As we worked on research for excellent companies, we were struck by the dominant use of story, slogan and legend as people tried to explain the characteristics of their own great institution. All the companies we interviewed, from Boeing to McDonald, were quite simply rich tapestries of anecdote, myth and fairy tales.
>
> (Peters and Waterman, 1982: 75)

Obviously great companies communicate well with their staff. The world-famous chocolate company Cadbury was built up over more than a century of close communication between management and workers at a time when this was rare. The Quaker Cadburys created a miniature welfare state at their Bourneville factory, involving themselves in their employees' education, medical care and leisure activities, as well as providing good quality, low-cost houses and gardens on the site, a far cry from the Birmingham slums where many workers had lived before. They created a powerful culture, much of which survives within the very different multinational world of Cadbury Schweppes. Great companies understand that it is management's responsibility not just to produce a few newsletters but to ensure that the culture is communicated and understood. Without good communication they will fail to motivate their staff and, without motivated staff, as businesses they will fail.

It is less obvious that, in order to communicate effectively, managers would choose to tell fairy stories. Such an approach demonstrates how enduring this method is. However, communication does not simply happen, and modern managers need to play a very active part in the creation of these meanings.

Great managers understand that their staff need to have some structure to their understanding of their organization and use a full range of techniques – 'stories and symbols' – to help the organization create meaning to make this happen. The link with Shakespeare is obvious. Shakespeare's essential task is to create a moving story by mobilizing symbols of words, plot and action. If the manager's task is also to create meaning for staff by using symbols, then why not learn from a master in the trade of creating symbols? Why struggle to understand the best way of moving people, when Shakespeare has already written some of the most moving language in world literature?

Shakespeare does something even more direct for modern managers. His plays portray leaders mobilizing meanings to move people. Throughout his plays Shakespeare uses symbols and language to move his audience, but he also demonstrates within his plays how his leaders, good and bad, use symbols and stories to provide a meaning that moves people in a certain direction. He describes how to do it (and how not to).

If Shakespeare had visited a modern corporation full of fairy tales and symbols that successfully motivated the staff, he would have recognized the method and success of managers who used symbols to create meaning for a workforce as he does for an audience.

Making meaning is what good managers must do for their staff. The meanings that work through their staff provide a meaning for the whole organization.

Sir John Harvey-Jones's closing of ICI's grand art deco board room and substituting shirt-sleeved meetings in armchairs in his office sent out a powerful signal that the chemical group's bureaucratic imperial past was history and that the old vertical channels of command would be flattened and made less formal. At the supermarket chain Asda, chairman Archie Norman introduced first-name badges for everyone – including himself – saying 'Happy to Help'. He also insisted that people stand up during meetings to get results more quickly.

Assuming the responsibility for managing change

Managers – at all levels – who take responsibility for the outcomes of their staff have to learn to take that responsibility without the *control* that is necessary to *guarantee* success. This is almost the original sin of the management experience. It's as if there were a time, long ago, when managers were 'allowed to manage', and they had all the power to do so.

This is a vital experience for managers. In her analysis of US management in the early 1980s Rosabeth Moss Kanter places it at the core of the problem for US managers:

> What has slipped away for many managers and executives is not just a sense of supremacy but a sense of control. That is what they find so unsettling, so frightening, so frustrating, so intolerable. They feel at the mercy of change or the threat of change in a world marked by turbulence, uncertainty and instability, because their comfort, let alone their success is dependent on many decisions of many players they can barely, if at all, influence.
>
> (Moss Kanter, 1983)

She claims that the experience of US management had been based upon a world of certainty. In historical fact this certainty took place in the limited time of the long boom from the Second World War to the oil shock of the 1970s. Most managers in most places for most of history have had to recognize that they cannot depend upon controlling everything. Managers both inside and outside the United States in the 1960s and 1970s have just had to get used to being unsettled, frustrated and frightened by trying to take responsibility for things they cannot control.

The real issue that confronts every manager when they wake up in the morning is taking responsibility without control. They know that they are responsible for the outcomes of their staff but they cannot be sure of controlling all of the things that will affect that output. This combination makes the manager anxious. The result of this tension is three different sorts of managers:

1. those who find their lack of control of everything makes it very difficult to take any responsibility at all;
2. those who forget they cannot control the world by acting as if they do;
3. those who live with the experience that they cannot control everything they need to in the world, but still take responsibility for the issues that their job describes.

The good manager lives with the anxiety, copes with it and continues to act. There are however two ways of denying that anxiety.

On the one hand bad managers look at the issues for which they should be responsible. They recognize that they cannot take control of enough of the world to guarantee that these things can happen, and the resultant tension leads them to deny any responsibility at all. This lack of omnipotence makes the manager so anxious that action is impossible. They are continually trying to take more and more power so that, if they get that extra bit of control, they will then have enough power to make things happen; but since they can never get control of everything to guarantee what will happen they cannot take responsibility for anything. They reject the responsibility that is inherent in their job and become immobilized.

The staff of such managers try to get a decision out of them, but time and again are refused. The managers think a decision is not possible because everything is not quite right at this precise moment – perhaps next week, when they have that extra bit of information, that extra bit of control, they will take the responsibility of giving an answer.

In Part 2 we explore three of Shakespeare's leaders who in different ways believe that having the title will on its own provide them with the authority to lead. We will see that, in different ways, King Lear, Richard II and Antony (of *Antony and Cleopatra*) all believe that their title, once granted by God or by Rome, gives them all the power they need. They fail.

On the other hand some managers, in coping with the fact that they don't control everything that affects their responsibility, will struggle to gain that control. These managers believe that they need to control everything in order to take responsibility and that managers can rule their whole world, and they act as if they do. Such managers continually come up against a world that reminds them they don't run everything. They ignore this and continue to act as if they do, they act as if they are a god.

The staff working for these managers are regularly assured that everything can be made OK. Their own bosses are also reassured that everything will be all right because they have a secret way of making everything OK – because after all they have the power to control everything. In reality of course that is impossible. The uncontrollable parts of the world keep crashing in on their godlike omnipotence. Until the crunch comes they never notice this problem because they cannot cope with the anxiety of a lack of control, so they blunder on as if the world is theirs to order about. They fail to do the things that they can because they cannot cope with the experience of not being able to do the things that they can't.

In Part 3 we explore three of Shakespeare's leaders who fit into this mould. Richard III, Macbeth and Coriolanus, to gain total control to meet their needs as leaders, all believe that they can manipulate the whole world. They fail.

Living with the tension of responsibility without control is the essence of a good manager. To achieve this managers have to know that they can manage their own experience of that tension. They take responsibility in the knowledge that they cannot control everything. As we shall see, throughout *Henry IV Parts 1* and *2*, the future Henry V learns about the language and culture of the people he will one day lead. He succeeds and ends the play named after him bestriding the kingdoms of England and France.

GENDER, SHAKESPEARE AND MODERN MANAGEMENT

There is one clear disjunction between Shakespeare's world and our own – the issue of gender equality in management. This issue concerns all organizations and managers and therefore its omission from this book requires some explanation.

Over the centuries men have usually carried out the leadership and management of organizations. For every Boadicea there have been a thousand Caesars, for every tribe of Amazons a hundred Huns and Tartars. Systematically, in nearly every society, for nearly all of the time, half of humanity has been excluded from leadership positions. Over the last few decades the modern world has recognized the absurdity of this exclusion and women are now included in the everyday work of modern management, although they are still under-represented.

Opening up leadership to women has not been, nor does it continue to be, easy. When any previously excluded group struggles to take their share of power, it inevitably involves conflict between the group and the people who have held the powerful positions. The conflict can be sharp, interspersed with periods of rumbling anger.

To the modern mind gender inequality in leadership positions is absurd. Unless you believe that there is a genetic gender differenti-ation, one that provides men with a management chromosome that is denied to women, there is no rational basis to this inequality. Yet at the turn of the millennium, in every country, the inequality of the distri-bution of power in the boardroom is acute. For the early years of the 21st century that inevitably means that the long march to include more women in positions of management power will have to continue. The fact that there is no logic behind the inequality does not make it any easier to overcome.

In terms of gender Shakespeare lived in a very different world and the theatre he wrote for was very different. There were no female actors in his theatre – the stage was an arena that only allowed men out to play. Playwrights write for the structure of the theatre of their day – and the theatre that Shakespeare wrote for only contained male actors. In every play all the female parts were played by men dressed as women. Whilst every group of players would have a specialist who would play women's parts, these were all men pretending to be women. However good these specialists were at pretending, they were not women.

That is one of the reasons why Shakespeare writes whole sections of women's parts where the women are pretending to be men. Portia, who in *The Merchant of Venice* delivers the famous speech concerning the quality of justice, makes the speech when she is pretending to be a man. As a male actor it was easier to be persuasive as a man playing a woman playing a man, than a man playing a woman. So in play after play Shakespeare writes parts where the male actor is playing a woman playing a man. This is a complex set of gender relationships to create, but it does make it easier for his male actors to be convincing for some of the time when they play women. (Indeed, in *As You Like It* there is a passage where a male actor is playing the part of a woman called Rosalind who, in the plot, for purposes of safety in the woods, plays a man who for purpose of the play then plays a woman – leaving the male actor playing a woman, playing a man, playing a woman. You have to be good at acting and understanding gender to achieve this.)

If women are completely absent from the whole enterprise of writing and performing plays, then their half of world experience can only be expressed in a second-hand way. This is how it was in Shakespeare's day. The plays were written, produced, directed and acted by men, with some women in the audience.

Men also dominated most of the world that Shakespeare lived in. In the 16th and 17th centuries the Church and the Army played a much greater role in running the country than they do today. The Church not only had a great deal of power, but dominated the way in which people thought about their personal and political world. Armies played a great role in determining who would win and who would lose power. Men dominated both institutions.

There was one shining and historic exception. Throughout most of Shakespeare's life there was a queen of England. Briefly under the Catholic Queen Mary and for most of the rest of his life under Queen Elizabeth I, the head of the English state was a woman. The monarch was the defining aspect of government. Their real and symbolic power seeped into every aspect of the life of the nation. So having a woman in charge had great meaning.

But even Shakespeare's experience of women in power was overlaid with considerable male strength. Elizabeth I's father, Henry VIII, had married six times to try and obtain a male heir to his throne. He was so worried by the prospect of only having female heirs that, in order to become divorced, he created the Church of England, destroying the historic link between the English state and the Roman Catholic church. To stop the chance of there being a female head of state meant that national institutions had to be completely transformed.

By the time Shakespeare wrote his plays Elizabeth had triumphed. She not only defeated all rebellions in England and Ireland, but by defeating the Spanish Armada she had seen off the greatest invasion threat to Britain between the 11th and 19th centuries. She had, by diplomacy, created an empire that would prove the basis for the biggest empire in world history. At home there was stability and the flowering of the first Elizabethan age. This was power and this was a powerful woman; Elizabeth I succeeded not only as a woman, but also as a single woman, making her own decisions for herself.

The only Shakespearean play about a powerful woman leader is *Antony and Cleopatra*. With the exception of Cleopatra, man after man struggles for and gains a throne, kills and lies for that throne. Yet many of the plays were written in the reign of the greatest monarch of her age. Shakespeare failed to take his cue from his queen, but he did take his cue from his wider society – apart from his queen there were virtually no female leaders. In writing this book I tried to bend this male-dominated canon of work about men in the direction of gender equality and lessons for management, but the results were very strained. There are lessons, but they are difficult to draw and would make the book something different from what it is intended to be.

How we learn and how managers can learn through this book

I want to conclude this part of the book by looking in more detail at how managers may actually learn from Shakespeare's leaders.

We sometimes learn from people who have very similar problems to ourselves. They persuade us to learn from their experience because we can see how their problems are the same as ours, and yet their way out of a problem is different. Some of this book operates that way. I will try and draw out from Shakespeare's characters the ways in which they solved problems and then 'sell' those solutions to the reader by trying to make Shakespeare's characters' problems look like theirs. For example, where Shakespeare is talking about the problem of communication with staff – modern managers have that problem – here is Shakespeare's solution, try it.

There is however a component of learning that starts from the experience of *different* worlds and then invites us to look at the world inventively. The way in which we learn to improve our actions does not necessarily come from the practice we want to improve. The best modern management writers take apart what is important in management theory and practice and relate it to other experiences.

A good teacher such as Charles Handy talks clearly to managers because he shows how their work is rather like some human experiences that are entirely outside management. He addresses managers as people. He talks to them directly, demonstrating that even when they are stuck, they can rethink their way out. His rethinking is based upon simple human analogies that are recognizable by managers since they can empathize with that aspect of the world. A manager can learn by standing on an analogy, looking back at their management practice and thinking that, whilst these are different parts of life, it is a bit like that. Not the same, but like it. What can I learn from living in the analogy to take back to the practice of management?

Handy makes us think through analogous experiences, and analogy gives us a chance to learn from outside management and apply inside management. In recent years a number of books have taken this stance, inviting the manager to go into the world of Winnie the Pooh or Sun Tzu. Once in that world they have used it to address management problems. Tens of thousands of people have read those books in an attempt to improve their practice through the experience of 'otherness'.

There is much evidence that we learn from *the other*, but on its own it is not a sufficient argument, because the other, in order to teach us anything about our own experience, must contain a similarity too. Jesus's parables work not because they are different stories from the difficult world of faith, but because they tell a story from a peasant's world that can be seen to be a link to the wider world of faith. The world of the analogy only works if *a* is a bit like *b* and individuals have a flicker of recognition.

We are left with the same problem. Even if we are teaching and learning through the experience of difference, how do I make out a case for the flash of recognition that exists between the worries of the modern manager and Shakespeare's plays? As I have said, at every stage when we see a play we see aspects of ourselves, and yet see lots of differences between the play and ourselves. It is that jointness that makes the learning successful.

This book therefore plans to use the 'other' aspects of Shakespeare by making them similar. As this section has shown I believe it is possible to build strong links between Shakespeare's plays and the modern world of management. Those links come from the recognition that whilst there are differences in the world of Shakespeare's plays and the 21st century world there are also similarities. These provide modern managers with the opportunity of learning about their work from some of the greatest literature ever written.

Part 2

❧❧

${\mathscr{A}}$uthority is not enough

Richard Burton as Antony in *Cleopatra* (source: Kobal Collection)

Chapter 2

$\mathcal{A}$RE LEADERS BORN OR MADE?

> 'Leaders are born, not made.' This is perhaps the most common assumption about leadership. Those who hold it maintain that there are certain in-built qualities such as initiative, courage, intelligence and honour, which together predicate a man to be a leader.
>
> (Adair, 1984: 5)

Over 400 years after Shakespeare's birth a significant management text recognizes that 'the most common assumption about leadership' is that leaders are born and not made. Adair goes on to attack this assumption for the rest of his book, but most people would probably agree with him. This means that, at the turn of the millennium, we live in a world where the most common assumption is that, from birth, people either know how to lead or they don't.

If this were true, for those of you without the 'breeding' there would be no point in reading further. You have either got it, or more likely you haven't, and therefore learning will not help. As Adair (1984: 5) goes on to point out, if we believe leaders are born then this 'approach is ill-suited to act as a basis for leadership training. Intrinsically, it hardly favours the idea of training at all, and instead encourages a concentration on selection. The ability to recognise a born leader becomes all important and attempts to "make" leaders are viewed with suspicion'. Of course I reject this view; otherwise writing a book that attempts to improve qualities of leadership would be a complete waste of time. However, Adair is correct to recognize that the view about leaders being born and not made is a common one, and one that nearly all management literature has to assault.

By the law of averages we can assume that many of the people who go and watch Shakespeare suffer from the same delusion. They look at his leaders and, since most of them are indeed kings, assume that they are good leaders and born to it. It must come as a shock when those leaders, in so many plays, fail miserably. This part of the book concerns one particular group who fail. They are all leaders who believe that being a leader, on its own, means you have the capacity and the power to lead.

The three Shakespearean leaders from whom I draw lessons in this chapter – Richard II, King Lear and Antony – all had plays named after them (even if Antony had to share his billing with Cleopatra). Shakespeare starts each of their plays with a great deal of power, and whilst the narratives of the plays are entirely different his conclusion is similar for each of them. The leaders not only die, but in various ways, by the end of the play, are completely humiliated.

Even given the very different stories, the trajectory from power to humiliation is a strong one. In none of the three narratives is it possible to understand any aspect of the play without comprehending this movement from success to failure. Each narrative is dominated by decline. It is from this decline that the specific lessons for modern managers are to be learnt.

At one level this is the simple human lesson you must remember when you are riding high. Even at the pinnacle of your success, you might fall. For these three leaders this lesson is not recognized, which makes the experience of collapse all the more problematic. The ancient Greek sin of hubris, the failure to recognize the fact that only gods can rule without let or hindrance, affects all three of these leaders. They believe that their personal hold over authority is boundless.

Shakespeare's lessons are much more specific than simply remembering downs as well as ups. All three of these leaders depend on their authority alone to give them the right to lead:

- For Richard II being king is enough. He has the title and, as someone anointed by God, people should just obey him.
- Lear, at the end of what appears a long and successful reign, believes, even when he has given his land away, that having royal blood gives him unlimited power.
- Antony believes that the power ascribed to him by Rome is actually his in his own person. Consequently, since he is Antony and Antony is power, he cannot lose.

Their loss, humiliation and failure are a result of their belief that having authority is enough to make things happen.

All work organizations have hierarchies, and all management presupposes a position within that hierarchy. Whilst there may be some organization theorists who assume that hierarchies should be based upon equal sets of relationships, and whilst some very inventive organizations may change the nature of hierarchy, it is still the case that anyone who works for Microsoft must remember that Bill Gates is boss.

My own definition of a manager as someone responsible for the output of others presupposes, for managers, two aspects of hierarchy. Managers are responsible for the output of those people beneath them as well as responsible to someone above them. The exact position of the manager within that hierarchy is very important if we are to understand their work. So hierarchies and the position of managers in them do matter.

Power within hierarchies comes in two different forms: a higher authority can ascribe it or the manager can achieve it alone. The modern organization believes that authority is achieved and not ascribed. Individual managers have to demonstrate that they can do the job, and gain their authority through the allegiance of their staff when they have proved they can do the job. Good managers achieve a great deal of authority by working well and bad managers fail because they cannot achieve that respect through their actions.

Charles Handy (1996: 5) portrays this very clearly: 'In machine organizations, power stems from one's position. In the new organization titles and roles carry very little weight until the leaders have proved their competence. All authority has to be earned before it is exercised.'

Handy poses this new manager against the manager whose authority is ascribed by the individual's position in the hierarchy. The latter have power not because of the success or failure of their actions, or relationship with the staff, but because of the title they have been given. It is the *title* that they believe makes people obey them. For such managers the size and extent of the title is vital. If they are deputy directors, then they will position all their work under their boss, and will gain their right to act from their job description and the power handed down to them by the director. If they are directors of specific departments (such as sales), then everything within their department is theirs to direct.

We have all worked with and for managers who depend upon their title to gain their authority. For them the trappings of authority are vital: the title, the size of the desk, the way in which their own managers treat them with respect are all very important. All of these attributes are talismanic for their approach to management power. When you work with or, worse, for such people, you are left wondering how they would manage if one day their desk and title were taken away.

In the most extreme cases, such as Richard II and Lear, their power as anointed kings was ascribed to them from birth. Antony was not born to such power, but in Shakespeare's previous play (*Julius Caesar*) he fought for his right to wield power.

Most modern managers gain their right to act from both sets of authority. On occasions even the best of managers, who achieve power from the respect of their staff and who work with their staff to achieve power, will depend upon their ascribed power in the hierarchy. On the other hand even the worst of managers, who depend upon their ascribed authority, will recognize that they achieve power from a few of their actions.

Tom Peters outlines the necessary relationship managers must develop with their followers to gain real power from them:

> The most effective leaders, political or corporate, empower others to act – and grow – in support of a cause that both leaders and followers find worthy. The leader's job is at once to articulate the empowering vision, and to stay in touch with followers to ensure that she or he is in tune with the needs of the real world where the vision is implemented.
>
> (Peters, 1989: 435)

This is a vital lesson for leaders, for it claims that if you lose touch with the world that your followers live in, you have lost touch with reality ('the real world where the vision is implemented'). Losing touch with reality will always destroy leaders, since they are trying to lead in a world that is not real. Reality always wins. The argument for being involved with followers goes beyond the ideological idea that it is good to work *with* people rather than order them about. It roots itself in the material necessity for authority to involve itself with followers or risk living in a fantasy. Involving leadership is a necessary guard against leaders losing touch and believing simply in their own power.

Modern business leaders may be set apart from reality because their reputation for brilliance or success prevents criticism or questioning within the organization. Martin Taylor, the former CEO of Barclays Bank, was universally regarded as an intellectual powerhouse whom no one could match. But under his strategy the bank lost massively in Russian investments, a fact he seemed to dismiss almost lightly in one television interview. There were other strategic problems and the board quite suddenly lost confidence in him – undoubtedly an unexpected and shattering blow to someone used to being adulated for his brainpower.

When leaders become cut off from the people in their organization they are cut off from reality. This is the main lesson to be drawn from all three of the leaders discussed in this chapter. In different ways they believe that, because of their titles, they can do it all. In different ways Shakespeare has them all fail totally.

Shakespeare's time was a time of change in the way in which authority was exercised. Before his time it was assumed that God granted power to kings and dukes alike, but this set of ideas about power was crumbling. There were many who still believed passionately that power could be handed down from on high. Richard II, King Lear and Antony are a part of this debate. They demonstrate different aspects of the belief that authority is handed down to a person for life, rather than having to be earned on a regular basis.

Their failure as leaders stems from their belief that their authority could be fixed to them as a person. How it became fixed is different in all three cases, but fixed it was. With all three Shakespeare demonstrates the weakness of a position that idealizes power. All three leaders lose out to armies or individuals that have a more rooted and materialist view of power. The lesson for all modern managers is stark. If you depend solely upon your job title and your job description to grant you the power to manage, you will eventually fail.

Shakespeare, the idea of being born to lead, and leadership

The 150 years prior to Shakespeare's time in the 16th century had seen kings and queens rapidly replaced by those who gained their crowns in battle rather than inheriting the crown from their parents. The link between God and king was no longer a constant. It is difficult to over-estimate the effect this had on how people thought about leadership. The dual elements of God and king interacted very strongly. Previously, when God and king were constant, the divine right of kings gave the king the legitimacy to rule. Imagine a society where God and king were constant and were feared. In that world the king, however good or bad, was the leader. He knew how to lead because God had anointed him at his coronation.

If you had a 'bad king', that was just bad luck. They were just as anointed as a 'good king', and had as much right to rule you. This affects the way in which subjects see their monarchs. If God and king are all-powerful, then the only way people can question good or bad behaviour by a monarch is to take on God as well as king. This is a difficult step to take.

For some time most monarchs had known they were not *really* an extension of gods. The Greeks and the Romans had learnt this, some-times the hard way. Emperors might be raised as gods, but they had a lot less power than 'real' gods.

The story of the English king, Canute, is even more striking. The tale would have us believe that his followers took this God/king relationship very seriously. They believed that the tides in the sea were his to command because, well, that was what a God-anointed king could do. Interestingly, Canute did not believe his power was this great and to prove it he sat on a beach as the tide came in. Having pretended to tell the sea to stop, when his feet and legs became soaked by the tide, his followers learnt the limitations of human leadership.

Most of us know that anyone who tried to challenge gravity or any of the other natural forces would fail. However, whilst any king might have known that he did not have a direct line to God, that did not stop him from using such a set of ideas to gain popular legitimacy for his actions. So the God/king relationship was important as a description of a reality – as the way in which the people were talked to about leadership.

This is hard to convey in the modern world. The completeness of such ideas means that there is no alternative way to think about leadership. Under these circumstances it would be very odd to find any literature about leadership or management. Those who are appointed by God lead, others follow.

The European world, which began to change in the two generations before Shakespeare, experienced accelerated change during his lifetime. Machiavelli gave his name to a new style of politics because for the first time you could question the hegemony that leadership was a God-given right of a few people alone. His textbook, as useful now to an aspiring manager as it was then, raised for the first time the question of how leaders learn how to lead.

In 1997 Lord McAlpine, previously head of an international construction firm, wrote a book in praise of Machiavelli. The revolutionary and shocking aspect about Machiavelli at the time was his philosophy that you could gain power and use it. McAlpine demonstrates some of the useful linkages between the very modern thinking of the 16th century Renaissance and today's world of modern management. Whilst Machiavelli did not write plays, he was part of the same modern thinking as Shakespeare about leadership. He was a part of the new world around Shakespeare.

SHAKESPEARE'S WRITING, HIS TIMES, CHANGE AND OUR TIMES

There is a very strong case for arguing that the world around us shapes our concerns and interests. We are not determined by the world around us, rather we act upon it and intervene. We are however affected a great deal by the social, economic and psychological conditions of our time. We are deeply affected by the world around us, and we deeply affect that world. Both things are true at once, and we cannot understand the human condition unless we hold both those truths in our head at once.

The conditions of Shakespeare's world were ones of turmoil. Throughout his life national politics, something he came to write a great deal about, was in flux. There was great change in the leadership of the state and its security.

Look at the national political events that occurred during Shakespeare's life. The king under whom he was born, Henry VIII, changed the entire constitution of the country. Henry VIII was only one generation away from the end of a civil war that had engulfed the safety of the entire nation. Henry's son Edward VI succeeded him but because he was under age and sickly throughout his reign, the regents who reigned in his stead tussled for power. A Catholic queen, Mary, followed, and persecuted the Protestant clergy who had themselves persecuted the Catholics before. She was replaced by Elizabeth I, who was an unmarried woman and a Protestant. She reigned for a long time but was, for most of it, under great attack from internal and external enemies. James I replaced her from a different dynasty, anxious about his capacity to continue to reign at all. Each succession was fraught with anxiety and each monarch was unsure about his or her ability to hang on to power.

On mainland Europe there were cruel and continuous wars between nations and religions. Internationally the equivalent of a world war was fought between the European nations in the Indian subcontinent, the Caribbean and parts of Africa. This conflict culminated in the Spanish Armada, a vast invading fleet and army sanctioned by the Pope, which threatened the nearest to invasion that Britain endured between 1066 and 1940.

Shakespeare's England was in great danger and constant political turmoil.

Below the court, there also was turmoil. One of the greatest landowners, the monasteries were dispossessed in the 1530s. This stripped the Church of enormous power and wealth and changed the land ownership of much of the country in the biggest upheaval for over 400 years. Many people were turned from their land and for the first time there were bands of sturdy beggars without any sense of place roaming the country.

Intellectually a series of changes also started at this time. We must remember that this is several centuries before the era of free speech. The change in ideas still did not allow people to express certain forms of opinion. The price of belief was higher than we can imagine. For example, if within this turmoil of change any person in public life was to admit to being an atheist execution would almost certainly follow. The fact that people would be severely punished for deviant thought drew a strong line between correct and incorrect thought. This is an important issue for Shakespeare because plays are about ideas. If the climate of opinion about some ideas could lead to death for those that held them, then the trade that Shakespeare dealt in was a dangerous one.

This was not an abstract threat. In Shakespeare's England there was a powerful secret police that would report deviant thoughts. Marlowe, one of Shakespeare's contemporary playwrights, was a police spy who was himself being spied upon. He was murdered, probably because of his espionage activities.

Shakespeare wrote about kings and queens at a time when there was a queen and then a king on the throne. On occasions both his real monarchs were the object of rebellions. Many of Shakespeare's plays were written about royal leaders who ended up being beaten in rebellion. In the politics of the time this was a dangerous thing to portray. The killing of Richard II by a usurper (Bolingbroke) was portrayed in the play as if it were a good thing for England. How would a reigning queen or a king feel about that?

In England in 1601 the Earl of Essex, ejected by the Queen from her court, decided to launch a rebellion. The afternoon before his coup his faction commissioned a performance of Shakespeare's *Richard II*. For many years before this particular performance the scene where Richard is killed had been censored from the text of the play. The Essex faction wanted the play to make a point and played the scene as a part of the lessons of the play. Their coup failed and the knight who commissioned the performance was sentenced to death. Shakespeare and his company managed to persuade the court that they were not a part of the rebellion. Had they failed to prove the point many of Shakespeare's plays would never have been written, as he would have been executed. Writing and performing plays in dangerous times can be a dangerous activity.

There are two sides to this coin of turmoil and threat. On the one hand deviant thought could be life-threatening. On the other, the history of the previous 100 years demonstrated that powerful ideas could rise and fall. Over time opposites could be believed – everyone did not have to think in the same way.

I want to suggest that writing plays at a time of change is different from writing at a time of constancy. Shakespeare wrote contemporary plays for an audience that was only just getting to grips with these changes. Many of the changes in the 16th and 17th centuries centred on the nature of religion. For those English people actively involved in religion at the beginning of the 16th century, it was normal to believe that wine in the confessional was turned into blood every Sunday. By the end of the century state religion in England had decreed that this did not in fact happen. These external changes had an internal impact on people and personalities. Plays that were concerned with the relationship between external change and internal emotion linked the dynamics of historical changes with the experience of internal emotional change.

As we know from changes in the present day, when large-scale external change takes place it does not lie within an individual's power to transform his or her personality completely. In our age, and at different times of our lives, we find change either wonderful or very difficult. We are left uncertain by changes in technology and society. Our personality lags behind the changes that are taking place, ensuring that at times of rapid change there is considerable psychological conflict.

All of Shakespeare's plays portray this relationship between historical change and personality. His characters try to come to terms with old ideas, new ways and different tasks. Most of his characters hesitate and struggle with this. A few are fanatics for the new and some try to hang on to the past. Everyone tries to make sense of the lag between their selves and the times.

Our new millennium is more full of rapid change, and we are even more full of the confusions in our internal selves when faced with it.

Our confused inner selves are linked to Shakespeare's characters by the similar impact of change upon our personality. Our personalities, then and now, are confused by change.

KINGS AND QUEENS, LORDS AND LADIES ARE HUMANS LIKE THE REST OF US (AND SO ARE MANAGERS)

It was this new world that shaped Shakespeare. For the first time, God did not directly appoint leaders and their skills of leadership were not God-given. Some of Shakespeare's leaders – for example Richard II – did believe that they were appointed 'God's deputy'. The truly modern aspect of Shakespeare is that he wrote his plays to demonstrate that such a view of kingship, in the modern world of the turn of the 17th century, did not work. Shakespeare makes most of his leaders more modern. These leaders lead, for the first time in history, as human beings, rather like the rest of us. Of course they are very different from the rest of us. More powerful, richer, with a very wide range of worries and responsibilities.

How, under these new sorts of leaders, is leadership carried out? Before a battle they will, like any soldier, worry that they might be killed. But unlike just any soldier they are also worried about their overall responsibility for thousands of others being killed. They also have to worry about losing the battle and what that will mean for the future. Like anyone they are afraid. Unlike everyone else, they worry for the future of thousands who are their responsibility. Like us they fall in love and worry about rejection, compatibility and whether love will work out. But unlike us they also worry about what will happen not just to their lives if the marriage doesn't work out, but to their two sets of lands if the relationship breaks down. They worry about love like us, but unlike us they worry about what will happen to thousands if their love is rejected.

This is the world that Shakespeare grew up in and that shapes the way in which his kings and leaders are written, shifting constantly between human doubts and affairs of state. To communicate this he develops leaders as people with characters, their own fears and their own hopes; but also as people with bigger lives than ordinary people. We are interested in them not only because they are leaders but also because they are human like us.

This is not an abstract idea about plot in Shakespeare's plays. It strikes to the core of how he represented the world. Unlike the plays of 300 years before, his plays were not peopled by 'everyman' characters representing the whole of humanity, but by individuals who were very different from each other. The whole structure of his plays depends upon the way in which individual characters are different from each other. Historically, by then it was becoming clear that each human being is different from another. History does not march through Shakespeare's plays as a series of automatons. History works through a series of human beings written as 'characters'. The essence of Shakespeare is this duality of human beings and leaders. His skill as a playwright is to link the narrative on leadership and the characters together.

For this book it is this conjuncture of people as leaders and leaders as people that provides us with another link between Shakespeare and management. This duality of leadership – on the one hand someone who fears, loves and cries like everyone else, on the other hand doing things that are very different from everyone else – provides us with the link to modern management.

Modern managers are human. Yet in the new millennium many believe that managers are born and not made. Most organizations I have worked for contain someone who really does believe that good managers are born to it. So the idea of the genetic basis of management so prevalent in Shakespeare's time is alive and well today. However, many people in the modern world know that managers are born like everyone else and, like everyone else, have to learn how to manage. We also know that managers, when they are managing, have responsibilities that others do not. Some seem to have crushing responsibilities for thousands of people's lives, and when they are doing this they are different from the rest of us.

Shakespeare's plays, in their very form as plays, encourage us to explore this duality of everyday humanness and unusual power. How did human beings do this at a time when they were only just learning how? How did a brilliant person write about this breakthrough? What does it mean for those of us today who manage both the ordinary and the extraordinary?

We can begin to explore these questions through the three Shakespearean leaders who best exemplify the old-fashioned ideology that leaders are born and not made.

Chapter 3

RICHARD II

Is being king enough?

Richard II chronologically starts Shakespeare's main English history plays, and represents the beginning of his British history of the eight plays of the War of the Roses cycle. The three plays of *Henry IV Parts 1* and *2* and *Henry V* follow on. Therefore if Shakespeare wants to make a point about chronological historical development, his *Richard II* will be the most 'old fashioned' and will be at the beginning of the process. If Shakespeare is making any points about the development of authority in British society some of the sharpest lessons will come from this play, since it is here that history starts with development from the 'past'.

Shakespeare's Richard II is usually portrayed as 'capricious', without a strong sense of direction; or weak, without a strong sense of leadership. He seems to move from appearing very strong to being very weak. Neither of these attributes are part of the personality that Shakespeare has written, but are a reflection of how Shakespeare's Richard believed he had the right to govern. He moved from great power as anointed king to virtually no power as a subject. He gambled all his power upon his belief in a set of ideas – that having the title of king was enough. He lost the bet when that belief came up against the modern materialist world.

Authority in the 14th century developed around individuals. This is a useful theme for Shakespeare, since he told his stories through the development of individuals and their characters. In fact Shakespeare's Richard is a study of the close interaction between person and position:

> In no other play of Shakespeare's is the office of kingship subjected to such intense scrutiny, from such a wide variety of angles. We see its ritual, quasi-religious significance, its practical underpinnings, and above all the importance of the man who holds it. Richard himself is one of Shakespeare's sharpest studies of a personality. Intensifying the scrutiny of the office, he was bound, it seems, to intensify the scrutiny of the man, and to test man and office against each other.
>
> (Leggatt, 1988: 59)

It is the interplay between the power of the individual and the power of the office that Shakespeare dissects to demonstrate to us that individuals cannot on their own wield power. This is a point that is made and remade throughout history.

For much of the play Richard is under siege from his cousin Bolingbroke, the future Henry IV. He is undoubtedly a more modern character who is struggling to impose a different view of authority on the kingdom. Half-way through the play Richard is besieged by Henry's superior army. At this moment, with his authority under attack not from ideas but from armed men, Richard explains where he believes his power comes from:

> *Not all the water in the rough rude sea*
> *Can wash the balm off from an anointed king;*
> *The breath of worldly men cannot depose*
> *The deputy elected by the Lord*:
> **Richard II**, Act 3 Scene 2 lines 54–57

These are beautiful images to have about power, and demonstrate from whence Shakespeare's Richard believes he gets his authority. Because he is the eldest son of his father, the king, he is God's 'elected' and therefore 'anointed' by him. In terms of hierarchy it is this process that makes a king, God's 'deputy'. This is also very powerful imagery, which in a religious society gathers much authority round it. If you are God's deputy and directly linked to Him you have almost unlimited power. The only way to question any of it is to question God and court eternal hell-fire.

Even if we find this idea difficult to believe today, being 'elected by God' does provide a powerful set of rights to act. The 'anointment with balm' comes directly from God Himself and can only take place if a king is actually touched by God. Anointment itself is a physical process, and whatever happens this cannot be washed away by the hand of a mere mortal. The only way you can become king is if God has touched you. Therefore if anyone challenges that power they are challenging God.

However beautiful a belief this may seem from the 17th century it is also 'old-fashioned'. Surely by the new millennium no one believes it any more, or there are only a few people who believe that monarchs gain all their authority from God. However, many people do feel that their right to act is given to them totally by the person above them. In the case of a king being God's deputy this is an obviously important link, but for many the chain of command that gives them the right to power goes right to the top of the organization, and it would be wrong to question it.

Shakespeare lived at a time when we think the 'few great leaders' still provided the real model for the rest of us. However, as we shall see, this is of particular importance for Shakespeare's Richard II, who systematically placed himself above everyone else because he was anointed by God and received his vast authority directly from the Deity. As we shall further see, this model did not work for Shakespeare's Richard – his aloofness and belief in the separation of leaders causes his downfall.

Shakespeare demonstrates in the rest of Richard's speech the problem with Richard's line of argument about power. His Richard believes that he cannot be 'unkinged' by any 'worldly man' – he cannot be deposed. Of course feeling impregnable as God's deputy is a strong position to feel that you are in. Yet, away from such fine thoughts, in the world of reality that Shakespeare has created alongside them, Richard is about to face a superior army under his cousin Bolingbroke. Even given this approaching nemesis he faces the opposing army with equanimity. After all, what can happen to God's anointed when faced by mere men? He continues his speech:

For every man that Bolingbroke hath press'd

To lift shrewd steel against our golden crown,
God for his Richard hath in heavenly pay
A glorious angel: then, if angels fight,
Weak men must fall, for heaven still guards the right.
Richard II, Act 3 Scene 2 lines 58–62

In this speech Shakespeare's Richard develops a strong image of where power really lies. A battle against an enemy with a powerful army is coming; in order to win that battle and retain his 'golden crown' Richard will need a better army. His power to be effective must match the opposition's power, on the battlefield where it matters. Therefore, for every man who 'lifts shrewd steel God [will] pay [for an] angel [who will vanquish] weak men'. This is an inevitable part of his notion of power. He believes that if an army comes against a king who is God's deputy then, because he is God's deputy, the opposition will find themselves fighting God's mercenaries, His paid angels. This is an image of strength and security, because surely he is correct. In a fight between 'weak men' and 'angels' the latter will win. It provides Richard, within his world-view, with some strength.

As the scene progresses and the battle comes nearer a number of the king's earthly supporters fail to come to his aid. Some have changed sides and some have been killed. Richard begins to face up to the fact that the angels may not be enough to win the battle against his enemy. He is forced by this reality to lament the loss of his real troops, but still he returns to the magic of authority:

I had forgot myself: am I not king?
Awake, thou coward majesty! … thou sleepest.
Is not the king's name twenty thousand names?
Arm, arm my name! … a puny subject strikes
At thy great glory … look not to the ground,
Ye favourites of a king: are we not high?
High be our thoughts:
Richard II, Act 3 Scene 2 lines 83–89

If there are no angels and no real troops then it is important for his followers to recognize that the 'king's name' on its own is worth 'twenty thousand' troops. Being the king will, through the very name, provide sufficient power and create allegiance from real people. This is a crucial point since it assumes people in the kingdom will follow their king because he is their king. The *name* itself, the title of his power, will call people forth. On its own that ascription can raise a large army. He has nothing to fear because he is 'high'; his 'thoughts' should be 'high'. Just being king is enough.

Given the traditional view of power this is not a mad thought for a king to have. If people give allegiance to a name then they will always follow the person who carries that name. This expectation that people will follow comes with the territory and can be depended on as an integral part of the relationship. If they don't follow then the whole structure of relationships falls down.

We have all worked for people who believe that their title forces us to give them total allegiance. They are after all our director, boss or manager and expect us, because of that title, to be directed by them. They believe that people's allegiance to them comes from their title, from their span of authority, and is owed to them because of that alone.

The scene continues and more and more 'real troops' fail to come to this king's aid. Quickly Richard realizes that he will not have an army, a real army, to fight for him. The angels disappear from his mind, the fiction of 20,000 men that will rally to the name of the king becomes just what it is, a fiction. Within a few minutes this realization crushes the fragile world of the king. In no time complete strength becomes very fragile.

> King Richard *No matter where; of comfort no man speak:*
> *Let's talk of graves, of worms and epitaphs; …*
> *Our lands, our lives and all are Bolingbroke's,*
> *And nothing can we call our own but death*
> *And that small model of the barren earth*
> *Which serves as paste and cover to our bones.*
> *For God's sake let us sit upon the ground*
> *And tell sad stories of the death of kings:*
> **Richard II**, Act 3 Scene 2 lines 144–45 and 151–56

What has Shakespeare made happen here? A king who believed that angels would be sent from God to join his army, and later believed that his name on its own would be worth 20,000 troops, has realized that he is short of real live troops to give him power on the ground. The opposing army is coming. Material reality comes crashing through the idealized view of power.

Shakespeare paints Richard as someone who suddenly realizes the limitations of what had until then appeared to be a powerful and all-encompassing set of ideas. It is a classic example of losing touch with reality. His lack of a relationship with followers, who live in the real world, separates him from that world. This separation allows Richard to retain an ideology that sounds strong, but in the crunch fails to grapple with reality at all. Under these circumstances his whole authority suddenly falls apart, leading to a collapse. He has lost 'our lands, our lives' and the only thing the king has left is his death, coupled with just enough of the land of his kingdom to provide a grave.

He goes further he sits down (that the anointed king sits in the company of his subjects is a recognition of human frailty), and talks with them about the death of kings. His authority, built so much around his unusual view of where the authority comes from, isn't only diminished by what happens, it collapses utterly. He becomes no different from anyone else and is seated amongst them.

This is not simply a battle between opposing armies, but a much bigger clash between whole world-views. Shakespeare's main character sets his view of his authority against Bolingbroke's view of power. Richard's whole kingdom is put at risk not just by a battle, but because it is based upon his belief that being a king is enough. Since there is no alternative to his view that he will win as God's king there can be no future of any kind.

What does Shakespeare make happen when this idealized view of power and authority is punctured? Once the ideal has gone there is nothing but loss and despair. Richard moves swiftly from being an unbeatable king with a whole country to having nothing but a patch of land big enough for a grave. From being a majesty anointed by God to sitting on the ground. He loses the battle without any battle taking place. His power was not based upon any form of material reality at all.

Shakespeare's Richard is written to teach his audience the limit of that view when it comes face to face with real material power. It is who wins in this battle between idealized and material power that makes Shakespeare a part of the modern world. From the 17th century Shakespeare's view of the 14th century points forward to a world where power on the ground decides who runs things. This is an important point. Looking back at Shakespeare from the turn of our millennium, we might expect him to tell stories that would praise the idealized moments of the past. He could construct a narrative containing a miracle by showing how God would intervene. The 20,000 angels could, in a play to make a different point, have turned up and won the day. His play could have made the point that this past was really all right, containing a world with a different reality than our own.

Shakespeare does the reverse. He stands with the modern world against the past. His Richard II is written to appear weak and capricious, demonstrating precisely what happens in the modern world when you just depend on ascribed authority to win battles against earthly troops. In fact, as the play continues the figure of Richard is painted as pathetic, moving from the appearance of total power to one of total powerlessness in no time at all. Shakespeare's Richard places his view of authority outside of common sense.

This is an important point for managers to take on board. If it was true at the turn of the 17th century it is even truer at the turn of the 20th. A belief in titles as the fount of all authority may, for a time, appear to provide strength. After all, being the director of sales does give you more authority than being the deputy director. People have to respect you more and more people have to do what you tell them. However, if this title is the only place from which you gain your power, if you fail to connect with the world of your staff, what appears to be strong is in fact very fragile.

History is full of changes where leaders felt they were secure because they had granted themselves titles and power, but suddenly their titles were swept away and what appeared unbeatable became weak. Similarly, managers who put their faith in their titles are not strong, but weak.

WITH ALL THOSE FANCY TITLES RICHARD STILL NEEDS MONEY

Earlier in the play, to make a point about leaders who believe in such unworldly views, Shakespeare also demonstrates that when he wants to Richard can be very worldly. If it is in his interest he can ignore the notion of power coming through birth. Shakespeare writes two scenes showing the clash between this idealized vision of Richard's and the real way in which he wields the power of his kingship. In the first act Richard is planning an invasion of Ireland to put down rebels. He plans to go there himself:

> *We will ourself in person to this war:*
> *And, for our coffers, with too great a court*
> *And liberal largess, are grown somewhat light,*
> *We are inforced to farm our royal realm:*
> *The revenue whereof shall furnish us*
> *For our affairs in hand: if that comes short,*
> *Our substitutes at home shall have blank charters:*
> *Whereto, when they shall know what men are rich,*
> *They shall subscribe them for large sums of gold*
> *And send them after to supply our wants;*
> **Richard II**, Act 1 Scene 4 lines 42–51

This is an illuminating speech. The anointed king is 'liberal' with the nation's funds and is keeping a large number of people at his court. This means that there is not the money in the exchequer to fight a war. So what is to be done? He will 'farm our royal realm'. This is an interesting metaphor for taxation, which sees the realm as a place to grow money for the use of the king and the court. It is a grubby activity for an anointed king.

In the next act one of the great Englishmen of this period, Gaunt, is dying, and amongst other truths he says to the king: 'Landlord of England art thou now, not king' (Act 2 Scene 1 line 93).

Gaunt poses two very different relationships between king and subject. Gaining money from his subjects as if they are tenants appears to be Richard's grand design as a landlord. It is a relationship, a far cry from the affairs of an anointed king, but it does provide a lot of money.

Later on in the scene, with Gaunt dead and Richard still needing money for his coffers, Richard decides:

> *Towards our assistance we do seize to us*
> *The plate, coin, revenues, and moveables,*
> *Whereof our uncle Gaunt did stand possess'd*
> **Richard II**, Act 2 Scene 1 lines 142–44

So to gain money he decides to simply disinherit Gaunt's son Hereford. But Richard's close supporter, York, points out the problem any disinheritance causes Richard in terms of his own position:

> *Take Hereford's rights away, and take from Time*
> *His charters and his customary rights;*
> *Let not to-morrow then ensue to-day;*
> *Be not thyself; for how art thou a king*
> *But by fair sequence and succession?*
> **Richard II**, Act 2 Scene 1 lines 178–82

York points out a contradiction here. Since Richard claims strongly to believe in the hereditary principle as the way in which he gains his own power as king, if he destroys the same principle between Gaunt and Hereford, will that not reflect on his own rights gained by 'sequence and succession?'

At the end of York's speech King Richard answers his plea:

> *Think what you will, we seize into our hands*
> *His plate, his goods, his money and his lands.*
> **Richard II**, Act 2 Scene 1 lines 192–93

This dismissal by Richard of the law of succession as simply a 'thought' of York's is a powerful image. He wants to get his hands on the money, so sweeps aside the ideology on which he bases his own power. His whole monarchy is based upon the rights and duties of succession. The only reason he is God's anointed is because his father was king. He believes he has the right to the throne before his younger brother because the right of succession goes through the eldest son. It is the cornerstone of his life, and yet when he needs some cash he sweeps it away.

Why does Shakespeare write this into Richard's actions? I believe he demonstrates that the idealistic view of power that Richard has about his own power is in fact a contingent view. This means that this view of the world is very helpful to him in the circumstances of his monarchy but it is not applicable in others. It is not a coherent view of his entire world, it is merely a useful way of justifying his own actions. The scene above, about stealing money from a dead man, is in complete contrast to the first speech I quoted. The same man, the same king, is involved in both actions. This only detracts from his believability as a king if he bases his monarchical power upon the anointed rule of succession – which he does.

Richard is eventually deposed and killed, an event that happens partly because, at crucial moments, he believed that being king was enough, and partly because he failed to carry through this world-view into all his actions. As he was warned above, stealing from Gaunt by denying the importance of blood inheritance puts his whole title to the throne at risk.

What direct lessons does this provide to modern managers? First, the simple belief in title appears to provide senior managers with a strong belief in authority. Handy (1996: 5) shows that the difference between modern and mechanical organizations creates very different authority forms. Richard exemplifies a mechanical view of power through title. Such a view has direct and important expectations of the way in which the rest of the organization will relate to that title. Such a view of authority demands total obedience.

However, if such a view of authority is ever called into question, what appears strong is in fact very weak. Robert (now Sir Robert) Horton, a former chief executive of British Petroleum, was a dominating – many thought arrogant – personality, widely regarded in the company as being totally in control, although there was much disagreement over his strategy for change. But his power collapsed when he was suddenly challenged by the board, led by a revolt among the non-executive directors, who duly ousted him.

It is this fragility that Shakespeare's Richard II demonstrates – a fragility that in the modern world, even that of the 16th century, demonstrates that such authority doesn't work. Managers need to recognize that their claim to authority, if it simply flows from their title, appears strong but is very fragile.

Second, in the real world of material power, other forms of power that go far beyond the nature of people's titles are vital. Richard loses not because he has insufficient authority, but because he has insufficient material power in the form of troops. Horton lost in the board room because he no longer had any power base amongst the directors.

Third, Shakespeare's Richard is inconsistent. His approach to his own rights to power is not mirrored by his approach to other aspects of power. When he wants money he denies the right to inheritance and in doing so undermines his only claim to power. Such inconsistency is a normal part of modern management, but in certain circumstances it can be as fatal as it was for Richard.

Chapter 4

⁓⁂⁓

ℋ(ING LEAR

Does giving up your kingdom necessarily stop you being king?

King Lear is a complex play that has been described as one that 'reaches down to the deepest concerns of the subconscious mind' (Wells, 1994: 273). What does Shakespeare's Lear tell us about the theme that authority on its own is not enough? One way of beginning to answer that question is to cheat and turn quickly to the ending of the play. This usually gives us a clue to some of the ideas that Shakespeare is trying to teach us. If we look at the end of *Richard II* we see a dead Richard and his cousin, an anxious Henry IV, on the throne.

King Lear ends like *Hamlet*, a stage full of bodies, with the last scene of both plays including the death of the eponymous hero. This ending is not so easy to read as there is not a final scene where one side ends up victorious and the other dead. In *King Lear* nearly every major protagonist dies. But there is still a message from this simple reading – that no one person in the play represents a way forward. Their death is the end, not only of their lives, but also of the world-view that their lives represent. They all have one thing in common – they are all a part of the world that Lear as king has created. If he was the only person who died the play could be read as a story, one which demonstrated the problems with his view of the world alone. Instead with so many deaths we have an ending that calls into question the entire nation that he, as king, has created. The entire world created by Shakespeare's Lear is deeply problematic.

In this play, as in all the plays about monarchs, there are very different views of power and how to use it. The dominant view of the play is Lear's, where authority is gained from the past and his personal power as king. No others have any part of power, and when he is on the throne they can be and are dismissed.

One of Shakespeare's clearest lessons is that when this much power is placed in one person there is a great chance that the power will be used in a capricious or whimsical way. If this happens what appears to be a very strong authority with a strong leader is in fact very fragile, with one absurd decision calling the whole structure into question. Where power resides in such a one-dimensional authority, the world can fall apart in chaos.

What picture is Shakespeare painting of this view of authority? A world that is so unstable that nearly everyone, with a range of different views, dies. This is a picture of a badly run and dangerous world. Painting a picture of what it was like living in a social order consigned to such tragedy was, throughout the ages, a horrible experience for Shakespeare's audience. This was not a world that people would want to live in.

Since this Part covers the question of failures in authority in Shakespeare, I want to concentrate on how authority fails in Lear. The play is difficult to read because the main action that involves Lear, that sets the scene for the whole play, takes place at the very beginning of the play. In the first scene Lear has to decide how to split up his kingdom amongst his three daughters. He decides to parcel out his kingdom based upon their capacity to prove, through their words, their love for him. This splits his kingdom, creating the chaos that people have to live with throughout the play.

Lear starts the play as an old king and we must suppose that he has had some long experience of running a nation. Yet the play starts with him doing something of stunning stupidity. In the first act he gathers his three daughters to him and says:

Give me the map there. Know that we have divided
In three our kingdom: and 'tis our fast intent
To shake all cares and business from our age;
Conferring them on younger strengths, while we
Unburthen'd crawl toward death…

Tell me, my daughters, –
Since now we will divest us, both of rule,
Interest of territory, cares of state, –
Which of you shall we say doth love us most?
That we our largest bounty may extend
Where nature doth with merit challenge.
King Lear, Act 1 Scene 1 lines 35–39 and 46–51

To modern eyes this seems a very odd thing to do. Lear starts the play with total power. He is king. The lands are his, to dispose of how he wants. He draws a map to cut up an entire kingdom. He decides now at this stage of his life that he is too old and wants to confer all his 'cares and business... on younger strengths'. If Shakespeare's Lear chooses to dispose of the lands in this way, that is his choice. He has the power to act this way. Before we turn to the outcome of this procedure, it is worth dwelling on what this total power and authority can mean.

King Lear opens within an undisputed authority. There is one person in charge and everyone knows what his being in charge means. He alone can decide how power shall be disposed. Shakespeare could have written this crucial decision as one that is carried out wisely and fairly. But instead all his audiences, from 1605 to the present day, are left feeling it is capricious. He is drawing our attention to the problem caused by total power. If one person can decide how to dispose of a nation entirely on his own whim then this amount of power is highly dangerous and can lead to the destruction of almost everything. Shakespeare writes the play to make that happen.

As the above speech shows, he has decided to split his kingdom between his three daughters Goneril, Regan and Cordelia. The test he sets them is to prove to him 'Which of you shall we say doth love us most?' The test is one of flattery. The sister who can claim in words to love her father dearest will get the best bit of Britain. The two eldest sisters play this game well. They flatter with a will, each of them claiming they love him first 'No less than life' and second 'I profess Myself an enemy to all other joys' (*King Lear*, Act 1 Scene 1 lines 56 and 71–72). The third sister though refuses to play the game of flattery. She says she 'cannot heave. My heart into my mouth', but 'I love your majesty According to my bond; nor more nor less' (*King Lear*, Act 1 Scene 1 lines 91–93).

Lear is enraged by his third daughter's response. Within a minute Lear disinherits her and splits the kingdom in two, giving all of it to his other two daughters. Lear has total power, and he therefore has total power over the outcome. In this first major action of the play he demonstrates that he has the authority to do whatever he wants.

As the scene continues his most faithful follower, Kent, tries to talk him out of this capricious decision to disinherit his daughter:

> *Be Kent unmannerly,*
> *When Lear is mad. What wilt thou do, old man?*
> *Thinks't thou that duty shall have dread to speak,*
> *When power to flattery bows? To plainness honour's bound,*
> *When majesty stoops to folly.*
> **King Lear**, Act 1 Scene 1 lines 151–55

This is a bold speech from a follower of such a powerful king. Kent goes so far as to suggest that 'Lear is mad' to make such a decision just because his daughter will not flatter him. He sees it as his 'duty … to speak' when *power bows* to *flattery*. He must speak *plainly*.

Lear's immediate reply is 'Kent, on thy life, no more' and later in the scene he goes on to explain to Kent that he should not to argue with him because:

> *To come between our sentence and our power,*
> *Which not our nature nor our place can bear,*
> *Our potency made good, take they reward.*
> **King Lear**, Act 1 Scene 1 lines 181–83

His reward for Kent is to exile his most loyal follower. The exile comes about because Kent tried arguing with him to change a very stupid decision, to come between a king's 'sentence and… power'. It is impossible for Lear, with his view of power, to cope with publicly changing his mind and changing a decision. His sentence on his youngest daughter for not flattering him must be backed up by his power. There must be nothing in between sentence and power, otherwise all his authority crumbles.

Shakespeare makes all of this happen in the first scene. He demonstrates the capacity for absolute power to act in an absurd way. He follows up that absurdity by showing that, given absolute power, it is impossible for Lear to retain power and change his mind. In an important way this demonstrates the fragility of Lear's total power. What appears to be very mighty is in fact very fragile. Once a decision is made it can never be unmade, and consequently he is forced to pile absurd decision on absurd decision.

This first scene is a demonstration by Shakespeare of the bad effects of concentrating power in the hands of one person.

What does this mean for modern management? Surely in the modern world nobody has the power to make such decisions, and if they did surely in the rational world they wouldn't make them in such an absurd way.

Well of course managers do. Shakespeare's point is as true now as it was then. Managers who occasionally achieve untrammelled power love to be unchecked by anything. Much of the time managers want to have as much power as they can possibly get their hands on – since the more power they have the more they can make things happen without involving other people.

One of the aims of ambitious managers is to get to a position where they can use their own judgement to run things unchecked by anyone else. In fact one of the definitions of moving up the managerial hierarchy can be the ability to make decisions that do not have to be checked with anyone. Under these circumstances managers can be tempted to demonstrate their power by showing to all their colleagues that they can take the decision in their own, their very own way. And if this is happening it is not advisable, even if you are the manager's oldest and most loyal supporter, to suggest they are doing something mad.

I would suggest that modern power could have this effect on managers as clearly as feudal power did. The attraction of being able to demonstrate that power is as great now as it was then; and the results for managers in this position, for themselves and their organizations are, I would suggest, likely to be the same as they were for Lear and his England.

As an example of a strong and apparently sure-footed chief executive making an absurd and quixotic mistake that destroys him, one need look no further than Gerald Ratner, the master of British jewellery retailing, who threw away a fortune and the family business by making some derogatory quips about his products at a conference of leading businessmen. His reputation never recovered, the business plummeted, Ratner was ousted and the company eventually sold to outsiders, who then changed its name. (It may have been poetic justice, because Ratner had earlier 'murdered his way to the top' by ousting his father from control of the company behind his back.)

The lessons from Shakespeare's *King Lear* do not end with this first scene. In the play different sorts of conflict run through every aspect of the plot and most of the main characters. After Lear has split his kingdom in two he obviously no longer has the capacity as king to make such decisions again. He sees the world through the eyes of someone with total power, but actually he no longer has any real power and quickly loses all its trappings – his knights, his followers and soon any shelter. Whilst he believes he has total power, the reality is total powerlessness. The world he lives in is the same as he used to live in, but he is now in the part of it where there is no power rather than the part where there is total power. The disjuncture between his belief about reality and the real world can only have one psychological outcome.

His madness comes in part from the inability of a very fixed view of power to come to terms with rapid change. The battle that is going on in Shakespeare's play is not between those who fight for one part of the kingdom and the other, but between those who are resisting change and those who are welcoming it. The king doesn't want to welcome the changes to the old order, but his two faithful retainers Kent and Gloucester do not help him.

Kent, having been exiled, keeps following the king (who is no longer king) so that he can protect him. The next time they meet they have the following exchange (Kent is in disguise):

Lear *What art thou?*
Kent *A very honest-hearted fellow, and as poor as the king.*
Lear *If thou be as poor for a subject as he is for a king, thou art poor enough. What wouldst thou?*
Kent *Service.*
Lear *Who wouldst thou serve?*
Kent *You.*
Lear *Dost thou know me, fellow?*

Kent *No, sir; but you have that in your countenance which I would fain call master.*
Lear *What's that?*
Kent *Authority.*
King Lear, Act 1 Scene 4 lines 17–27

Kent's role in life, despite being treated so badly, is to serve. The king, having given away his land, is fast losing real power but he still has something in his 'countenance' that people would 'fain call master'. 'Authority' shines from his face. Here the old order is being reinforced. People serve those who have authority stamped on their faces. It is what happens in this world. Or rather it is what used to happen in the whole world and now increasingly happens only in that part of the world that Lear and his friends inhabit. Everywhere else there is change.

Shakespeare writes very early in the play about the changes that have been happening in England at the time it is set. These changes are not just in the narrative of the play, but in speeches about other events. Gloucester, Lear's other great supporter, laments the amount of change going on. In the scene after the fracture with Cordelia and Kent Gloucester notes:

These late eclipses in the sun and moon portend no good to us: though the wisdom of nature can reason it thus and thus, yet nature finds itself scourged by the sequent effects: love cools, friendship falls off, brothers divide: in cities, mutinies; in countries, discord; in palaces, treason; and the bond cracked 'twixt son and father... the king falls from bias of nature; there's father against child. We have seen the best of our time: machinations, hollowness, treachery, and all ruinous disorders, follow us disquietly to our graves... And the noble and true-hearted Kent banished! his offence honesty! 'Tis strange.
King Lear, Act 1 Scene 2 lines 103–19, 111–14 and 116–17

''Tis strange' indeed. What a lament about change! Such a lament has been heard from conservatives in every generation. All of these new things are happening but the nearest Gloucester can get to a 'cause' is to be found in the eclipses of sun and moon. We will return in a minute to a different perception of these changes, from Gloucester's bastard son Edmund, who welcomes them. Here though it is important to stress the resistance to change felt by conservative authority figures such as Lear, Kent and Gloucester. In the past they had 'the best of our time'.

Now all they are offered for the future is 'hollowness' of change from the certainty of a strict authority by the king.

Lear has been in charge of this world for some considerable time and his attitude to change permeates his followers and their world. Lear's form of authority has turned change into an enemy, something that can be characterized only as creating discord. Since change changes things, and everything happening at the moment is to be defended, then change can only bring discord.

Kent is banished and still follows the king. Later in the play Gloucester has his eyes put out for helping the king. The three of them continue their way through appalling physical and mental pain, hanging on to the truths of their past. Their world disintegrates, but they cling strongly to the only values that they know, and these values depend upon the certainty of a single strong authority.

The tragedy in the real Shakespearean sense is that it is exactly these values of absolute power that have created the crisis that brings about the disintegration of their world. If Lear had not had absolute power, and had not used it capriciously, then their world would have continued. Absolute power has destroyed the world of absolute power. To watch three noble leaders clinging on to the very ideas that have led them to such awfulness is genuinely tragic.

The world of the new millennium contains a great deal more change than the world of Shakespeare's Lear. An organization or a manager that fails to keep up with the modernity of the changes around them will find survival hard. Managers have to learn to recognize the rapidity of what is going on around them. Sometimes they will defend their organization against that change, often because they are defending themselves against that change. This is often a dreadful mistake, since they are building rigidity into their actions and their organizations that will be problematic. Whilst very few people think the stars and the moon are the creators of change there are far too many managers who fear change in the same way as Gloucester does.

In the modern world this view of authority and change is not unusual. There are many managers who believe that it is their task to defend the *status quo* and act as the stewards of the resources they are given to manage. For these people management is 'looking after' the existing conditions and, for them, all change is discord.

Tom Peters has harsh words about such managers:

> Lately I've been ending my speeches with a snide observation which directly concerns this prescription: 'If you are interested in keeping your jobs, ask yourself at the end of the day, every day, "What exactly and precisely and explicitly is being done in my work area differently from the way it was done when I came to work in the morning?"' The average manager starts each day as an expense item... not a revenue enhancer. ... The only way to do so is by making things different and better. Different and better today can only mean, acted upon... It's tough medicine. The manager, in today's world, doesn't get paid to be a 'steward of resources', a favoured term not so many years ago. He or she gets paid for one and only one thing – to make things better (incrementally and dramatically), to change things, to act – today.
>
> (Peters, 1989: 469)

The stewardship of resources is a really good phrase for conservative management. The really important thing for stewards is to protect themselves and their organizations from change. Yet time and again the message of management theorists is to bring about change, although the managers they are talking to see their role as 'stewarding resources', and not bringing about change. The manager does not simply have to welcome change but to bring it about, to act on it. Stewarding resources was the policy followed by Lord Weinstock, architect of Britain's General Electric Company, which for years sat on a massive cash mountain while financial analysts speculated what he would do with it to develop the group. Weinstock seemed to lose the will to use this powerful instrument of acquisition; instead, under his successor, George Simpson, GEC's technological jewel, Marconi, has been divested.

Under Lord Blakenham, the Pearson Group was maintained as a cluster of prestige businesses including the *Financial Times*, classic French vineyards, Lazard's merchant bank and Madame Tussaud's, but there was no synergy to the famous names. Executive control has now passed to a feisty US manager, Marjorie Scardino, who is paring down the group to its core media interests.

Shakespeare's Lear is someone committed to stewarding resources and demonstrating his power through that stewardship. He resists change, but throughout the play is engulfed by it. Lear cannot stop it – he wants to but is completely taken over by it.

The lessons from Lear are hard ones. Protect yourself and your organization from change and you will fail. The more you protect it, the more you will fail by being engulfed by forces that you thought you could simply stop.

There is, however, another analysis of authority and change that Shakespeare creates in this play. Edmund is Gloucester's illegitimate son. As such Edmund will not only inherit nothing from his father, but is also beyond the normal bounds of control. He is portrayed as a manipulative and treacherous character from the beginning to the end. He does not believe in fixed authority, and is contemptuous of his father's explanation of change to be found in the sun and the moon. After Gloucester's speech quoted above, he provides a very different analysis. It is important to note that he does not disagree with Gloucester that all of these changes are happening, but he has a different set of reasons to explain them:

> *This is the excellent foppery of the world, that, when we are sick in fortune – often the surfeit of our own behaviour – we make guilty of our disasters the sun, the moon, and the stars: as if we were villains by necessity, fools by heavenly compulsion; knaves, thieves, and treachers, by spherical predominance; drunkards, liars, and adulterers, by an enforced obedience of planetary influence; and all that we are evil in, by a divine thrusting on:*
> **King Lear**, Act 1 Scene 2 lines 118–26

Edmund is sarcastic about his father's railing against change, and his antique belief that eclipses have caused all these changes. He laughs at those who believe that the stars cause bad luck, when in fact it is caused by your own 'behaviour'. This is a modern view of the world and is in conflict with that of Lear, Gloucester and Kent. What is important about Shakespeare's character of Edmund is that he demonstrates that within Lear's England there is a very sharp clash of worldviews. The explanations that Lear has for what is happening to him and his times are not the only ones around. This clash of explanations is included to demonstrate that Lear and his friends continue to see the world that way because they choose to. They are 'old-fashioned' and, as their world disintegrated, they could if they wanted have had a different explanation, but they choose not to.

Edmund believes that it is possible to move away from behaviour caused by the stars to a world where we take responsibility for our own actions – when we are 'sick in fortune' it is often the result 'of our own behaviour'. Recognizing our own responsibility is exciting for Edmund and contains a very different theory of change from that of his father.

This redoubles the lesson to be learnt about change. The three people who run the organization that is England not only fail to recognize the changes that are taking place but fail to recognize that there are more rational explanations for what is happening in their world. This is a 'double blindness' that stops them from recognizing change in its new, more rational guise. In modern organizations managers sometimes not only fail to recognize the changes that are taking place but can fail to keep up to date with modern methods of explanation.

Chapter 5

ANTONY

Whose power did he wield – Rome's or Antony's?

Shakespeare's Antony provides complex lessons about leadership. First, as with Richard III and Henry V, he appears in more than one play. He is a major Shakespearean character. In *Julius Caesar* he gives the funeral oration that turns the crowd against Caesar's assassins. He then wins victory after victory, and kills his opponents. Finally, he is one of the main players in *Antony and Cleopatra*, a play that seems to 'follow on' from *Julius Caesar*.

> But in spite of their common source [in Plutarch] the plays are very different. As a story, *Antony and Cleopatra* is as much a sequel to *Julius Caesar* as *Henry V* is to *Henry IV Part 2*, and there are a few references to the events of the earlier play; but the differences of tone, structure and ethos make it difficult to think of one as a continuation of the other, and unlike the English history plays, they are rarely performed together.
>
> (Wells, 1994: 301)

Given these differences it is difficult to treat Shakespeare's Antony in *Antony and Cleopatra* as a continuation of the same man from *Julius Caesar*. There are however some important and contextual continuities between the two plays. It is, for example, important that Antony is older in the second play. We know that his Cleopatra was the lover of Julius Caesar, whose assassins Antony killed in the first play. There are references in the second play to his great generalship in the first. However the separateness of the play for our purposes seems to create two different sets of lessons about Antony. In this second play he starts as one of the three leaders of the whole world. He ends the play in defeat and disaster. There are specific lessons to be drawn from this trajectory.

Antony and Cleopatra is also a play about sex. It is as good an erotic story as *Romeo and Juliet* (and better if you are of an age when you find it difficult to empathize with the first love of young teenagers). It is much more a play about power. The two protagonists are leading large areas of the world. One is a great Roman general, the other an empress. This same empress had previously had a relationship with an even greater Roman general, Julius Caesar. This 'love' takes place through the politics of power of the whole 'known world'. As the play unfolds it covers not only the African and the European sides of the Mediterranean but the Middle East. There are battles taking place involving armies a thousand miles away from Rome.

Shakespeare's play is set at the time of consolidation of this power of Rome. As Octavius Caesar says before one of the last battles of the play:

> *The time of universal peace is near:*
> *Prove this a prosperous day, the three-nook'd world*
> *Shall bear the olive freely.*
> **Antony and Cleopatra**, Act 4 Scene 6 lines 5–7

Shakespeare's Octavius Caesar is making the point that if he can win this battle then a long period of peace will come to the world. Of course this will not be an abstract peace, but one that has been won by the Romans, for the Romans. What was known as *Pax Romanus* means that they have colonized the world. There will be no rebellion.

The fact that the action of the play takes place in the years just before the *Pax Romanus* explains the sexual relationship between Antony and Cleopatra. It was clear by this stage of history that the Romans had the organizational and military might to run the world. How did an empress, a part of the Roman world that wanted to maintain national independence, obtain sufficient power to hold off that Roman strength? The only way to maintain that independence was to make an alliance with some parts of Rome against the rest.

Cleopatra needed Antony not as an individual but as a part of the triumvirate that ruled the Roman world (together with Lepidus and Octavius Caesar). Antony is introduced to the play in its very first scene in this way:

> Philo *Look, where they come:*
> *Take but good note, and you shall see in him*
> *The triple pillar of the world transform'd*
> *Into a strumpet's fool:*
> **Antony and Cleopatra**, Act 1 Scene 1 lines 10–13

Shakespeare's Antony starts the play having been degraded from running a third of the world to his lover's fool. He is of course both. He still has the power granted from Rome to be 'the triple pillar of the world', but he is also 'a strumpet's fool'. Later in the scene Philo confirms this dual nature of Antony:

> *Sir, sometimes, when he is not Antony,*
> *He comes too short of that great property*
> *Which still should go with Antony.*
> **Antony and Cleopatra**, Act 1 Scene 1 lines 61–63

Shakespeare's Antony as an individual human being is both 'Antony' and 'not Antony'. When he is 'not Antony' he falls 'short' of being the 'Antony' that everyone in Rome remembers as the real 'Antony'! Shakespeare has written a very tight dialectic here but it is worth unpicking since it provides the key to Antony's trajectory throughout the play.

Antony has gone to Egypt as a part of his leadership duties for Rome. He is responsible for a third of the empire, authority granted to him by the power of Rome. He has power to make things happen in Egypt only as a part of the power structure of Rome. He is a Roman and has been a part of that power structure for some time. He has gained power through his capacity as a military general. He defeats the assassins of Julius Caesar and 'Antony' is an integral part of Rome's power structure. The only reason that Antony is in Egypt is to carry out Roman power. The Romans respect 'Antony' because of this power.

'Not Antony' is a part of Egypt. Not only is he in love with its queen but he has taken on board the hopes and fears of Cleopatra as queen of Egypt. Earlier in this scene he talks of he and Cleopatra wandering through the streets and noting the qualities of Egyptian people. He is at home there. The Egyptians respect 'not Antony'.

This is a complex duality. Throughout the play, act by act, Antony is clearly both the Roman 'Antony' and the Egyptian 'not Antony'. He moves scene by scene from being one or the other. It is usually possible for individuals to be different things. It is not however possible for individuals to maintain for very long being two things that are in direct opposition to each other. He cannot serve both Rome and Egypt. Rome will not allow it. This is obvious, so why does it prove so difficult for the Antony that Shakespeare writes to understand that it is impossible to use that power on both sides?

Antony believes that the power conferred upon him by Rome is his to carry out in his own capacity, in other words that he has been granted it as an individual. His greatness in battle has meant that when Rome grants him power it is his to wield as an individual. He believes that his place in history is to wield that power on his own, as his personal power. In a way he believes he created that power in the wars following Julius Caesar's death and, believing this, when he was in fact given it he thinks it is his. If he chooses to wield it in one direction or another then that is his choice, since it is his power.

This can never be the case. Power in Roman times, as now, is constructed through a set of organizational structures. It may be granted to an individual with some power in that organization, but it can also be taken away. Douglas McGregor has provided a critique of this personal view of power:

> There are four major variables now known to be involved in leadership: 1) the characteristics of the leader; 2) the attitudes, needs, and other personal characteristics of the followers; 3) characteristics of the organization, such as its purpose, its structure, the nature of the tasks to be performed; and 4) the social, economic and political milieu. The personal characteristics required for effective performance as a leader vary, depending on the other factors. This is an important research finding. It means that leadership is not a property of the individual, but a complex relationship among these variables...

Research findings to date suggest, then, that it is more fruitful to consider leadership as a relationship between the leader and the situation than as a universal pattern of characteristics possessed by certain people.

(McGregor, 1966: 73)

These are important points for any manager to take on board. Too many managers believe that they themselves have the individual characteristics to manage and to lead and that these characteristics can be removed from the situation they are in and the organizations they help to run.

Shakespeare's Antony is the story of what happens if you forget that the individual does not gain authority through his or her individual self, but through a constant relationship with a particular set of power structures. The power of Antony was made by Rome, and when he decided to wield that power to other ends it could and did unmake him.

This is the clearest lesson that managers can learn from Shakespeare's Antony. He confuses his power as a person with the authority of his position. He feels so secure in his position that he feels he can do whatever he wants with it.

This is not an uncommon problem within the management of organizations. Individuals who are granted power feel that it is theirs to use. Having been granted it they feel they have in some way earned it for their own designs and their own aims. To a certain extent the tension between personal and organizational goals can be lived with by an organization. The drift between the two lessens the effectiveness of an organization, but will not disable it. However, if individuals feel that the organizational power to achieve things is in any way based in their individual selves the likelihood is that sooner or later they will use it to bolster that error.

There is of course nothing wrong with being an individual in an organization. Most modern organizations recognize that they cannot work with automatons, but cherish the individual character of their managers and their staff. But the organization is not something with which individuals can do what they want. When they try they must be stripped of the power that was conferred on them not as individuals, but as posts within the organization.

Whilst Cleopatra may love Antony as an individual it is as a Roman general and as an empress that they relate. Cleopatra needs some

Roman power to maintain Egypt's independence, something she could
not achieve on her own. So Cleopatra needs an individual who is
firmly linked to Roman power; but she also needs an individual who
will use that power in favour of Egypt against Rome. She therefore
needs 'Antony' and 'not Antony' to hold on to this duality. The Antony
of Egypt, the Antony of the present, must be able to find himelf in the
Antony of the past, the Roman general.

In the first half of the play Roman power and Cleopatra join in the
battle that is going on inside Antony as to whether his power belongs to
Rome or himself. In the second act Antony is recalled to Rome to meet
the two other members of the triumvirate who rule the world,
Octavius Caesar and Lepidus. A rebellion is being led by Pompey
against Rome and therefore a solution to Antony's allegiance is
pressing. 'Antony' supports Rome but 'not Antony' supports Egypt.
Rome needs to know where it stands.

The triumvirate meets. The meeting starts with a warning from
Caesar that puts forward the problem of the split that is taking place
within Antony between his allegiance to Rome and his belief that he
holds the power for himself.

> Antony *My being in Egypt, Caesar,*
> *What was't to you?*
> Caesar *No more than my residing here at Rome*
> *Might be to you in Egypt: yet, if you there*
> *Did practise on my state, your being in Egypt*
> *Might be my question.*
> **Antony and Cleopatra**, Act 2 Scene 2 lines 39–44

This precisely explains Antony's problem to himself. If you are a
Roman general living in Egypt and your allegiance is to where your
power came from, then it does not matter where you live. If on the
other hand you think your power is separate from Rome, then being in
Egypt is a problem.

Octavius Caesar seeks a solution to this. He says:

> *Yet, if I knew*
> *What hoop should hold us stanch, from edge to edge*
> *O' the world I would pursue it.*
> **Antony and Cleopatra**, Act 2 Scene 2 lines 119–21

His general Agrippa finds a 'hoop' that will 'hold' them together. Octavius has a sister Octavia, and Agrippa says:

To hold you in perpetual amity,
To make you brothers, and to knit your hearts
With an unslipping knot, take Antony
Octavia to his wife;
Antony and Cleopatra, Act 2 Scene 2 lines 130–33

It is expected that the marriage to Octavia will bind Antony to Rome with 'an unslipping knot'. Both the hoop and the knot are an attempt to ensure that the split that is developing between Antony and the source of his power is re-bound. Antony agrees wholeheartedly. He wants to be whole and to use his power in such a way as to become one with its source in Rome. In celebration of this oneness he goes off and defeats Pompey. All of his old brilliance as a general returns when he is at one with its source.

The specific hoop that Octavius uses to bind Antony is an emperor's sister, and it appears enough to re-bind Antony to Rome. The hoop involves sex with an important woman, and since it is the emperor's sister it appears indestructible. However we know that this particular form of hoop also creates a contradiction for Antony since it is precisely that hoop, sex with an important woman, that binds him to Egypt and Cleopatra.

It is not surprising that the hoop that binds Antony does not please Cleopatra. She and her nation's future need an Antony who will wield his power in *their* interests and not in Rome's. She represents this conflict:

Let him for ever go: – let him not – Charmian,
Though he be painted one way like a Gorgon,
The other way's a Mars.
Antony and Cleopatra, Act 2 Scene 5 lines 115–17

Let him go but stop him. He is a devil and a brilliant general at the same time. He is Rome, but he is also Egypt. She needs that conflict.

Gradually as the play progresses the Antony who believes that his power is represented in his self takes over from the Antony of the past, who recognized he needed Rome, and he loses his power. Act by act he loses his Roman power back to those who gave it to him, Rome. He fights bravely as an individual but as a leader and as a general is inept. He makes strategic and tactical errors, and in the mistakes that are made in the second half of the play it is impossible to recognize the brilliant general of the earlier war.

Cleopatra fights against this disempowerment with everything she has. But there is a problem, since she needs a powerful Antony and since Antony's power springs from Rome, all that she has are her hopes and dreams for how he might be in her own view of him.

Towards the end of the play, when Antony is dead, Cleopatra is still dreaming of him with massive power:

> *I dream'd there was an Emperor Antony:*
> *O, such another sleep, that I might see*
> *But such another man! …*
> *His legs bestrid the ocean: his rear'd arm*
> *Crested the world: his voice was propertied*
> *As all the tuned spheres, and that to friends;*
> *But when he meant to quail and shake the orb,*
> *He was as rattling thunder…*
>   *in his livery*
> *Walk'd crowns and crownets; realms and islands were*
> *As plates dropp'd from his pocket.*
> **Antony and Cleopatra**, Act 5 Scene 2 lines 78–81, 82–86 and 89–91

This image of him is one that would be able to defeat Rome and defend Egypt. In her dream he had so much power that 'realms and islands' dropped from his pocket and with his legs 'bestrid the ocean' he could walk across the Mediterranean and destroy Rome. Ultimately the last lesson from *Antony and Cleopatra* about the battle within 'Antony' and 'not Antony' is that dreams cannot conquer Roman legions.

Shakespeare's Antony as a character has been created by a set of Roman power relationships. However, Antony makes the mistake of believing that his power is founded in himself. He believes that he has this power within himself as an individual. Consequently he believes he can take the power with him away from the organizational relationships that created them. However the power is not personal but still resides in the relationships that created it and in fact is still wielded there. Without those original relationships Antony is simply a very good soldier, not a leader. Without them he is of no real use to Cleopatra to fend off the Romans.

However as far as Antony is concerned, such is the relationship between Antony and the Rome that constituted his power that their political and personal identities are bound together. When they separate Antony disintegrates.

Modern managers need to recognize the strong relationship between the individual and the post. The post gains its powers from the organization, they do not reside in individuals on their own. Sometimes managers make this mistake and believe the power comes not from the organization but from themselves. This causes problems on a similar scale to those experienced by Antony.

There is a further insight into the relationship between leader and led in Shakespeare's Antony, in which Shakespeare demonstrates that Antony's relationship with his troops is problematic.

At the beginning of the third act Antony's troops have just defeated a Middle Eastern army of Pathians. Silius is congratulating his fellow officer Ventidius on a successful campaign. Given Ventidius's success, it is not surprising that Silius expects praise and rewards for him from their captain Antony.

Silius *Whilst yet with Parthian blood thy sword is warm, ...*
The routed fly: so thy grand captain Antony
Shall set thee on triumphant chariots, and
Put garlands on thy head.
Ventidius *O Silius, Silius,*
I have done enough; a lower place, note well,
May make too great an act: for learn this, Silius;
Better to leave undone, than by our deed
Acquire too high a fame when him we serve's away.
Caesar and Antony have ever won
More in their officer than person: Sossius,
One of my place in Syria, his lieutenant,
For quick accumulation of renown,
Which he achieved by the minute, lost his favour.
Who does i' the wars more than his captain can

Becomes his captain's captain: …
I could do more to do Antonius good,
But 'twould offend him; and in his offence
Should my performance perish.
Antony and Cleopatra, Act 3 Scene 1 lines 7, 11–22 and 25–28

Shakespeare writes a whole scene simply to give us an insight into how Antony is seen by his troops. Given the victory Ventidius should expect garlands, but not so. Shakespeare paints a picture of Antony's troops afraid to take credit for their actions in case they appear to build themselves up above their leader. Ventidius tells a story of where this happened to an officer called Sossius who achieved more than his leader Antony and lost favour. It is obviously dangerous in Antony's army to achieve more than Antony can. The merit of good action within Antony's army counts for nothing, In fact if you do achieve a lot it is important to hide it from the leader or you will suffer for it.

Where does such a set of relationships lead? It is clear to Ventidius that it restricts his capacity to help the army achieve its goals. For he 'could do more to do Antonius good', but 'twould offend him;' and 'in this offence. Should my performance perish'. The outcome is clear. Antony's leading officers will underperform rather than do better than their leader. Such a set of relationships automatically restricts the efficiency of the army from trying their best. Looked at organizationally it is an error of some importance since it would mean officers were looking over their shoulders, worrying not that they were performing too little, but that they were achieving too much. If the officers do achieve a lot then it is important that it is hidden from Antony, who must never find out that he has won more through his officer than through his person. Consequently a conspiracy has to take place to hide the truth from him.

Shakespeare writes this scene to give us an insight into the relationships between 'great men' and their officers. These 'great men' seem to have fragile egos that cannot cope with having successful people beneath them. It is not possible to read any aspects of this scene as flattering for Antony, since Shakespeare so obviously displays a weakness in Antony's make-up. Instead it is a clear warning that a fragile ego in a leader can have a strong impact on the nature and efficiency of an organization. Antony loses because his army is frightened of doing too well. If they do well Antony punishes them.

It does however complement the major lesson we have drawn from Shakespeare's Antony. If managers personalize their power and abstract it from the organization that gave it to them then they are very likely to be jealous of others encroaching on it in any way. Power personalized and abstracted in this way is very fragile, partly because it gives the impression to other individuals in the organization that it can be transferred without any problem from one individual to another. If power resides in an individual and has no organized base then it is dispensed on a very casual basis. Consequently, people who see power this way are themselves nervous that others can simply remove some of their power and hand it to another.

Such a set of relationships does nothing for building teams or creating organizational strengths away from individual power.

If a manager makes it clear to subordinates that he or she has to lead all the successes in an organization it will restrict the capacity of the organization enormously. Senior managers whose egos are this fragile will have a powerful, limiting effect upon their staff's actions.

All management theorists make the point that managers are going to have real long-term problems with their organization if they fail to work successfully with good staff. Over 40 years ago Peter Drucker (1954: 19) warned: 'Don't be afraid of strength in your organisation. This is the besetting sin of people who run organisations. Of course able people are ambitious. But you run far less risk of having people around you who want to push you out, than you risk by being served by mediocrity.'

If managers are frightened of talent beneath them they will reward mediocrity and the organization will falter. If the manager rewards talent then it is possible that a talented person may want the manager's job, but since the organization will be bursting with rewarded talent, it will do well.

Antony was frightened of rewarding talent. His talented people had to hide their success and pretend all the time it was Antony's.

CONCLUSIONS TO PART 2

These three failed leaders all provide dramatic lessons for today. In different ways they all reflect the movement away from what has in the past been considered a natural order of things. The modern world has shaken that order and called all of the thinking behind it into question. It is clear now that organizations cannot simply operate in a linear up and down way, but exist in a much more complex and collegial way. As Helgein (1996: 24) says: 'As we come to recognize the dynamic connectedness of the various parts within a whole, top-down structures begin to seem less a reflection of any natural order and more a way of arranging our human world to reflect outmoded perceptions.'

Once we realize that 'the natural order' of hierarchy is no longer natural we understand that those people who hang on to seeing organizations that way do so because of personal preference. The 'natural' order is in fact like any other order, and it is a matter of choice to see the world that way. It is not 'natural' for leaders to believe that leaders are born and not made, it is a belief like any other. When someone tries to support that view with the argument that it follows nature, they are wrong and have to support the argument like any other.

Yet still people claim support for some organizational forms as if God created them and they are therefore not open to question. Time and again in the modern, real world of organizations you hear managers claim that simple hierarchy is God-given, as if that concludes the argument. Shakespeare shows us that such a view is not given by God, but is constructed by men to bolster their own view of power.

Despite appearances it is not a strong view of power, but a very weak one, and the real world of much more complex organizations comes flooding in to prove that being king is not enough.

Part 3

Having all the power is not enough

Al Pacino as Richard III in *Looking for Richard* (source: Kobal Collection)

INTRODUCTION TO PART 3

Vaulting ambition, which o'erleaps itself
And falls on the other.
Macbeth, Act 1 Scene 7 lines 25–28

It may seem odd for this book to have another part dealing with the failure of leadership, but it is important to recognize that there are more failures than successes in Shakespeare's leaders. Indeed the near constancy with which, in play after play, leaders fail to thrive or even survive does leave us with the impression that Shakespeare really didn't like leaders. It's as if there were a 10-part series on TV about great modern managers, seven of whom not only failed but their companies went bust and the families appeared in the series to complain about how awful they were. This is an important analogy because such a series would be hugely popular, especially compared to a series about how great managers were. That wouldn't last beyond the trailer.

Failure and defeat make a better story, and Shakespeare was writing stories. But there is a further point. Those of us who want to convey information to managers recognize that there is always much more to learn from failure than from success. It is somehow easier to pick up on lessons from people who did badly than from those who shine with success. Mark Twain, always with an eye for an aphorism, put this brilliantly with his view that 'There is nothing so annoying as a good example'. Good examples represent a tyranny, since it's never really possible to be 'as good' as they are.

Shakespeare's failed leaders are useful to learn from. He wrote the characters of kings and would-be kings who, time and again, overreach themselves. But what can we learn from failure?

I start from the position that being a manager, running something, is inherently very difficult, whether it's a Roman war or a modern company. There are always issues beyond your control. Everyone has high expectations, and a large number of people need you to succeed for their wealth and happiness. So when, again and again, Shakespeare shows us failure and difficulty, he is describing in a range of different settings, in Rome, in Scotland or England, on imaginary islands, how really hard it is to run anything. I still find this the great unsaid truth about managers and management, that to really be good at it, to move your organization along, takes an enormous amount of skill, activity and energy. Under these circumstances, you *are* much more likely to fail than to be a great leader.

Shakespeare is telling us something about power – that it is not easy, and if you want to have it and you want history to like you for it, you have to be very good at it.

Equally, as we shall see from Part 4 of this book, on Henry V, even for a successful leader success and failure exist, both as an integral part of the experience in the same person. It is also the case that in this part of the book, whilst the three leaders fail badly in the end, in each play there is for some time considerable success:

- against the odds Shakespeare's Richard III does become King of England and reigns for some time;
- against expectations, his Macbeth does become King of Scotland; and
- for most of the play, Shakespeare's Coriolanus is unbeatable when he has a sword in his hand.

Despite the fact that each play ends in tears, we need to recognize that these people are *not* underachievers. They make it to the peak of their profession. What makes Shakespeare a great writer is that their success, the reason they make it to the top, is also the reason that they fail humiliatingly.

The lesson from each character is a harsh one. If you do it this way, it may work for a while, but in the end it will be a disaster. Each drama is a warning against the short-term effects of a very good set of tactics that undermine themselves in the long term. Each of these plays, read only to the half-way mark, would give the opposite lesson to the one that must be drawn from the final scene:

- for Richard III it would demonstrate that brilliant manipulation, coupled with action, can get you everything you want;
- for Macbeth, one decisive act can achieve your ambition; and
- for Coriolanus, sticking to being an aloof and powerful leader will get you the throne.

But by the end of each play each strength has become a weakness and the leaders fail.

POWER AND AMBITION IN THE WORKPLACE

Every organization in the world suffers from office politics. Sometimes it is a mild irritant to the smooth running of the organization, but occasionally it takes over its aims and perverts its every action. What I mean by 'office politics' covers the way in which individuals and groups pursue their own power games within the organization. They can use politics to pursue small issues such as where their desk will be, or to pervert the entire organization or to improve their own position.

It is the job of managers to manage the effects of office politics alongside every other activity within their area of responsibility. It is therefore essential for managers to know what it means both in general and in practice within their organization. The higher they move up the organizational ladder the more important will be the stakes in office politics and the more difficult will be the managers' work.

It is essential not to be naïve about the existence of office and organizational politics. Managers must expect politics to take place below the surface all the time and they must learn how to manage it. They can only do this by understanding that the appearance of authority is shot through with smaller and darker themes. They must not simply understand their task through the appearance of the organization. If they do, they may manage that part well but still fail overall.

In this book most of the Shakespeare plays contain powerful themes about politics. Sometimes the politics covers the aims of organizations or nations as they struggle for control. Given the way in which Shakespeare uses individual characters to paint his wider picture, much more often the narrative covers the way in which individuals and groups create history for their own ends. Detailed and brilliantly written stories of individual treachery and betrayal run through all the plays. He tells 'big history' through the narratives of individuals and groups.

This is intrinsic to the way in which Shakespeare wrote and is one of the reasons he remains so popular. He tells his stories through characterization. As I outlined in the Introduction,

Shakespeare wrote his plays through individual characters. The stories move along because individuals move them. We experience *people* making things happen, not abstractions. This means that there are no 'abstractions' in Shakespeare's plays. Nations do not do anything. Armies do not march through history but are led by and composed of individuals. 'History' does not change, it is changed by individuals.

In this way Shakespeare is particularly helpful in teaching managers about the nature of power in organizations. Because he tells his large historical stories through the individual characters who are vying for their own personal power, he teaches his audience that the large narratives of history can only be understood through the small politics of individual and group ambition. The manager is therefore forced to understand the lesson that power is fought over and distributed through what appear to be background activities. Shakespeare teaches us that these small narratives dominate the bigger narrative of the organization level. It is essential that managers understand these different levels.

Since Shakespeare addresses these smaller, more personal human narratives I want to use this style of address, this analysis of human knowledge, to critique the established management literature. In the Introduction I claimed that management was about emotions. Of course it is not *only* about emotions, but it would be impossible to outline accurately an important episode of management in a company without seeing the emotions that are involved. Fear, anger, loyalty, betrayal and ambition take place within real management all the time. Management literature that fails to recognize that, that stresses the way in which managers are simply rational beings, will fail to address managers and their work and will therefore fail to teach them lessons that they need to learn.

Reaching people, helping them give that extra ounce of effort, motivating them to really believe the organization's vision, can only happen if their managers are genuinely in touch with them. People can only be moved in this way through some form of emotional relationship. Similarly, too much management literature analyses organizations in an abstract form and fails to address the real issues of practice that individuals need to know about. This abstraction away from real activity and real life is one of the outcomes of an alienation of human activity and analysis that affects most academic analysis.

Shakespeare can never be accused of furthering this alienation between real people, their activity and change. His plays are full of real human characters, who carry out recognizable actions and who in turn make history. Whilst we cannot sometimes see ourselves carrying out those particular actions, we can understand why others perform them and can reflect back on our own action.

This has an important impact on the content of this part of the book. Office politics and power in the workplace are activities and organizational issues that affect every manager. Office politics can however be written as a set of abstractions external to the work of the manager. This is not helpful to managers because they are not drawn into seeing themselves and their emotions in the abstractions. To be helpful, all management literature must address the lived experience of individual managers.

This part of the book addresses that lived experience of power in the workplace by talking directly to the emotion of ambition. Ambition leads to action, perhaps not immediately, but it is difficult to understand how ambition would not at some stage lead to activity of some kind. Ambition is an emotion frowned on by a few but understood by many, and most managers are ambitious.

Ambition is one of the main drivers for the individual distribution of power within organizations. People may want to get on in an organization because they want more personal recognition, a bigger salary or more power to push people around. But they may also be ambitious for a position with more power to achieve other things, to make the organization a more moral one, to ensure that the organization helps more people or to stop amoral people getting on.

This makes ambition a necessary part of the analysis of power; further, it is an emotion that all managers (to a greater or lesser extent) will recognize in themselves. Senior managers rely on ambition as one of the main drivers for change and development within their organization. Managers below them in the hierarchy want to improve their positions, and therefore need to take the values and aims of their organization to heart and work within them. The organization depends, in part, upon individual ambition to ensure that people take its values into their work. The organization 'buys' that loyalty because it recognizes that people are ambitious. Indeed it is difficult to imagine how organizations would move and change at all without the strength of a member's individual ambition.

Most of the managers reading this book will want to get on and get a better job. They probably have a view of their career that involves a bigger job with a better salary at some time in the future. Their activity follows their goals, and in many ways their emotion to do better drives the way in which they work and manage.

Much of management activity concerns managers taking responsibility for a set of activities in a world that they themselves do not control. Richard III and Macbeth try to overcome this by trying to control the whole world through the manipulation of leadership. They use 'vaulting ambition' to drive themselves to the very top of their organizations under the illusion that this will provide them with total control. Before they gain the throne they find they cannot live with the contradiction between control and responsibility so they try to control everything.

Psychologically, they are both driven to get to the top because they cannot live with the tension of not controlling everything. Shakespeare portrays these characters as *driven* by ambition. We recognize the psychological disturbance that springs from individuals who have no choice – they have to get to the top to resolve their inner tension. The activity that springs from their ambition is manipulation – because they cannot live with the experience of the lack of control they try to manipulate the whole world to fit in with their ends.

The drive to manipulate the world to fit in with an individual's desires is a painful form of psychological need. Some of us will recognize this need for control in our relationship with our parents, children or loved ones. We need to control them and in order to achieve this we manipulate them. At work some managers need to manipulate their teams so as to give themselves the feeling of control.

Richard III and Macbeth need to manipulate their entire nations to try to make themselves psychologically whole. At no stage in this process, either as they strive for the top or when they reach the throne, can either of them be described as 'happy'. Driven people rarely are.

We can thrill to their ambition and the behaviour that springs from it, but it is not attractive.

I argued earlier that Shakespeare wrote in a world that was undergoing great change. In the 16th century, the modern world was slowly beginning to grow. That slow growth has continued throughout the last four centuries and continues today. It is across this bridge of modernity that Shakespeare's meaning comes to us.

Shakespeare's time had just come to terms with a round world, but it is likely that most people still thought it flat. Nowadays few people in Britain think the world is flat, but quite a few believe that the stars control their destiny. The influence of astrology at the heart of Reagan's government in the 1980s gives us a hint of the distance we still have to travel.

Let me take another example from the core of Shakespeare's work, an important aspect of one of the plays I deal with here: the magic in *Macbeth*. Famously the play starts with the three witches on the heath who lead Macbeth to believe, in very allegorical terms, that he will one day be king. They and their apparent magical ability to see into the future are a vital part of the plot. Yet 400 years ago what was the status of the magic they were engaged in? In Shakespeare's day, were the witches in *Macbeth* seen by the audience as real witches or were they seen as allegories? We will never know whether Shakespeare thought his audience believed in magic or not. It is likely that some thought witches were real and some allegorical. We can easily imagine a prolonged discussion after the play about the nature of the witches' predictions.

Magic drifts into and out of Shakespeare's plays and, in Shakespeare's period, for the first time in history, magic was not simply true. But nor was it completely allegorical. For Shakespeare and for his collective audience *it was both*. Sufficient people in his audience would still believe in witchcraft to give its reality credibility. But there were sufficient 'moderns' in the audience to see the witches as allegories. Shakespeare could and did 'play' with this ambivalence. Today, when the mists flow across the heath, and as Macbeth approaches the crones, there will be fewer people (but still some) in the audience who believe that these witches possess real magic. The growth in rationality that started in Shakespeare's generation continues with our own, but it still has some way to go. Modernism has not completed its journey through all our lives.

This is especially true in the realm of leadership and authority. As I argue in the rest of the book, the successful amongst Shakespeare's leaders led as modern people. But many of his leaders, especially the worst, were also full of older ideas. Shakespeare 'plays' with these conflicting ideas about modernity and leadership.

Today fewer people still believe in those God-given rights to lead, although there are some who believe that managers are born and not made. We are linked across the centuries not just by senses, ideas and emotions but by one of the major strains of thought about leadership and management that still drives our lives today. Today most people believe that the world is there to be made by women and men and is not a series of God-given experiences. This growth in the recognition that men and women can play a role in making events happen has a particular resonance for managers. If we live in a world that is made for us, that is pre-ordained, then there is little that managers can achieve. If, however, we live in the modern world that can be made, then our work and our actions have an effect. For managers that means that ambition, and the tactics and strategies of action, are worthwhile.

Manipulation as management

Shakespeare's *Richard III* and *Macbeth* are stories of extreme ambition, with extreme methods employed to achieve the goals of the protagonists. The moral of Shakespeare's stories is that there are appalling outcomes for those who try to gain leadership through murder. Both Shakespeare's Richard III and Macbeth are famous for their attempts to manipulate events to make things happen – murder being the simplest way of getting rid of opposition. Richard manipulates people and parts of the organization throughout the whole play, from the first speech to nearly his last. He is world famous for it.

Many people follow on from this emphasis on manipulation in management to believe that management is an unpleasant activity that is best carried out by unpleasant people. The feeling is that nice people have difficulty managing because it contains some very nasty activities and nasty outputs; for example, when a manager starts the job they need to be prepared to sack people. More often they need to be able to discipline their staff. Many people would find that hard. Therefore it is understandable that the view is that the people who become managers had better be a bit unpleasant. Whilst everyone may acknowledge that it's a job that needs to be done since, at the very least, it helps make the trains run on time, some say that the people who do it have to be a bit unpleasant.

This 'characteristic' of unpleasantness can take different forms. However, to most people, manipulation of people, and often events, appears necessary to make things happen. Within this context a successful manager must be able to treat events, people and institutions as other people would treat pieces in a chess game, moving them about in order to win the game. It would appear that a manager does not worry that these are 'real' people.

Thus if managers have to improve the productivity of their teams they will have to ensure that everyone works harder. To make that happen they will have to change people's behaviour. Initially this may appear to involve something that people want, such as training, but they are 'only doing that in order to achieve something else'. After the training comes the reorganization and after the reorganization comes the complete change in the job description. Within the bounds of work-related behaviour the end for the manager will justify the means.

So much for appearances; for the managers themselves these are difficult issues. Much of the job is about making decisions that are both emotionally and intellectually difficult. Very often managers find themselves making change in a way that is manipulative – even though they know they shouldn't. It's just an easier way of doing it, of making things happen. Sometimes it is very hard to envisage how you might bring about a change in your part of the organization if you were genuinely open. There are always pressures and manipulation may appear to be the easy way round them.

In both *Richard III* and *Macbeth* Shakespeare describes the extremes of manipulative leadership. On a grand scale he demonstrates that individuals can lie, cheat and even kill their way to the top. These plays demonstrate how some leaders see other people as dispensable, to be killed as necessary. Even on this grand scale Shakespeare's lesson could not be clearer – manipulation of the world for your own ends may succeed for a while, but in the end it fails catastrophically.

BEING AMBITIOUS IS NOT ENOUGH

Ambition is one of the main themes of Shakespeare's plays. He recognizes it as an emotion that can link the activities of famous kings and queens to the hopes and fears of ordinary people. His characters who want to be monarchs want, like us, to get on. And whilst we may want to 'get on' by being a bit more financially secure and getting our immediate boss's job, they may want to 'get on' by becoming a king or an emperor. Our ambition for improvement in our own lives may dominate how we think about our life and work; for these Shakespearean leaders their ambition dominates not just their work, but the life of their kingdom.

Shakespeare demonstrates through these characters how entire civil wars are fought to the death of a nation through the normal emotion of ambition that we each have inside ourselves. He uses the common emotion of ambition as the driving force of history. If these large historical stories develop because of individual ambition, we can better understand our own emotion of ambition, even though it is expressed on a smaller scale.

Here I emphasize the problems and the dark side of ambition. It should be stressed that this does not exhaust Shakespeare's lessons on the subject. In *Henry IV Part 1*, for instance, we see the young Prince of Wales having ambition as a necessary part of being a great king. In Part 2 of this book we saw failures in leadership without ambition. Ambition is not in itself a bad thing, but all of the characters outlined below became dominated by it.

Shakespeare's Richard III and Macbeth are driven by the emotion of ambition, and in different ways have become talismans for this emotion and what it drives people to. The play's audience has demonstrated to them the full trajectory of where ambition gets you; they see its mechanisms, learn how it is carried out, bask in its success, but are led, in the end, to recognize its catastrophic failure. Even though the failure comes at the end of the plays, the audience is left, when they leave the theatre or finish reading the play, with the darkness of that failure dominating not only their experience of the whole play but their experience of the dominating character the play is named after as well.

Coriolanus is driven in a different way. As a leader he believes he can only truly lead his people by removing all traces of humanity from his life. To lead he needs to act as an inanimate object (he asks to be made into a 'sword' to defend his people). This deliberate absence of humanity appears to make him a great leader and for a while this lack of humanity brings him success. However, just as vaulting ambition gained Richard III and Macbeth their kingdom but in the end destroyed them, so does Coriolanus's lack of humanity. He cannot sustain his position and is finally undone by his own success.

As with most major lessons from Shakespeare about human life, being left with this overriding lesson is not an accident. The death and destruction with which these plays end say one thing clearly. Powerful ambition, carried out and acted on in such a way as to dominate all activity in your life, will ruin not only your own life but the lives of people around you.

All three plays in this Part have become bywords for failure and tragedy but, as we shall see, they are also demonstrations of how, for a limited while, ambition can be successful. These monarchs have a detailed analysis of the tactics and strategy necessary to become a monarch. They could provide a textbook for every ambitious manager who doesn't mind breaking a few rules. Throughout the plays there is an excitement about how you can break and bend rules to get on, but they leave you with a sure knowledge of what will happen if you do succeed with such techniques.

They therefore teach modern managers a number of very clear lessons – lessons in how to succeed, how to plan actions and carry them out in such a way as not to get the blame, and how to live with the fruits of your success, but also how, by succeeding through certain strategies, to fail totally.

Chapter 6

RICHARD III

His own man, with ambition for a nation

Shakespeare's Richard III is an exciting character. He is rarely likeable but always interesting. Not only does he have an entire play named after him, he is also a powerful character in the sequence of plays that, in real history, precede his own (*Henry VI Parts 1, 2* and *3*). These three plays portray a nation at the height of civil war. The whole country is a killing field, as families exact revenge for previous slaughter in a series of battles. Richard is in the leading family of one camp, that of York. His main enemy is the Lancastrian camp, the head of which is Henry VI, the present king. In growing up throughout this bloodbath Richard learns the power of force as an agent of change. Even more in tune with our own modern times, he recognizes that those who today run the organization can be quickly changed for others.

During Richard's life, given the speed of change from king to king, it was very difficult to believe in the divine right of kings. It was power that made things happen – if you didn't happen to be a leader at the moment you could become one in the future. During his life Richard learns that history is not fixed, it can be made by your own actions.

In Act 3 of *Henry VI Part 3* Richard explains what this means to him:

Why, then, I do but dream on sovereignty;
Like one that stands upon a promontory,

And spies a far-off shore where he would tread,
Wishing his foot were equal with his eye,
And chides the sea that sunders him from thence,
Saying, he'll lade it dry to have his way:
Henry VI Part 3, Act 3 Scene 2 lines 134–39

Here he can see on 'a far-off shore' the crown of England, but since he cannot walk on water and 'wishing his foot were equal with his eye,' he will have to act – he will ladle the entire sea dry so that he can reach his goal. These are powerful images of action. If he wants to become king he is going to have to work very hard to get there.

It is true that there is a long way between him and the crown, not only his enemy the present king Henry VI, but Henry's son Edward. From his own family there are his two elder brothers and the two princes, the sons of his eldest brother. Six people between Richard and the throne is a large sea to ladle dry. Six men of good health and various ages, who are fighting on both sides of the war. Over the next play and a half we see him 'ladle' them aside and, through their deaths, he reaches his crown.

There are many ambitious managers who, having looked at the hierarchy above them, know they could carry out the work of the CEO with greater skill and verve than the present occupant. Sometimes there may be as many as six people between that goal and yourself, but in a dreamy moment it is possible to think of things that will happen to all six.

The chief executive is up for retirement, and his deputy will have to go when he goes because everyone knows he is not up to it. It is true that his assistant will get the job, but she won't last long. The scandal that you know covers your boss and her boss will come out in the next few months, and they will have to go. That still leaves one person between yourself and the top job. That's not so bad. He can be dealt with.

The difference between Richard and our manager is that the former realizes that his personal action is the only way to really get there. He cannot wait for fate to intervene. *He* will have to make it all happen. Action is needed to make history happen in order for Richard to get what he wants. And he will have to cause violent death in order to get there.

Leaving aside the method, all of this manipulation and action makes Richard a very modern man. He takes the modern way of making his own fate rather than relying on others to make it for him: the sea between him and his ambition will not simply run dry, but will have to be ladled by him out of the way. The crown is there to be grabbed by his own activity. The point of ambition is not just yearning after something that you want but taking action to bring it nearer. If you really want something, go and make it happen.

In the soliloquy just quoted he uses two other images which are a very telling description of ambition:

> *And I, – like one lost in a thorny wood,*
> *That rends the thorns and is rent with the thorns,*
> *Seeking a way and straying from the way;*
> *Not knowing how to find the open air,*
> *But toiling desperately to find it out, –*
> *Torment myself to catch the English crown:*
> *And from that torment I will free myself,*
> *Or hew my way out with a bloody axe.*
> **Henry VI Part 3**, Act 3 Scene 2 lines 174–81

If you have ever been really overwhelmed by ambition you will recognize this beautiful description, which clearly describes the pain of wanting. Even if it has not happened to you, we have all at some time known someone who has been taken over by an ambition. The experience gives us moments of clarity but, for most of the time, it is the emotion of wanting, of need, that traps us in its thrall.

When this happens two things take place at the same time. It is vital to go forward, but equally, on occasion, you are not quite sure where forward is. It is vital to act, but every action may be wrong. Trapped by a lack of clarity, and stung by the thorns of action, it is not a pleasant place to be. The way to get through is by plotting the detail of a sequence of complex activity. If I do this, then that will happen, opening up a small gap that will allow me to do this, that will in turn possibly... etc. But it isn't easy to find your way. For many, including Richard, it is tempting to cut your way through with action – hack the thorns and barriers out of the way.

In the final battle of Henry VI's reign Richard starts his drive to the top by killing Henry VI and his son Edward. In some way their deaths are acceptable. Henry VI and Edward were Richard's enemies and he was a warrior killing them in the name of a righteous quarrel between different parts of the kingdom. This could be painted as just another horror of war, but we know that a couple of acts before Richard told us that these two deaths would be the beginning of a long line of murder. However, they take place in a battle, and are therefore somewhat masked, not appearing to be about his personal ambition. They look as if they spring from a bigger quarrel between his family of York and its enemy, Lancaster. Indeed, because of this killing, Richard gains credibility with his own family, who see him as their warrior, creating a future for all of them, when in fact he is his own man, creating his own future.

Murder aside, this scenario can be seen in the world of management. Individual ambition can be masked by apparent loyalty to a wider group. Individuals can appear to be working for a common organizational objective, but are using that allegiance to mask their real, personally driven activity. As with Richard this appears to be a good strategy: we can help ourselves, but not appear to do so, because it looks as if we are helping others. The *we* covers up the actions of the *I*.

However, Shakespeare suggests that this takes place at a cost, not only a moral cost but confusion about the reasons for action. Individual ambition, and actions that further that ambition, rarely fit exactly with the wider good of a wider group. This leads to confusion about why we are doing things, not just in ourselves but in everyone around us. The mask of the collective action rarely covers the reality of the personal action completely.

Our colleagues can become confused by this. They will be expecting to judge our actions as a part of the collective activity of the organization. Sometimes this will fit, and our individual action will disappear within a common vision. But at other times it will diverge, leaving everyone else puzzled by what looks like a sudden outburst of individual activity. As with Richard's family, this can be very destructive of the collective will.

Shakespeare's Richard opens his eponymous play with a famous and moving speech about the end of battle and the emergence of his brother Edward as successful Yorkist king (this son – sun – of York):

Now is the winter of our discontent
Made glorious summer by this sun of York;
And all the clouds that lour'd upon our house
in the deep bosom of the ocean buried.
Now are our brows bound with victorious wreaths;
Our bruised arms hung up for monuments;
Richard III, Act 1 Scene 1 lines 1–6

It is impossible not to let one of Shakespeare's great puns go by without comment. Richard is celebrating his elder brother's accession to the throne as the son of the Duke of York. In bringing to the end the winter of war, he welcomes the warmth brought about by the sun of the new king.

The play opens with this promise of peace and the hanging up of arms, yet from the quote from *Henry VI Part 3* on pages 95–96 we already know Richard is planning the deaths of his own relatives. In this way, starting in the first scene of the play, he is separated from the victory of his family by his own personal ambition. It is this separation from everyone that in the end brings about his downfall. He cannot enjoy these peaceful times because of his nature. He demonstrates this as he continues the same soliloquy:

And therefore, since I cannot prove a lover,
To entertain these fair well-spoken days,
I am determined to prove a villain
And hate the idle pleasures of these days.
Plots have I laid, inductions dangerous,
By drunken prophecies, libels and dreams,
To set my brother Clarence and the king
In deadly hate the one against the other:
And if King Edward be as true and just
As I am subtle, false and treacherous,
This day should Clarence closely be mew'd up,
Richard III, Act 1 Scene 1 lines 28–38

Within minutes of celebrating that all the clouds are buried at the bottom of the ocean he is plotting to turn his brother Edward the king (who is 'true and just') against his brother Clarence. He plots to ensure that by the end of that day Clarence will be 'mew'd up' or incarcerated in the Tower of London. From the very first speech in the play, Richard's plots develop thick and fast.

At the start of this play Shakespeare's Richard explains what is going on to the audience in asides, Shakespeare's only main character who does this. In dramatic terms he acts as his own 'chorus', explaining everything directly to the audience. In sharing his strategies with the audience he is further separating himself from the characters around him. We, the audience, know what is going on but they, the characters in the same play, don't. This separation continues throughout the play, until Richard is entirely on his own. Indeed, it is this increasing separation that marks the play. As Richard wins the crown, bringing his full ambition to fruition, he is completely alone.

Shakespeare's Richard III is a leader with great skill and vision. He organizes himself and others around that skill, achieving very much more than most. However, the vision and the leadership is personalized and is shared by very few. As the play progresses and he gains in power the vision is shared by fewer and fewer. Richard spends very little time even trying to share his vision, except with a very few individuals whom he uses brazenly to help him to gain his personal goals. In fact the way in which he pursues his vision separates him from other people rather than includes them.

As this separation continues Shakespeare demonstrates through Richard's actions that it is highly dangerous to be close to anyone who is this ambitious. Richard's elder brother Clarence (who is therefore nearer the throne than him) is murdered in prison under Richard's orders. His eldest brother King Edward dies. For a while Richard is the protector of the realm. He is in charge of the nation, but because his elder brother Edward's two sons are still alive, under the rules of succession he is not king but is merely keeping the throne warm for his nephews.

In the following scene a group of the great and the good of England, chaired by Richard, are planning the coronation of the eldest prince. This is a typical committee scene. The committee has to prepare for the coronation, but the most important person on the committee, Richard, the Lord Protector, does not turn up on time. So the others have to try and make a decision without knowing Richard's choice. In his absence they speculate about what Richard may want.

Hastings *My lords, at once: the cause why we are met*
Is, to determine of the coronation.
In God's name, speak: when is the royal day?
Buckingham *Are all things fitting for that royal time?*
Derby *It is, and wants but nomination.*
Ely *To-morrow, then, I judge a happy day.*
Buckingham *Who knows the lord protector's mind herein?*
Who is most inward with the noble duke?
Ely *Your grace, we think, should soonest know his mind.*
Buckingham *Who, I, my lord! we know each other's faces,*
But for our hearts, he knows no more of mine,
Than I of yours;
Nor I no more of his, than you of mine.
Lord Hastings, you and he are near in love.
Richard III, Act 3 Scene 4 lines 1–14

These are Richard's closest allies, but they are all terrified of what might happen. Half-way through the play none of them, in the public of a committee, dares to hazard a guess at what he thinks. The Bishop of Ely is right – Buckingham is Richard's closest ally, yet what does Buckingham say about all of their relationships? He is realistic and says that that they may 'know each other's faces' but not their *hearts*. Those closest to Richard do not know each other well enough to say what the others want. In this world trust has gone completely. Buckingham goes on to say that he, as the person closest to Richard, doesn't know Richard's mind and, importantly, Richard does not know his (Buckingham's). Hastings does not know the bishop's mind, nor does the bishop know his. Buckingham concludes by passing the buck and saying that surely Hastings, as the man closest to Richard, must tell them all what Richard thinks. By the end of the day Hastings has been killed by Richard. The price of proximity in the world of Richard's ambition can be high.

Richard's problem is caused by his ambition separating his own hopes and actions from those around him, most particularly the family for whom he has fought. The play starts with a claim about the success of the Yorks as a collective, but within seconds degenerates into Richard's personal plotting for ambition. As the play progresses Richard rises and succeeds, but as he succeeds most people, including his very closest allies, trust him less and less. For their part this lack of trust may seem a wise precaution.

In terms of a management strategy this separation creates a real problem since, through his own actions, Richard becomes more and more isolated. No one really knows, not even those closest to him, what he will do next. Whatever it is it will be in his own personal interest of gaining the crown and not in anyone else's interest. Robert Maxwell, a bullying entrepreneur whose descent into crime was masked partly by his associates' (and his sons') unwillingness to challenge him openly, is a prime example of this. He raided his employees' pension funds to finance loss-making businesses and eventually died, either by suicide or misadventure, just as his chicanery was about to be exposed.

THE IMPORTANCE OF TRUST

Given the importance of communication in modern management, it is vital that people believe what their senior manager is telling them. It is difficult to motivate people around a vision if people can't really believe anything you tell them. This means trust is an essential part of successful management. If staff do not trust you they don't believe you; and if they don't believe you then they cannot be motivated by you, they cannot act on your goals.

Rosabeth Moss Kanter has expressed this clearly:

> The doing more with less strategies place an even greater premium on trust than did the adversarial protective business practices of the traditional corporation. Business collaborations, joint ventures, labour management partnerships and other stakeholder alliances all involve the element of trust – a commitment of strategic information or key resources to the partners.
>
> (Moss Kanter, 1988: 362)

Richard is engaged in what has been a 'joint venture', to place him on the throne. Despite all his brilliant activity on his own behalf he couldn't achieve this on his own, so he needs other people in the organization to help him achieve his goals. He needs them to have a 'commitment' and to provide him with 'resources' and 'information'. A leader with an eye to these needs would have ensured that trust had been maintained within at least that inner circle of allies. But the whole climate of plot and murder created as the main driver for change in Richard's world undermines his relationship with even his closest allies. By this stage the trust and his allies have gone completely and he is left alone, and a lot less effective than he would have been had some trust been maintained between him and his supporters. It is the very success of the way he follows his ambition that creates a climate of mistrust.

Once trust begins to evaporate a leader loses relationships essential to the normal running of an organization. You communicate, but because nobody trusts what you say your organization will not tell you the truth about what is going on. They keep quiet because they are terrified of you.

> The organisation that fails to make it happen is best characterised by a lack of truthfulness and openness. Bad news in organisations is seldom received with much enthusiasm. The reality of life is, of course, that it is the bad news messenger who should be the most prized... but those who will stand up and tell you 'hopefully tactfully' that things are not really the way that everyone else thinks, they are pearls beyond price.
>
> (Harvey-Jones, 1988: 51–52)

In terms of receiving any information about the real world, the climate of mistrust and fear characterized by the committee meeting quoted earlier demonstrates the problem that Richard now has. In this climate it is impossible to imagine someone being able to give him the difficult news that any leader needs to hear. You can see how managers can cut themselves off from information from below and from being believed when giving out information to those below them.

Jack Welch of General Electric was once told by Walter Wriston, chairman of Citicorp and a member of the GE board: 'Jack, you're always going to be the last one to know the critical things that need to be done in your organization. Everyone else already knows.' Welch determined that he would not be the last to know, and from then on he used Crotonville, GE's internal forum and business school, to engage with GE managers in a regular, uninhibited exchange of questions and answers where he would find out what others in the organization really thought and knew.

The final impediment to Richard's ambition are Edward's two boys. When the two princes in the Tower are killed under Richard's orders he becomes king. Yet having achieved his ambition, in Shakespeare's play this is not a happy time for Richard. In terms of the real history of England, Richard III reigned for two years. In Shakespeare's play there is no time when he is wearing the crown he has worked and killed for that he is at all happy. Immediately after he is crowned there are plots against him. His method of gaining power simultaneously creates its own fear that the same method can be used to take it from him. This is the most straightforward lesson Shakespeare teaches. You know that if you have lied and cheated your way to the top others can lie and cheat their way to the top, and there is nothing you can do or say about it. Immoral activity in gaining power brings its own anxiety, since you know what is possible for others to do to you.

In Richard's case these plots eventually lead to an enormous army led by the future Henry VII (and in real life the grandfather of Elizabeth I, still on the throne when Shakespeare was writing this play).

The night before the last scene in the play, when the future Henry VII's army is arrayed against him, Richard is revisited by the ghosts of all of the people he has killed. Unsurprisingly, they curse him and hope that the battle the next day goes badly for him. This is not a good way to spend the night before a decisive battle. The ghosts frighten him about the future and demonstrate that past misdeeds are never fully in the past. When you break moral rules to get to the top of your organization, then those rules and that morality will come back to haunt you. You cannot affect your history without it affecting the way in which you wield the power obtained through immoral means.

Richard wakes up from his dreams full of anguish:

Cold fearful drops stand on my trembling flesh,
What? Do I fear myself? there's none else by:
Richard loves Richard; that is, I am I.
Is there a murderer here? …
no soul shall pity me:
Nay, wherefore should they, since that I myself
Find in myself no pity to myself?
Richard III, Act 5 Scene 3 lines 182–85 and 202–04

This is the final result of all Richard's plotting. When he is alone, and he has killed or banished all his enemies and scared everyone else who might oppose him, who can there be left to fear? Actually the most dangerous person in the kingdom is still there when no one else is around – Richard himself. In killing his way to the crown his activities have brought about such havoc that he would be mad not to be afraid of the most dangerous man in the country, even if it is Richard himself. This may seem odd, but Richard knows more than anyone else what he is capable of and that he is in the company of the most dangerous man around. After all everyone else has either been killed by him or deserted him. As if this fear of himself as his own potential murderer was not bad enough, he recognizes that, like all the ghosts of the people he has killed, he does not even pity himself. He has had no pity for his brother and the two princes, all of whom he has killed, so why should he feel pity for their killer?

By the time of his last battle Richard is on his own. Each action in his short cut to the top has estranged him from some group or ally that would now, given the coming battle, be very useful. He has succeeded in getting to run the country but he is alone; because he is alone he must fail.

The next day he loses the battle and his last words famously demonstrate how much the kingdom that he has been killing for all his life is worth. At that moment all he would be prepared to exchange it for is a horse. The end of the play does not simply end with his death, since in Shakespeare's time death in itself did not 'teach a sufficient lesson'. He dies humiliatingly, showing the fruitlessness of all that ambition.

It is even more poignant that Richard had been born into a class that was never short of horses to ride. Yet at the end of all his successful plotting, ambition and killing he is prepared to plead to exchange the results for something that he has always had in any case. In concluding with the phrase 'my kingdom for a horse!' Shakespeare demonstrates the futility of Richard's ambition.

The isolation of Richard's ambition is extreme, but the process we have traced is of some importance for all modern managers to understand. We cannot simply claim that 'ambition is bad' – that is much too simple. However, we have seen that an encompassing ambition, one that excludes others from its hopes and actions, will isolate. The combination of ambition and pure individualism creates the isolation. Shakespeare's

Richard shows us that a clear ambition, combined with an extreme will to act under all circumstances can, against all the odds, succeed. Six people between you and the crown can all in various ways and at various times die or be killed. But this process means you are left with so little trust that nobody really knows what you are thinking and what you are going to do next. When you have threatened everybody you are isolated.

Shakespeare wanted to show that such a path to power may 'work' but would be ultimately self-defeating. Power, even monarchical power, cannot be used without other people who trust you. Power, even 400 years ago, needed other people to help the ambitious to hold on to it. Individualized ambition can bring success, but at the same time it brings disaster.

The same is even more true with power at the turn of the new millennium. Managers can climb a greasy pole to the top and can achieve a great deal of power this way. On the way up, as they achieve their goal, it is very easy to lose everyone's trust. As each individual's trust, as each relationship, is lost, it appears that each one on its own doesn't matter. But when the goal is achieved you are alone and cannot wield the power on your own.

Modern management theorists emphasize how leaders create succesful relationships with followers:

> Leadership is many things. It is patient, usually boring coalition building. It is the purposeful seeding of cabals that one hopes will result in the appropriate ferment in the bowels of the organisation, It is meticulously shifting the attention of the institution through the mundane language of management systems. It is altering agendas so that new priorities get enough attention. It is being visible when things are going awry, and invisible when they are working well. It's building a loyal team at the top that speaks more or less with one voice. It's listening carefully much of the time, frequently speaking with encouragement, and reinforcing words with believable action.
>
> (Peters and Waterman, 1982: 82)

Peters and Waterman list the small, difficult things that a leader must do to have any followers and to shape history. By the end of Shakespeare's *Richard III* we are left with a very clear picture of what happens if you fail to follow this slow, meticulous work of building relationships.

Chapter 7

*M*ACBETH

'To know my deed 'twere best not know myself'

Shakespeare's Macbeth also kills his way to a throne. The play was written nine years after *Richard III* but there are many similarities, as Wells (1994: 282) notes: 'Macbeth himself is more like Richard III than any of the intervening protagonists. Both men are great warriors who come to the throne not by warfare but by murder.'

They are both isolated leaders who change history, not for others, not for their supporters, but for themselves. They are classic cases of leaders who place their own selves above everything. This is an important issue for leadership. The common sense version that we all have of how to be a great leader is to be a powerful individual. Since leadership, at some time or another, must become enshrined in an individual, then it is important that that individual has the personal capacity and charisma to carry it off. What is interesting both about Shakespeare's leaders and about the way in which modern management talks about leadership is that the individual character who enshrines leadership, whilst being a strength, is also a great problem.

Peter Drucker sums up this type of manager:

The leaders who work most effectively, it seems to me, never say 'I'. And that is not because they have trained themselves not to say 'I'. They don't think 'I'. They think 'we'; and they think 'team'. They understand their job to be to make the team function. They accept the responsibility and don't side-step it, but 'we' gets the credit. There is an identification (very often, quite unconscious) with the task and with the group. This is what creates trust, what enables you to get the task done.

(Drucker, 1990: 14)

This is a very important lesson because it is counter-intuitive. All leaders are usually painted as individuals who above all else have a clear and arrogant sense of their selves. Drucker demonstrates why this must not be the case, but interestingly so does Shakespeare 400 years earlier. Shakespeare's Macbeth demonstrates just how bad it gets if the leader only understands what it is to be an 'I'.

Whilst I will explore some of the similarities between the two Shakespearean characters there are also some important differences. Richard starts his play plotting to take the crown. Shakespeare's Macbeth starts the play as a king's loyal subject. He appears to have spent his life in valued and loyal service.

Shakespeare introduces Macbeth in the second scene in his absence. He has just put down a rebellion against the king and then immediately destroyed an invasion from Norway. Both of these he achieves with extreme and bloody personal violence. A sergeant reports that in the rebellion Macbeth cut through the rebel army in search of the rebel leader:

> *Till he faced the slave;*
> *Which ne'er shook hands, nor bade farewell to him,*
> *Till he unseam'd him from the nave to the chaps,*
> *And fix'd his head upon our battlements*
> **Macbeth**, Act 1 Scene 2 lines 21–24

And then when he attacks the Norwegian force Macbeth is reported as being covered in others' blood ('they meant to bathe in reeking wounds' *Macbeth*, Act 1 Scene 2, line 40).

These two pictures describe a brave man but they also describe someone who is steeped in violence and blood. Shakespeare writes these two reports at the very beginning of the play to let us know the measure of the Macbeth he is describing. This Macbeth doesn't just kill opponents but cuts them from their navel to their jaw. He doesn't just fight to win but bathes in the blood of the wounds of the people he has vanquished. It was not necessary for Shakespeare to use such language. He could have reported on Macbeth's bravery and left it at that. Instead he selects these images to ensure that we link Macbeth with violence and the love of violence.

At the beginning of the play Macbeth uses this violence for the king. He slaughters people, and his enjoyment of this slaughter doesn't seem to worry people because he is killing out of loyalty. No one worries that he really loves killing. As a result of this loyal slaughter the king gives him a new title, thereby encouraging his lust for blood.

Macbeth *The service and the loyalty I owe,*
In doing it, pays itself. Your highness' part
Is to receive our duties; and our duties
Are to your throne and state, children and servants,
Which do but what they should, by doing every thing
Safe towards your love and honour
Macbeth, Act 1 Scene 4 lines 23–28

The payment Macbeth expects for his violent service to the king is to be found in loyalty being its own reward. Shakespeare paints Macbeth's king as a great man, symbolizing all that is good about being a monarch.

The king's greatness is emphasized later in the play when Macbeth has killed him. Macduff, having found the king's body, describes what has happened apocalyptically:

Confusion now hath made his masterpiece!
Most sacrilegious murder hath broke ope
The Lord's anointed temple and stole thence
The life o' the building!
Macbeth, Act 2 Scene 3 lines 73–76

The death of the true king is sacrilegious. It is a masterpiece of confusion and will steal the life from the building. This death turns the world upside-down, yet we know it was committed by someone who starts the play as the epitome of loyalty.

So how does Macbeth turn from being a bloody but loyal follower of a true and great king to being his murderer? First, as I have already hinted, Macbeth is steeped in blood and seems to enjoy killing. Since he has this relationship with violence, at any time he has the means at hand to kill the king. This is not a little matter. If killing is simply routine for someone then they can learn to kill inappropriately. Enjoying slashing someone in two with a sword may mean that you end up not really minding who you do it to at all. Macbeth's king made Macbeth a killer and the king was able to use that killing for his own kingdom. Macbeth's king dies because he has created Macbeth's love of killing.

In a modern organization leaders at the top may well encourage their middle managers to break all sorts of taboos and rules for the good of the organization. Occasionally, under such guidance from the top, middle managers may become expert at immoral or rule-breaking behaviour. Senior managers may well feel that such behaviour is all right as long as it achieves the organization's goals. If their subordinates have to break the odd rule to gain that, all is well.

Further, one of the middle managers may well become an expert in this sort of rule breaking. Such expertise in the service of the company will be celebrated and may even be rewarded (as was Macbeth's). Within such a set of organizational incentives something potentially destructive is being constructed. Nick Leeson, the rogue trader in Baring's Singapore operation, was richly rewarded for his behaviour – for a time – but destruction quickly followed.

Second, and famously, the witches predict that Macbeth will be king. They put the thought of ambition into his head, but the thought remains just that – a possibility. Macbeth is different from Richard III because he does not, from the very first, set out to plot his gaining of the crown. Instead he starts loyal but becomes confused by the prospect of perhaps one day being king:

> *This supernatural soliciting*
> *Cannot be ill, cannot be good…*
> *that function*
> *Is smother'd in surmise, and nothing is*
> *But what is not.*
> **Macbeth**, Act 1 Scene 3 lines 130–31 and 140–41

What he has been told will happen by the witches ('supernatural soliciting') is that he will become king. For Macbeth this is both 'ill' and 'good'. He doesn't know what will happen, and knows less what to do when 'nothing is But what is not'. It is difficult to imagine a more ambivalent set of sentences. The thing that he wants to become is real in his mind (it *is*) but is not real in the world (it *is not*). It exists in both those states at once. In this way two futures exist side by side for a while. He doesn't spring from loyalty to treachery in one bound – he is really confused. This is partly because of the nature of where the thought has come from. There was a confusion in Shakespeare's day about witches and what they do as there is a modern confusion about predictions and star signs.

If your star sign says you are going to have a wonderful day and make a lot of money, what is confusing is whether you personally have to do anything about it or whether it's just going to happen. Surely a prediction is something that will just happen? But wouldn't it be a good idea to do something like the lottery to help the prediction on its way? If you stay in bed all day will it still come true?

The witches say Macbeth will be king. Does he have to do anything at all? Will it happen without his actions? He continues his thoughts:

If chance will have me king, why, chance may crown me,
Without my stir…
Come what come may,
Time and the hour runs through the roughest day.
Macbeth, Act 1 Scene 3 lines 143–44 and 145–46

This is a sharp difference from Richard III. Richard knew from the very beginning that if he was to become king he would have to kill several people. The notion did not enter his head that he would become king without his *stir*ring. But for Macbeth there is the hope that chance will have him king and he will have to do nothing. He ends thinking come what may, time will pass ('time and the hour runs through the roughest day') and the passage of time will make things happen.

The conflict between the picture the witches held up to him of himself as future king and his loyalty to the king continues for several scenes. It is true that Lady Macbeth is on one side in this debate – she wants Macbeth to become king by any means – but he remains ambivalent right up to the killing and even after he has killed the king. His actions are the same as Richard's, become king by any means (including slaughter), but with Richard there is no ambivalence. The outcome is the same, but the ambivalence is entirely different. In the end the deed is done for reasons that he really never understands, except ambition. This may seem an obvious point to make about leaders and leadership, but good leaders have to be able to sustain a great deal of stress in making very difficult decisions.

Being emotionally secure and strong provides the basis for open and useful interpersonal interactions. Leaders who aren't find such interactions hard and can, as we shall see with Macbeth, get blown off course. Shakespeare's Macbeth demonstrates what happens if a leader has no integrity.

People will not follow people who they think have no integrity. This is not simply a moral matter – that followers won't like people who lack integrity – but a material one. When you follow people you follow their judgement. If this looks as if it can be moved around by events then it is dangerous to give them any credibility since you may find yourself following people who do odd things.

It is difficult to give Macbeth much credibility for his integrity. His life is changed by ambition, and that ambition takes root because some witches tell him something is going to happen. His whole life is changed because of something he is told that feeds his ambition. Such changed activity does not give confidence.

In the speech just before he kills the king he weighs up the arguments on either side. He starts by reflecting on the reasons for his loyalty to the king, since he is not only king but a guest in Macbeth's household.

> *He's here in double trust;*
> *First, as I am his kinsman and his subject,*
> *Strong both against the deed; then, as his host,*
> *Who should against his murderer shut the door,*
> *Not bear the knife myself. Besides, this Duncan*
> *Hath borne his faculties so meek, hath been*
> *So clear in his great office, that his virtues*
> *Will plead like angels, trumpet-tongued, against*
> *The deep damnation of his taking-off;*
> **Macbeth**, Act 1 Scene 7 lines 12–20

So there are many reasons not to kill the king: Macbeth is related to the king, is his subject and is his host. On top of that Duncan has not only been a a great king but has also been a nice man. So why kill him? Macbeth continues:

> *I have no spur*
> *To prick the sides of my intent, but only*
> *Vaulting ambition, which o'erleaps itself*
> *And falls on the other.*
> **Macbeth**, Act 1 Scene 7 lines 25–27

So the only reason he can find on this side of the argument is his ambition. Fuelled by witches and his wife, that side of him wins the argument and he kills the king.

The ambivalence about this murder could be construed as a manager making a careful decision and weighing up the pros and cons, as evidenced by the two aspects of this speech. But in fact this crucial decision that will change Macbeth's life and the nation's is not well made.

Leaders and managers have to make decisions all the time – this represents one of their main activities. Management literature has a variety of different ways of describing this, but there are usually several steps involved:

> Among writers on decision making there is broad agreement on the main phases or steps of the process.
> *Making the decision*: the analytic, synthetic and valuing methods of thinking then get to work exploring and weighing the different courses of action. The facets of doing this are listing the advantages and disadvantages; examining the consequences of each course; measuring against standard criteria and values; testing beside the yardstick of the aim or objective; weighing the risks against the expected gain.
> *Implementing the decision*: the process is not complete unless it is *implemented*.
> (Adair, 1984: 108)

The quite straightforward injunctions to managers to undertake decision analysis demonstrate how Shakespeare writes Macbeth as failing. Readers may think it is harsh to judge a medieval Scottish noble by such criteria, but let us not forget that Shakespeare's Macbeth is making a decision that will bring him to the throne of a kingdom. Once there he will have to run an entire country – day after day he will make decisions that will affect thousands of people. This particular decision he keeps putting off making and, in the end, after going round and round, seems to make it out of carelessness. This is the most important decision of his life but he can't really seem to bring himself to make it except in an offhand way.

So how does he measure up the injunctions of:

1. specifying the aim;
2. examining the consequences of each course;
3. measuring against standard criteria and values;
4. testing beside the yardstick of the aim or objective;
5. weighing the risks against the expected gain; and
6. implementing the decision?

Specifying the aim

It is true that Macbeth specifies the aim clearly. He wants to be king and he also specifies the way of getting there, by killing the king.

Examining the consequences of each course

He considers in the last speech quoted above the list of consequences on both sides of the decision and comes to the conclusion that the only reason for killing the king is that he, Macbeth, is ambitious. So, even in private discussion with himself, he is going ahead, not because he thinks he will make a better king for Scotland, not because his country needs him, but simply because he wants to have this job.

There seems to be very little thought of how he will run the country and how the country will be run without the dead king. His analysis of what factors are necessary for the choice to succeed are very limited indeed. He seems to give no thought at all to what will happen once the king is dead and he is king. What is it all for? What does he want to do with Scotland? Very little except be king it would seem, which is why Shakespeare gives him such a difficult time when he becomes king. The only thing he wanted to do was to sit on Duncan's throne, and that is about all he does.

Measuring against standard criteria and values

This is very weak indeed. Against any set of values this action is wrong. It will not only look bad but everybody will know it is bad. Duncan is a good king and a good man – it is not as if Macbeth can pretend he is a tyrant or selling out the nation to the Norwegians. Since the only reason Macbeth can find for killing him is that he, Macbeth, is ambitious, this will never be a good deed.

Testing beside the yardstick of the aim or objective

Testing the decision and its implementation against the objective is also a very big problem. Since the decision is to become a king by killing a king, once you have become a king in this way you are only a murder away from losing the throne yourself. This method of getting there undermines the security of being a king. There are many decisions like this, for example wanting to gain a period of stability and calm in an organization, but doing so through a firestorm of instability and anxiety. If it worked then the method would undermine the calm by opening up the possibility of somebody else doing it.

Weighing the risks against the expected gain

Macbeth's analysis of the risks inherent in the decision is poor. He only thinks of an alibi at the very moment he has killed the king. He just seems to assume that once he is king everything will be all right. Later in the play he seems surprised that he has to go on killing in order to keep the throne. Everyone who might know about his killing of the king has in turn to be slaughtered. His life disintegrates into a sort of long surprise at the mistake that he made. This lack of foresight into the future is, again, not unusual amongst managers. It is sometimes impossible to see beyond the decision itself to what will happen afterwards – yet the only point in making the decision is to get to the point after it has been achieved.

Implementing the decision

Macbeth is clearest, crystal clear, about the kind of action that is necessary to bring about the decision. Indeed it is this that dominates the whole decision. It is as if he is known for one thing, for one skill that overrides all others – he is good at killing people – so to carry out this decision he chooses his best skill to become king. It is possible that there were other ways of getting there. Obviously the king felt Macbeth was a great warrior. His kingdom depended upon Macbeth's skills as a warrior – so why not discuss sharing the kingdom? Why not become the king's heir? These were possibilities, but such a method of making the change would have needed someone with a much broader range of skills. For Macbeth there is only one method – murder – and in the end the outcome of the decision, running Scotland, is completely overwhelmed by this simple method of getting there. This is not uncommon. Managers make the decision to get somewhere by a certain route and the means completely dominate the end when they get there. If you are good at a particular means of getting somewhere then you might as well use that means to get to all sorts of different places.

For Macbeth this failure to link the method of carrying out the decision – murder – which he seems to find easy, with the making of the decision and life afterwards – both of which he seems to find very difficult – ruins his life. Even immediately after he has killed the king he remains ambivalent:

> *To know my deed, 'twere best not know myself.*
> *Wake Duncan with thy knocking! I would thou couldst!*
> **Macbeth**, Act 2 Scene 2 lines 73–74

This is very extreme ambivalence and beautifully put by Shakespeare. Having thought about it for some time, he has just murdered the king. But the moment after the killing he recognizes that he must now not know himself – he must change completely. He must become the person that the deed dictates he is. His life is redefined by that act. He starts by believing that he is defining the act, he is in charge of the decision, but in fact he becomes defined by the act and by the decision and through this becomes another person.

After the deed has been done Shakespeare still has him acting for some time as someone who has very little idea why he did it. From that moment he has to live the rest of his life in a different world. He seems very unprepared for the kingship that he has killed for.

There is a further difference from Richard's killing. Richard barely hid his killings. He chose not to hide evidence of his hired assassins. His power and ideas were outside the moral universe of others and therefore fear would stop any real retribution.

Macbeth's killing of the king is different because he is ambivalent about the action. He also frames the murdered king's sons for the murder and hopes that the investigation will believe that they did it. He then continues the slaughter by killing anyone who knew, including his closest friend Banquo and Macduff's wife and children. In this he is doing what he knows how to do well, that is kill. By the time his wife dies and the end is beckoning he seems to care little about his life or the future:

> *She should have died hereafter;*
> *There would have been a time for such a word.*
> *To-morrow, and to-morrow, and to-morrow,*
> *Creeps in this petty pace from day to day*
> *To the last syllable of recorded time,*
> *And all our yesterdays have lighted fools*
> *The way to dusty death. Out, out, brief candle!*
> *Life's but a walking shadow, a poor player*
> *That struts and frets his hour upon the stage*
> *And then is heard no more: it is a tale*
> *Told by an idiot, full of sound and fury,*
> *Signifying nothing.*
> **Macbeth**, Act 5 Scene 5 lines 17–28

So at the end of this story of ambition Shakespeare writes a conclusion that not only leaves Macbeth killed, but his wife too. He ends up believing that his life has been a tale 'told by an idiot, full of sound and fury' but 'signifying nothing' at all. It is difficult to think of a more empty way of looking at the life of a king than 'signifying nothing', especially when at one stage of your life you had 'vaulting ambition' for the job.

What is Shakespeare telling us about the results of Macbeth's ambition and the methods of his gaining the kingship? Whilst it is about ambition, the nature of the ambition and the actions that flow from it are very different from those of Richard III, who spent years trying to manipulate the world to make himself king. His rise was plotted by him actively year by year, whilst Macbeth is casual. He is living a life within social boundaries loyal to his king, whom he admires, when suddenly it is suggested to him that one day he will be king and he begins to dwell on that possibility. As the ambition grows he hopes he may gain his goal by doing nothing; he is unsure whether to act on the suggestions, and in the end does so. Although the turning point of the play, this is undertaken very casually. The only reason for killing the king is simple ambition – he is grabbed strongly by something, but has no real reason apart from his ambition for carrying it out. Just before the act and afterwards he *is* thinking of not doing it – but once it is done his life is changed. He gains what he wants but the method of his achieving his ambition turns his life into nothing.

It is difficult to imagine Shakespeare writing this play without intending these twin messages to be the core of the narrative: the power of ambition taking over someone who seems happy enough, and then the casualness of an awful deed like murder. It would be easy for someone to casually murder someone else having spent most of their life killing people and bathing in blood. So the ability to transgress in this particular way, that is killing someone, comes from previous experience. Macbeth does what he has always done well, but in a new context. He kills a king and ruins his life.

What lessons are there for modern managers? There are three main issues. First, Shakespeare demonstrates the immense power ambition has to change your life and potentially ruin it. The portrayal of ambition here is like a malignant growth in Macbeth, once it has touched him it eventually takes him over. There are similar experiences in modern organizations. A casual remark about the possibilities of managers progressing up the organization, can catch hold of them and transform their lives. They begin to think of little else, and unless they control the ambition it will take over their working life and in some cases render them useless. Given the extent to which individual ambition is a ubiquitous part of the modern organization the chances of being 'touched' by it are quite high.

Second, once managers are in this frame of mind they can act against their long-term interests very easily and quite casually. Ambition is a dangerous thing with which to be walking around an organization, since a manager can quite easily find an opportunity to use the emotion. If the manager is ambitious it is important to keep it in check and not give in to it capriciously.

Third, as we outlined above, once an organization has encouraged a manager to become skilled in at best a morally dubious and at worst a morally wrong activity, that skill can easily be turned to inappropriate ends.

Chapter 8

CORIOLANUS

Leading from the front is not enough

Coriolanus is a play about conflict: between nations, between parts of a nation, between members of a family and, most importantly, within the character after whom the play was named. This conflict is carried out both in battles and in words and is unremitting, with very few 'soft' scenes or characters.

Much of management is about conflict. Not about battles but about organizations, groups and individuals trying to achieve goals that are in conflict with others. I find it difficult to imagine how managers can ever be successful if they are afraid of conflict, yet for some the moment conflict appears it knocks them off course. Yet we all recognize that it is a normal part of the context within which we work. Managers must expect conflict to be a part of their day in the same way that time and its passage is a part of any day at work. And just as a manager has to be able to factor time into all of his or her activities, so it is essential to be able to do the same with conflict. A successful manager's knowledge that different periods of time have very different consequences for a project or the success of an organization applies equally to conflict.

Shakespeare's *Coriolanus* is worth reading as a story because it highlights the way in which conflict talks place and, like watching newsreel footage of a real battle, it makes you realize just how nasty it can get. In showing how bad it can get it almost prepares you for what it is like. Of course nothing can prepare you for what you will feel when you are engaged in real, clashing conflict, but good drama can nearly achieve that. As someone who has never shot at anyone, or been shot at, I can only guess what it is like. If one day I knew I had to do it, apart from spending a few hours shooting at targets and learning how to keep my head down, I would spend some time reading *Coriolanus* to prepare me for the moment when I might have to kill (or be killed).

LEARNING TO LIVE WITH THE MANAGEMENT OF CONFLICT OR LEARNING TO LOVE IT

In management terms I have been involved in a lot of conflict. Sometimes it gets very sharp and, whilst not life threatening, it is scary. It is important to remember that it's probably very wise to be scared – your reputation and sometimes your job are at stake, and if you get blasé about that you will inevitably make mistakes. In most large organizations there are people who are only happy if they are engaged in a row – and, crucially, if there isn't one going on at the time they will make it happen. So whilst it is vital to learn to live with managing conflict, beware what happens if you learn to love it.

Shakespeare's Coriolanus is someone who fails to make the distinction between living with conflict and loving it. As we shall see, he is only happy in a battle – in modern parlance he has become a conflict 'junkie' who cannot operate without it. When confronted with some quite simple management activities outside of a raging battle he cannot cope. He is a great leader, but one who can only lead with a single mode of operation; if that changes he is lost.

The play is not simply about conflict, but also about being responsible, not just for playing a part in conflict but in leading it. As I have said, in management conflict arises all the time and we have to get used to it. Egos and organizations clash and we have to deal with the waves when that occurs. However, conflict is a very different experience when you are responsible for it, when you are making it happen, when you are making it work. Working within it is one problem, taking the responsibility for starting it and implementing it is another. Under these circumstances the responsibility for success and failure is all yours. When the occasion arises *you* decide whether to keep it going or, if that is impossible, stop it. In Act 4, before the battle of Agincourt, Henry V has to think not only of his own death but of the deaths of thousands and the possible loss of his nation to a foreign power. That is because he is leading a conflict and not just being a part of it.

Most of Shakespeare's plays about conflict contain important insights into what life is like for ordinary people caught in the middle of these conflicts. Their continuing concern is about the actions and feelings of those who are leading the conflict and, in the case of Coriolanus, a character who not only relishes the experience but is diminished when it stops.

The entire play, *Coriolanus*, is all about the leader, how he behaves and what he thinks. Coriolanus is written as a great wartime leader. As such when the battle is raging he is always actively involved in the bloodiest part. Whilst we never see some of Shakespeare's other leaders actually fighting and killing people on the battlefield, Coriolanus is on several occasions covered in the blood of his dead enemies.

This particular form of leadership means that there are two main ways in which Coriolanus could be described. In modern terms people would say: 1) he leads from the front; and 2) he leads by example. Both these descriptions of management styles are usually seen as good, providing as they do active leadership and a good model for change. Why Shakespeare's Coriolanus is such an important play for managers is that his portrayal of these styles is very clear. But the play also shows what happens if the example and the leading from the front lead to a separation from your organization, its 'troops' and its humanity. Leadership without sufficient contact with the followers ends up being purely by example, and not by being involved with the lives and aspirations of the followers. The problem then is separation from the lives of people who are expected to follow. The end result of leaders just doing this is fatal both for them and their cause. Coriolanus chose to lead by personal example. However, his example of extra personal bravery is impossible to follow.

Coriolanus is represented as an individual leader of almost supernatural proportions. In the play we see him as a warrior-leader brilliantly motivating his troops to almost impossible victories. We see it and therefore we believe it, but it is *almost* unbelievable since he reaches such godlike heights. From the early part of the play this is also how people talk about him, for example:

Cominius *It is held*
That valour is the chiefest virtue, and
Most dignifies the haver: if it be,
The man I speak of cannot in the world
Be singly counterpoised.
Coriolanus, Act 2 Scene 2 lines 88–92

Valour is the best virtue to have and this man has it more than any other. In fact since none in the world has more of it he must be outside of the world to be that good: Coriolanus is so good at what he does he must be a god; because he is a god he is separate from us. His success as a godlike exemplary leader means that none of us can really be like him since we are mere mortals.

So there are problems with up-front, visionary leaders. Tom Peters outlines the various components that all have to coexist if such leaders are going to work:

Visions are aesthetic and moral – as well as strategically sound. Visions come from within – as well as from outside. They are personal – and group centred. Developing a vision and values is a messy, artistic process. Living it convincingly is a passionate one, beyond any doubt. Posters and wallet-sized cards declaring the visions and corporate values may be helpful, but they may not be. In fact, they can hinder and make a mockery of the process if the vision and values are merely proclaimed, but not lived convincingly.

(Peters, 1989: 401)

There are four components of leading through vision:

1. The vision has to be important and not ephemeral.
2. It has to be lived and not simply external to the organization.
3. Creating clear visions is a messy process.
4. The vision must involve followers as well as leaders in its construction and implementation.

We are used to seeing leadership as primarily about the first two. Great, passionate people leading by example, living their lives and actions around clear, articulated goals that they believe in. When this happens, people follow. Peters suggests that for success it is crucial to add the other two elements to this process.

Leaders must involve the people who they expect to live the vision with them. People will not follow something through thick and thin that they have had no part in creating, and this process of creating a vision is a difficult and messy one.

So, given the personal involvement of Coriolanus in winning battles, given his clear personal leadership, is he a great leader to learn from? Despite the way in which Coriolanus as a war leader wins victory after victory Shakespeare has him ending the play with not only his death but his complete humiliation. We need therefore to understand the whole lesson that Shakespeare is giving us through his Coriolanus. If there is something to learn from the totality of Shakespeare's Coriolanus it is important to think through the reasons for his failure. As we shall see he is very good at leading, but appalling at involving his followers, for whom he has no regard at all.

LEADING BY UNREASONABLE EXAMPLE WILL LEAD TO SEPARATION FROM YOUR STAFF

Coriolanus not only leads from the front but he leads with his own body in the battle. In modern terms we would say that he definitely 'walked the talk'. The description of him after a battle is used to personify the victory. This speech explains how he had turned a retreat into a victory by stopping his men from fleeing.

Cominius *he stopp'd the fliers;*
And by his rare example made the coward
Turn terror into sport: as weeds before
A vessel under sail, so men obey'd
And fell below his stem: his sword, death's stamp,
Where it did mark, it took; from face to foot
He was a thing of blood, whose every motion
Was timed with dying cries: alone he enter'd
The mortal gate of the city, which he painted
With shunless destiny; aidless came off,

And with a sudden re-inforcement struck
Corioli like a planet:
Coriolanus, Act 2 Scene 2 lines 108–19

This is an awesome picture. By his 'rare example' he stops his men from retreating and, with his sword, cuts the enemy in two 'from face to foot'. He wins a big battle single handed and, just in case you miss out on his personal involvement in the slaughter, Shakespeare has him leading by example and becoming 'a thing of blood'.

We have already seen these deeds – this speech reports action that has already been on stage, so Shakespeare, who rarely wasted a major speech or scene by writing them twice, must have been underlining the point about his main character. First, we know it is no exaggeration. It is not just that Coriolanus fights bravely and with great danger to himself, but he leads through these actions. Through his personal actions he really changes events. This is not simply a great general but one who shares with his troops the arduous nature of battle.

At the beginning of the above speech Cominius finds it difficult to find words to describe what the play's audience (although not the audience on the stage) has already seen:

I shall lack voice: the deeds of Coriolanus
Should not be utter'd feebly.
Coriolanus, Act 2 Scene 2 lines 86–88

His relationship as a fellow leader of Rome with Coriolanus is that the latter's actions are so special that he will not have words to describe him. He 'lacks voice' to describe what has happened. Coriolanus's actions as a warrior are almost beyond words – he is so much greater than other people that human words cannot really encompass him.

Cominius's speech goes on to describe the main attribute that Coriolanus as a leader is given throughout the play. He is virtuous, a characteristic that is above all others, and there is nobody in the world who can compare with his virtuousness (be 'singly counterpoised'). So he has more virtue than anyone else, and is a bolder fighter. Surely this is the perfect characteristic for a leader. It is important that Shakespeare's Coriolanus is built up to such heights because it is these very characteristics as a leader that will cause him such problems and in the end lead to his humiliation and death.

Again and again Shakespeare paints Coriolanus as a valiant battle leader who does not believe in retreat or defeat. Since he does not believe in retreat he does not allow his troops to do so. Marcius[1] says:

> *Are you Lords o' the field?*
> *If not, why cease you till you are so?*
> **Coriolanus**, Act 1 Scene 6 lines 47–48

So Coriolanus is saying stay and fight, and as a good leader and in nearly every battle he shows how to do it with his own body. But his appeal to his soldiers is always from a very separate person, a person whose very valour separates him from his troops. Even at moments when he is physically close to his soldiers, when he is going into battle, he asks his troops to turn him into a weapon, and thus underlines his difference from them: 'O me alone! make you a sword of me?' (*Coriolanus*, Act 1 Scene 6, line 76).

As he says he 'alone' can do these things, he 'alone' can be made into a sword to slaughter the enemy. These are incredibly strong images of a particular style of leadership. He urges the troops to turn him into an instrument that they can use to slaughter their opponents and when he becomes such an instrument he is obviously not a man like others.

Throughout the play others pick up on the importance that this separation plays in his leadership. A soldier describes him:

> *he is himself alone,*
> *To answer all the city.*
> **Coriolanus**, Act 1 Scene 4 lines 50–51

Coriolanus underlines the other aspect of this separation by rallying his troops with insults and abuse.

---

1. Coriolanus starts the play with the name 'Marcius'. Owing to his bravery at the battle of Corioles, he is awarded the name 'Coriolanus'.

Marcius *You shames of Rome! you herd of – Boils and plagues*
Plaster you o'er, that you may be abhorr'd
Further than seen and one infect another
Against the wind a mile! You souls of geese,
That bear the shapes of men, how have you run
From slaves that apes would beat!
Coriolanus, Act 1 Scene 4 lines 30–36

These words demonstrate to his troops (and crucially to the audience) the fact that he is different from them. This difference is not only concerned with that between the leader and the led, but shows that for Coriolanus the difference is a chasm between himself and his troops. Look at the images here. Coriolanus is referred to by others as a god. He refers to his troops as boils, plagues, geese and less than apes. These are deliberate and considered subhuman images. As a form of motivation it may work in the short term but surely does so by diminishing the people who should be motivated by it in the longer term.

Compare this speech at a turning point of a battle to Henry V in the next Part before the walls of Harfleur. Henry raises his troops to his equal, Coriolanus diminishes them to several levels of the food chain beneath him. Coriolanus demonstrates that he believes in his own separateness from them; Henry, their close relationship.

As early as the first scene, when talking to his troops, he underlines this separation:

Marcius *He that will give good words to thee will flatter*
Beneath abhorring. What would you have, you curs,
That like not peace nor war? the one affrights you,
The other makes you proud. He that trusts to you,
Where he should find you lions, finds you hares;
Where foxes, geese: …
He that depends
Upon your favours swims with fins of lead
Coriolanus, Act 1 Scene 1 lines 165–70 and 177–78

Coriolanus is outlining his hatred for the people: they are cowards in war, they are fickle, they favour the undeserving, and they need to be kept in awe or they prey on one another. He lets the audience know that he despises the very people he is fighting for and the troops that he leads so bravely.

Every modern approach to leadership and management demonstrates that this relationship with followers based upon control simply does not work:

> The philosophy of management by direction and control – regardless of whether it is hard or soft – is inadequate to motivate because the human needs on which this approach relies are relatively unimportant motivators of behaviour in our society today. Direction and control are of limited value in motivating people whose important needs are social and egotistic.
>
> (McGregor, 1966: 73)

Many managers have very simple relationships with the people they manage: they tell them what to do. This direction is based upon a very simple view of motivation with a very pre-modern notion of man. McGregor points out that modern people, with a wider set of social and personal motivations, cannot be simply told what to do. Compared to the wider experiences of the social and personal world of the ego, direction has only a limited use. Yet it still remains one of the main ways in which managers try and motivate people.

In an earlier book Peter Drucker (1954: 297) complements this point by pointing out the other great motivator used by leaders through the ages: 'What we need is to replace the externally imposed spur of fear with an internal self-motivation for performance.' If we think of people as essentially a simple bundle of responses to stimuli, then fear seems like a really great motivator. Historically, it has always been one of the main ways in which leaders think they can manage people, but Shakespeare in Coriolanus points out how limited it is.

Why, then, if he doesn't like the people he is fighting for, does he fight? Shakespeare portrays Coriolanus as a driven person who again and again has to demonstrate his capacity to win battles; time and again he has to show how brave he is. A citizen says of him: 'though softconscienced men can be content to say it was for his country, he did it to please his mother, and to be partly proud which he is even to the altitude of his virtue' (*Coriolanus*, Act 1 Scene 1 lines 36–39).

As an explanation for continually leading armies into very dangerous situations, doing it to please your mother is of psychological but not historical importance. It is an example of Shakespeare's ability to make a very telling point that two acts later he has Coriolanus's mother demonstrating that in terms of their real relationship he did not have to be so driven:

> Volumnia *You might have been enough the man you are,*
> *With striving less to be so.*
> **Coriolanus**, Act 3 Scene 2 lines 19–20

His mother is saying forcefully that, my son you are mistaken, you didn't have to strive so much to get my love, you would have been just as big a man without all that blood, all those battles. Although Coriolanus may have felt that he had to do all these things to gain his mother's approval, in fact he didn't. She provides this insight in reply to his view of his own personality and his own role in the play:

> Coriolanus *Would you have me*
> *False to my nature? Rather say I play*
> *The man I am.*
> **Coriolanus**, Act 3 Scene 2 lines 14–16

One of Shakespeare's best points is the way in which he has his roles explaining to an audience that they are just that – roles. Coriolanus, in defensive reply to his mother's questioning, says he is the man he is, he can be no other. He does what he does because of who he is.

He is a driven person who leads the troops he despises into battle after battle; whilst he wins the battles he does so by an unreasonable refusal to recognize his troops' humanity and their fear. To dehumanize them we noted above that he classes them as subhuman things. As for himself, he can be no other than what he is; unlike others he cannot 'play another role'.

THE PROBLEM OF THE DRIVEN LEADER

We can recognize this unbending nature in managers we work with. They appear to be brilliant at leadership, they win and win again; but when they talk about their staff they demonstrate their separation and the way in which they despise them. Working with such managers is hard because they are so unreasonable about their expectations of their staff. They return to the fray again and again and you get the distinct impression that they are only happy in conflict, demonstrating their fearlessness.

To many people this looks like great leadership. But we know how fragile it really is. Such leaders are not in charge of themselves, and because they are not in charge of themselves they cannot in the long term strategically create events. So they search for fight after fight and even create fights, not because the organization needs them, but to meet their own psychological needs. Leaders that are driven, however good they are, are out of control.

Organizations cannot survive for long when they are led in this way. Modern management theorists all underline the importance of collegial relationships within the organization and how dangerous separation is.

> Dialogue can occur only when a group of people see each other as colleagues in a mutual quest for deeper insight and clarity. Thinking of each other as colleagues is important because thought is participative. The conscious act of thinking of each other as colleagues contributes toward interacting as colleagues. This may sound simple, but it can make a profound difference.
>
> (Senge, 1992: 245)

Peter Senge's point is that organizations cannot learn from the people inside them if authority relations separate the people from each other. His whole approach to the learning organization is a recognition that an organization can only really learn when there is mutual respect for other people's knowledge, wherever you are in the hierarchy. To achieve this needs a *conscious act* of thinking of each other as colleagues, and to achieve that people need to work at it.

Within Coriolanus's army there seem to be three groups in a hierarchy. The leader as a god, occasionally followers as men, and third, occasionally followers as worse than apes. These are not collegial relationships and consequently the organization has no capacity whatsoever to learn from its members.

WHAT HAPPENS TO CORIOLANUS?

How does Shakespeare deal with the end of Coriolanus? How does he portray the outcome of a godlike driven leader? Coriolanus spends most of the play defending Rome against the Volsci – on several occasions scattering Rome's enemies without mercy. However he feels slighted by the Romans and changes sides. He gathers a new army of his old enemies, the Volsci, around him and marches on Rome. Once more he is an automaton, attacking his old city without mercy – doing the thing he does best, but in the opposite direction from the way he used to do it.

The Romans send out emissaries of his old friends to try to persuade him not to slaughter them all. His mother and her friends plead with him, on their knees. For the first time in the play the common bond of humanity floods into Coriolanus from these women. The older women overturn his implacability and he turns back from the gates of Rome. But the experience is so very new to him that he cannot cope. For the rest of the play he sleepwalks through the action. There are no more battles, no more victories; he is undone by humanity. As one of his allies in the attack on Rome, Aufidius, says:

> *At a few drops of women's rheum, which are*
> *As cheap as lies, he sold the blood and labour*
> *Of our great action:*
> **Coriolanus**, Act 5 Scene 6 lines 46–48

A few women's tears destroy a great warrior because he was not at all prepared for the emotions that they let loose. To turn himself into a warrior he separates himself from human feelings. He lifts the seige of Rome and on his return to the Volsci he invites his own death. He is killed and he ends up with his body being stood on.

Touched just briefly by the humanity that he thought he was separated from, all his separation evaporates and he cannot operate at all. He is destroyed by the contact with the very relationship that he denied could affect him.

Shakespeare's lesson for the driven manager is a powerful one. Centuries before Freud he uncovers the relationship between being very driven and your mother. He makes the point that when you are driven you can achieve many things, many victories, and change events. But sooner or later humanity will burst through and at that stage humanity, a mother's tears, will destroy you as if it were an alien virus. It has been made an alien virus by the way in which you have denied its ability to affect you. Shakespeare paints the most powerful human link he can think of – a mother on her knees in front of her son, pleading with him for her own and her friends' lives. Imagine such a powerful human event.

In the face of this Coriolanus cannot cope. He links leadership with distance from humanity, so when he can no longer defend against humanity he cannot lead.

The most straightforward lesson concerns the dangers of this separation from humanity. It would appear that as a warrior-leader Coriolanus was brilliant precisely because he was separated from humanity. We can imagine people saying of him that because he was driven and single minded, without any concessions to human feeling, he would lead and manage clearly and with strength. In fact such managers are very weak, because sooner or later a small emotion will come crashing in and destroy their ability to manage at all.

CONCLUSIONS TO PART 3
SEPARATION FAILS FOR LEADERS

In many ways these three leaders are all modern men. They know that the world has to be made to work and that people and organizations need to be led to change that world. Whilst their main field of activity is war they all have an appreciation of the necessity to organize action.

Each of these characters has a specific lesson for modern managers, but taken as a trio they also raise a number of important issues. However beguiling the short-term success is for Richard III, Macbeth and Coriolanus, collapse and ruin lie ahead for them and their cause. Whilst they all seem to have successful styles for 'getting there' the leadership styles that bring them their success also bring them the inevitability of failure.

If they were analysed as case studies by modern management theorists each would be used to teach modern managers the dangers of authoritarianism. More than anything else Shakespeare wrote exciting but cautionary tales of how leaders turn to authoritarianism to make things happen quickly. In each of these plays the leaders believe they can only really do things if they have all the power to themselves. This need for personalized, total power and the need to get it through authoritarianism is successful, but it is also corrosive and must end in failure. It must end in failure because even if you have all the power of a monarch you cannot control everything, you cannot make everything do what it is told. This makes Shakespeare one of the most modern of management theorists, since his critique of authoritarianism is a major part of modern thought.

If Shakespeare had constantly to tell stories of leaders overreaching themselves through the dangers of authoritarianism, then this must have been one of the important features of leadership – how leaders actually worked. It would have been recognizable to his audiences as the way in which people tried to run things. Of course this is still true today – organizations suffer continually from managers trying to find an easy way of achieving something by simply telling people to do it. Time and again in modern organizations we experience this as a failing, but managers continue to turn to authoritarianism just to make things happen. Under pressure there seems to be a belief that shouting at the world to 'just do it' will work.

Much of modern management literature has this implicit critique of authoritarianism and, like Shakespeare, paints stories of its failure. Being authoritarian is something that managers will fall into if they don't stick to the higher and better systems and styles of management. It is a residual category of bad management:

> [Leaders] must be able to help people understand the systemic forces that shape change. It is not enough to intuitively grasp these forces. Many 'visionary strategists' have rich intuitions about the cause of change, intuitions they cannot explain. They end up being authoritarian leaders, imposing their strategies and policies or continuously interfering in decisions. They fall into this fate, even if their values are contrary to authoritarian leadership – because only they see the decisions that need to be made.
>
> (Senge,1992: 340)

Senge paints a picture that everyone who has ever worked in an organization can recognize in some managers: those who increasingly paint themselves into an authoritarian corner and because of that fail. In that way Richard III, Macbeth and Coriolanus still stand as examples of how to get there, but having got there *that way,* how to fail.

Part 4

*L*earning to be a heroic leader

Kenneth Branagh as Henry V (source: Kobal Collection)

Chapter 9

HENRY V

'All things are ready, if our minds be so'

Henry V is Shakespeare's great heroic leader. His character develops at the centre of three plays, culminating in his becoming the great national leader, so much so that in the dark days of the Second World War *Henry V* was made into a lavish film to remind the British of past patriotism and success. His is the one clear Shakespearean character to show us how to be a popular and successful leader. Much of this part of the book will chart the growth of this success and popularity and the lessons we can draw from it for modern management.

Above all the lessons for managers from Shakespeare's Henry concern his management of *people*. He listens to and talks with his troops in such a way as to motivate them to ever higher deeds of daring. This is a vital part of management. Despite all of the management theory and training underlining the importance of people to organizations this still remains the one issue managers flee from.

> In my experience, people can face almost any problem except the problems of people. They can work long hours, face declining business, face loss of jobs, but not the problems of people. Faced with problems of people (management included) management in my experience go into a state of paralysis, taking refuge in formation of QC Circles, and groups for EI, EP and QWL (Employee Involvement, Employee

Participation, and Quality of Work Life). These groups predictably disintegrate within a few months from frustration, finding themselves unwilling parties to a cruel hoax, unable to accomplish anything, for the simple reason that no one in management will take action on suggestions for improvement.

(Deming, 1982: 85)

We can all recognize the creation of the alphabet soup that is employee involvement, which can exist simply in order to distance managers from the people who work for them.

Managing people is hard because, however much managers would like their staff to act as if they were automatons, all staff have the real and difficult attributes of human beings: they think, feel and react all the time, and through every thought, emotion and action they add and subtract something to and from their manager's wishes. Unlike machines, no one does exactly what he or she is told. It is this interactivity that makes managers fearful of managing people since, unlike money or information, people talk back.

Told to do something, at the very least, they will end up asking why. At the very worst for an anxious manager they will come up with six compelling reasons why what you have asked them to do is wrong. Deming is right. Most managers recognize that managing people is very hard and too many of them try to duck it. That is why managers need all the help they can get in the management of people.

Shakespeare's Henry is a great leader because he recognizes that nothing can be achieved without the people he manages and leads. He recognizes too that he is in their hands, and at crucial moments if they don't perform well then he is bound to fail. Before turning to Henry's ability as a leader it is important to provide a note of caution about Shakespeare and heroics, one that can often be missed in all the yearning for simple hero worship.

Everyone wants to see their hero as purely good and great. We would all, in our dreams, wish to manage power and authority with no downside, to run our organizations with victories and roses all the way. As managers we want to be like that. Yet we recognize that, in our own difficult, compromised lives, we cannot be like that. As managers we struggle to perform unpleasant and difficult actions. It is inevitable that in place of this reality we want our heroes to be one-dimensional, beautiful and without complication. We turn to Shakespeare's Henry to provide that. After the dross and difficulties of his other leaders, we appear to have a one-dimensional hero who is 'the ideal image of the potentialities of the English character' (Mack, 1965: xxxv).

During the plays that concern his father's reign (*Henry IV Parts 1* and *2*) and that introduce Henry, he is often referred to as Prince Hal. One of their main themes concerns the way in which Hal develops into a great leader. This, together with all of *Henry V*, provides Shakespeare with the opportunity to develop a character not only rich in detail, but unfolding over 10 hours of drama. Over the three plays this appears to be a simple movement from evil to good. For managers in the real world development is not like that. Even at the pinnacle of success there are problems, anxieties and hard, nagging decisions to be made. The past can never be forgotten. What, in that past, was never pure wrong can never become pure right. Managers do grow and develop but they never become 'purely' good. We recognize that we are full of contradictions between good and bad, and that the way in which we veer between these two makes our work even more fraught. Our world of work is messy, complex and claims few shining heroic moments.

The first lesson I want to draw from Shakespeare's Henry is that this messy world is the world of Shakespeare's hero too. Shakespeare, even when writing a popular blockbuster like *Henry V*, never lets the audience fail to recognize compromise and contradiction. His cleanest heroes know that at their most heroic moment they carry out morally difficult and murky actions and deal with them in ambiguous ways. There are many lessons from Shakespeare's Hal about how to be a great leader, but don't look to Shakespeare for simple heroics about leadership. His message is hard: even if you reach the top, even if you defeat your enemies against all the odds, even if you get the girl as well, there are very dark moments. And they are at the core of senior management. Power is not clean. Even in success expect anguish, pain and compromise.

Great heroic success is not straightforward. Shakespeare's view is that when people wield power it is never clean and simple. Having power means getting yourself dirty, and exercising great power even at the cleanest moments of victory is to get yourself very dirty. As a manager, even when you win, expect sleepless nights, and compromises with bad and sad activity, with consequent moral ambiguities. If you expect anything else you do not live in the real world of power and you should not seek it out. Moral ambiguity, contradictions about action and compromised outcomes are normal. This stress on ambiguity is why Shakespeare is a great writer and has so much to teach us about how we manage large modern organizations. He demonstrates that management and organizations are never straightforward:

> The ambivalent practice and effect of Shakespeare's *Henry V* is by now a critical commonplace... the play's shifting portrayal of political power provides the fulcrum of its affective structure; the state appears alternately as beneficent or coercive.
>
> (Clare McEachern, 1995: 292)

It is not just the state and government that shift from dark to light, from one form to another throughout the play. Shakespeare writes of a leader who changes himself in order to be able to manage organizations and events that are good and bad. These are not simply abstract changes in the way in which Henry's realm works, the state and government in Shakespeare's plays are personified through the character of Henry V. Therefore it is this character who moves from light to dark, who sometimes leads like a knight in shining armour and sometimes like a wicked wizard.

As is usual with Shakespeare, the plot is played out through the characters in the narrative, leaving us as audience to learn, not in an abstract way, but through the way in which another individual works. There are three clear examples of the 'awfulness of power' and all come from the height of Henry's power in the play *Henry V*. They all take place in Henry's successful military campaign across northern France, and involve his leadership in life or death situations.

FROM HONOUR TO BARBARISM IN ONE DAY

I have already suggested that the main leadership activity Henry engages in is the management of people. In *Henry V* we see this taking place through a variety of activities, the most dramatic being his speeches to his troops around the battles they are involved in. These are not only some of the most famous passages in English literature, but are good examples of how to communicate very important messages at very difficult times. As we shall see Shakespeare develops the character of Henry in such a way as to ensure that he fully understands the culture of his troops. Henry builds upon his knowledge of his troops to suggest they can achieve great things. Each battle he fights is a complex organizational task that can only be fully achieved by really stretching his troops, which in turn can only be achieved by communicating complex management ideas about their coming activities in the battle. Above all he must communicate motivation. After all, it is likely that in the forthcoming battle some of his soldiers will die, and many will be expected to kill or maim others. Under these circumstances it is important that they want to follow him a great deal – motivation must be high.

John Harvey-Jones recognizes the importance of managers not only communicating to their staff but doing so in a way that stretches them:

> The art of 'growing people' lies to a great degree in this stretching process. First everybody in a well-run organisation should feel himself under some pressure... People's self-confidence grows when they achieve more. Each time they achieve more, an even more ambitious or difficult target needs to be set. I am firmly of the belief that most people in this world achieve only a fraction of what they are capable of... It is the responsibility of the leadership and management to give opportunities and put demands on people which enable them to grow as human beings in their work environment.
>
> (Harvey-Jones, 1988: 62)

This extract argues that the role of the good manager is one of 'growing people', and Harvey-Jones has no doubt that the only way to achieve this is by stretching them fully in their work situation to make them achieve a great deal more than they think they can. This view of human nature has important implications for how managers act. Such a view means that managers who set 'easy targets' for their staff will fail them as human beings because they would fail to fully develop their potential. A good manager ensures that staff aim high, higher sometimes than they think they can achieve. The two main battles in *Henry V* are accompanied by great speeches, both aimed at growing Henry's troops.

The first is before the walls of the French town of Harfleur, where Henry's army is besieging the town. The siege has been difficult and Henry is impatient. Shakespeare's Henry V personally leads his army with great valour and, with a brilliant speech – one of the greatest speeches in world literature – joins his followers to his project. In the heat of a battle that has no sure outcome Henry rallies his troops and places his leadership and his life with them on the line:

And you, good yeomen,
Whose limbs were made in England, show us here
The mettle of your pasture; let us swear
That you are worth your breeding; which I doubt not;
For there is none of you so mean and base,
That hath not noble lustre in your eyes.
I see you stand like greyhounds in the slips,
Straining upon the start. The game's afoot:
Follow your spirit, and upon this charge
Cry 'God for Harry, England, and Saint George!'
Henry V, Act 3 Scene 1 lines 25–34

His assumption about his troops – that they are straining to get stuck into the battle like greyhounds in the slips – creates very high expectations of them. He expects them to work very hard and bravely for him, and assumes they will have these high aspirations for themselves.

At times of conflict between ourselves and a foe, this is the speech that all managers want to make to their staff. It starts with a challenge for Henry's troops to 'show [their] mettle'. This makes them realize that, whilst we are leaders and they are staff, we come from the same place and have the same interests. It claims that everyone, even those 'mean and base' has 'noble lustre in [their] eyes' and that they are worth their breeding. These are all very important aspects of motivation for soldiers to hear, especially spoken by a king. It assumes that they are desperate to fight side by side for the same objective as their leader, and to prove it you put yourself with them in the thick of it. You include your body and your name, 'Harry', at the centre of this fight.

All of us who have managed staff engaged in conflict know how important their support is. Equally we recognize how dangerous it is for a leader to set off on a charge into danger, because it is always possible that half-way through the charge, when you turn around and look, they have not followed – you find yourself on your own. It is one thing, in John Harvey-Jones's terms, to stretch people; it is another to know them well enough to know that they can achieve what you expect. Henry knew his troops would follow him. His speech and his knowledge come together in a great piece of leadership.

Shakespeare's Henry's speeches, both before the walls of Harfleur and later, before Agincourt, are masterpieces of communicated vision. Every modern management theorist talks about vision, and most underline the importance of a close relationship between the vision of the leader and that of the led.

Over 40 years ago Philip Selznick (1957: 149) underlined this process as one that transforms the technical relationship that takes place in most organizations into one that genuinely moves people: 'The inbuilding of purpose is a challenge to creativity because it involves transferring men and groups from neutral, technical units into participants who have a particular stamp, sensitivity and involvement'. This combines a number of important points. I have repeatedly stressed that too many ideas in management suppose a formal, rational, logical and essentially unemotional relationship to the tasks. Yet the really important part of a vision and a visionary leader is to transform what is neutral and technical into sensitivity and involvement. In fact the whole point of modern management is to involve people in the organization beyond their technical relationship. The point of good leadership is to break staff away from that neutrality of 'only working here'.

Selznick (1957: 149–50) continues: 'To institutionalise is to infuse with value beyond the technical requirements of the task in hand... From the standpoint of the committed person, the organisation is changed from an expendable tool into a valued source of personal satisfaction.' When organizations move people to commit themselves as individuals rather than a neutral unit the organization gains a personal commitment that is transformative. Organizations without this commitment are expendable to the people who work in them. They can be replaced by another organization, equally able to meet technical needs for pay and pension. This aim of good leadership is to enthuse and drive the staff member beyond a technical achievement.

Before the walls of Harfleur Henry could have appealed to his soldiers as good technicians. The Welsh archers could have been praised for their accuracy, the cavalry for their ability to carry out dressage. In the fight to come such skills were undoubtedly important, but it wasn't those skills that really mattered. What mattered was to link the particular task in hand to transformative visions that the men would be able to feel – their valour, their equality with the king and their country. Shakespeare's Henry is genuinely transformative in his vision – the men he addresses become different soldiers, they become a part of something wider when they have heard him speak. He demonstrates to managers that if you want your people to 'go that extra mile' it is necessary to enthuse and move them.

This is not the only lesson from the battle of Harfleur, however. After this speech Henry and his troops fight to storm the town, but it is not a simple victory – the charge he led does not win the battle. It continues with Henry in the vanguard fighting side by side with 'his yeomen'. In a break in the battle the citizens of Harfleur come anxiously to the tops of the wall around the town to see what is happening. Henry shouts at them to surrender and warns them, in the next speech, what will happen if they do not give in. He starts with a recognition of his warlike persona:

> *as I am a soldier,*
> *A name that in my thoughts becomes me best …*
> *The gates of mercy shall be all shut up,*
> *And the flesh'd soldier, rough and hard of heart,*
> *In liberty of bloody hand shall range*
> *With conscience wide as hell, mowing like grass*
> *Your fresh-fair virgins, and your flowering infants.*
> *What is it then to me, if impious war,*
> *Array'd in flames like to the prince of fiends,*
> *Do, with his smirch'd complexion, all fell feats*
> *Enlink'd to waste and desolation?*
> *What is't to me, when you yourselves are cause,*
> *If your pure maidens fall into the hand*
> *Of hot and forcing violation?*
> **Henry V**, Act 3 Scene 3 lines 5–6 and 10–21

This is different. Henry is a national military leader. He is in charge of a powerful army and standing before the walls of a battered small town. He is clearly and obviously threatening civilians with rape, infanticide and rape again in case they missed the first threat. To threaten parents with their infants being 'mow[n] like grass' is quite hideous.

This is a speech and a threat that none of us as managers would ever want to see ourselves making, even in our worst nightmares. This is a powerful lesson. Shakespeare is saying that we move from the highest point of the best moment of leadership to the worst point of our nightmares, simultaneously making the point that the same person does this in one day. At one moment Henry is a great leader; at the next he is a great leader who threatens to rape teenagers and kill babies.

Power in front of Harfleur is in both speeches awful (as in leaving us full of awe). In the 15th century if you went to war and led a campaign this was what it was like. In the new millennium if you exercise power there will be moments of great moral difficulty. Being a manager means that you will certainly have to threaten to sack people, or close down a part of your organization; at times managers have to act in such a way as to make ordinary people very unhappy. These actions might come hard on the manager's heels of the moments of greatest moral clarity. Be prepared, or your management will falter with the shock and surprise of moving so quickly from the light to the dark side.

Such a variety of actions from the same leader in the same battle raises important questions of morality for senior managers. How far will you go to achieve the goals of your organization? Unless managers have clear answers to this question they may find themselves swept along by events. In 15th-century warfare, without some moral clarity it was apparently perfectly acceptable for great leaders to threaten to kill children. Managers need to have some idea of the moral limits they are prepared to go to in order to achieve contemporary goals.

Back in the play, the civilians of Harfleur give in. Before Henry leaves the city he orders his governor Exeter to 'use mercy to them all' (*Henry V*, Act 3 Scene 3 line 54). Once more, in victory, the gentleman.

Power, friendship and action

In Henry's army there are some soldiers who, just a few years before, had been his close friends. He drank and partied with them and even joined them in a form of 15th-century mugging. They were close friends for many years. As we shall see he used this friendship to learn both about his similarity to ordinary people and his differences. They form one of the bases for his management style.

After winning the town of Harfleur Henry's sick and depleted army moves across northern France, aiming for the port of Calais and the short sea journey home. However it is important to Henry to make the point that France is not a foreign country he is invading, since he is claiming that this is his nation, that he is coming back to rule. If people do not fight him he will be good to them and he bans all stealing and looting by his army. Yet one of his ex-drinking partners, Bardolph, steals a crucifix. In the previous two plays we saw that Bardolph and his friends steal things for fun. In both *Henry IV Parts 1* and *2* stealing is normalized. However a few years later in northern France the time and the place allow no exception to a new set of rules. Henry condemns his old friend to death and he is hanged.

> Henry *We would have all such offenders so cut off: and we give express charge, that in our marches through the country, there be nothing compelled from the villages, nothing taken but paid for, none of the French upbraided or abused in disdainful language; for when lenity and cruelty play for a kingdom, the gentler gamester is the soonest winner.*
> **Henry V**, Act 3 Scene 6 lines 104–10

On Henry's orders a close friend is hanged, and for the purpose of the invasion necessarily so – the politics of an invading army compel it. He will lose fewer troops in battle if his friend is hanged for looting. The invasion will go easier with 'the gentlest gamester [being] the soonest winner'. This is the politics of power winning over the experience of loyalty in friendship with a cruel vengeance.

No modern managers are in the position to execute a friend. But many of us have had to make a decision in such a way as to forget some past personal relationship. This is hard, always hard, sometimes almost as hard as in this example; but if you want to have power you must be prepared to do it. In a new set of circumstances a friend carrying out the same activity that you used to carry out together is now doing something wrong. What was right for you then is wrong now; what was celebrated then is punished now.

Shakespeare is teaching us a greater point on a wider field. Each decision is not just a decision in its own right, but is in public terms a lesson for others. The execution of a friend makes a number of points with great clarity:

- If I am prepared to hang him, since you know he is my friend, then the rest of you had better behave.
- If I am prepared to hang him, since you know he is my friend, this is an important principle.
- If I am prepared to hang him, then the army is doing something much more important than what we all normally think of as important, that is friendship.

Equally Shakespeare is portraying Henry as saying to his army (and audience), on pain of death, I will not have the French upbraided or abused in disdainful language since it is politic to be nice to them. A little while earlier this same leader in front of Harfleur was personally abusing the citizens by threatening to kill their babies and rape their daughters.

Shakespeare is telling us that great leaders do not lead simple lives of principle. Winning a difficult campaign will call for stratagems that call forth very different activities at different times. Shakespeare lays out before us very starkly a lesson in open contradiction: be a great leader by being fearful one day and kind the next. Indeed, when you are being kind, be prepared (as with Bardolph) to be ruthless. It is difficult to 'read off' from Shakespeare a one-dimensional view of power here.

- Is it heroic to kill a friend?
- Is it heroic to threaten?
- Is it heroic to be kind to civilians?

The difficult lesson that Shakespeare paints is that at times, if you want to be a great manager, all these things are necessary. Henry is a great and heroic leader because he manages that situation. The morality is not an abstract code of behaviour, but a set of learnt and shared experiences. Abstract principles don't seem very useful. A great leader will make hard decisions and will trust what he has learnt in his life. He will have the nerve to place himself and his own life at hazard by those decisions at Harfleur and at Agincourt. But his greatness will not spring from any simple set of heroic principles, whether of the chivalrous 14th century that Henry lived in, Shakespeare's Elizabethan age or our own new millennium.

KILL ALL THE PRISONERS

The pinnacle of Henry's success, the high point of *Henry V*, is at the battle of Agincourt. As we shall see, the French troops outnumber his British army by 10 to 1. His troops are sick and tired. He and they are frightened for their lives. The battle gets under way and the French, full of vanity and expecting an easy victory, badly misjudge the battle. They are losing and losing badly. To gain one easy aspect of a victory the French cavalry descends on Henry's camp, behind and away from the English army, and kills all of the boys who were left in the camp to look after the baggage. Henry returns to the camp, sees the dead boys, and is rightly outraged. Even though within a few minutes it is clear that he is winning the battle, he takes swift retribution:

> *I was not angry since I came to France*
> *Until this instant...*
> *Besides, we'll cut the throats of those we have,*
> *And not a man of them that we shall take*
> *Shall taste our mercy.*
> **Henry V**, Act 4 Scene 7 lines 53–54 and 61–63

A terrible retribution is unleashed. If there is a principle from Shakespeare here it is the principle of two wrongs making a right. The French kill our boys, so we slaughter their unarmed prisoners. Within minutes the battle is seen to be won, but the prisoners for those moments are to be slaughtered in retribution. Again, is this a heroic piece of leadership? Do we remember Henry because he orders the slaughter of unarmed prisoners? No, we remember him because he was noble, chivalrous and brave. But we also remember him because he won.

Shakespeare could have simply painted him as a shining hero. Shakespeare could have left out all of the above three scenes, and we would have had this clear and straightforward vision of a heroic leader. What would we have learnt from that? We would we have learnt that it is necessary to be brave, good and courageous, and if you behave that way you will be a great leader.

Emphatically that is not Shakespeare's lesson. He writes a very different character since he knows that it is not true. Great leaders, and great portrayals of great leaders, live in the world of difficult and compromised decisions. Shakespeare decides, even when writing the story of his greatest hero, that all leaders must be portrayed as managing contradictions and difficulties. The greatness of the play is that leadership is not simple, but full of ambiguities. The greatness of Shakespeare's leaders is that they are also full of ambiguities.

Don't come to Shakespeare, even at the heroic moment, expecting simple lessons. Expect to have to work hard learning how to manage hard. The lessons he draws from the leadership ambiguities of the 16th century fit in with the management contradictions of our modern world.

As we have seen, some of Shakespeare's leaders fail to appreciate this and try and be one-dimensional. Richard II believed that being king was enough. He felt that being king he did not have to struggle with contradictions, since his kingship gave him power. It didn't. Coriolanus believed that being a valiant warrior was enough. But when he needed to manage men in peace as well as in war his one-dimensional capacity as a valiant soldier meant this could not work. Shakespeare in other settings does give us one-dimensional leaders, but only in order to show us how they fail.

To succeed in providing leadership you have to learn to grapple with the ambiguities of power like Henry. Ambiguities do not make a flawed leader, quite the reverse – a leader who pretends that there are no ambiguities achieves that.

Learning to lead, not born to it

Shakespeare's Henry V takes three plays to emerge as a great leader. In the 16th century this is more than simply a dramatic device. It gives the character time to learn and develop different ways of managing events. Let's not forget that other leaders in Shakespeare believed they could lead because they were born to it.

The historical thrust of the whole of Shakespeare's English history plays goes against the idea of a king being born to rule. It is interesting to note that queens and kings in Shakespeare's lifetime were very concerned with their right to rule through bloodline. It is therefore odd to the point of being dangerous for Shakespeare to write plays about history that accentuate a very different point.

> This seems to be the point... of Bolingbroke's successful challenge to Richard II, but particularly of Hal's defeat of Hotspur and his subsequent victory as king over the French. In each case, State authority does not descend directly through blood. Rather it pursues a disrupted and discontinuous course through history, arising out of conflicts within the reigning oligarchy as to which bloodline shall legitimately rule.
>
> (Tennenhouse, 1994: 21)

Richard II came to the throne as the eldest son of his parents and as rightful heir to the throne. His cousin Bolingbroke kills him to gain the throne and become Henry IV. Shakespeare's plays on this subject, and his highlighting of such a false succession, demonstrate that the divine succession of kings does not work. Human actions make monarchs.

Prince Hal has a particular point to make here. His father killed a king who was king through bloodline. At the end of *Henry IV Part 1* Prince Hal kills Hotspur, who has a greater bloodline right to be king. So Henry V only becomes king because he and his father slaughter men who were kings or had greater right to be kings. Consequently, if Shakespeare's Henry V believes that people were born to be king then he should not be one, since his father murdered to be king and was not born to it. He wastes little time on such thoughts, but his father is more worried by his own regicide. Throughout the two plays named after him Henry IV is anxious about his right to be king. His murder of a fairly useless Richard II may have been necessary to modernize the country, but the guilt he lives with undermines that project.

Throughout both plays Henry IV is obsessed with his guilt, and in one of Shakespeare's most famous lines Henry shows his difficult experience as king: 'Uneasy lies the head that wears a crown' (*Henry IV Part 2*, Act 3 Scene 1 line 31).

Bolingbroke wants to be king so much that he deposes his cousin, the king, and then to make sure there is no comeback has him killed. From that moment Bolingbroke is uneasy.

Price Hal has no such problem. As we shall see from his first soliloquy in Act 1 Scene 2 of *Henry IV Part 1*, he is preparing to be king. To this end, and very specifically to the end of becoming a *great* king, he spends his time moving between the different worlds of an East End tavern and the king's court. For those of us interested in lessons for managers this is an important scene, where Prince Hal not only demonstrates his ability to associate with both the common people and the monarchy, but lets the audience into his reasons for doing so. On his very first appearance on Shakespeare's stage Prince Hal, Falstaff and Poins (his lowlife mates) have just decided to carry out a complex robbery. After the others leave Prince Hal remains and speaks of his real intentions:

> *So, when this loose behaviour I throw off*
> *And pay the debt I never promised,*
> *By how much better than my word I am,*
> *By so much shall I falsify men's hopes*
> *And like bright metal on a sullen ground,*
> *My reformation, glittering o'er my fault,*
> *Shall show more goodly and attract more eyes*
> *Than that which hath no foil to set it off.*
> *I'll so offend, to make offence a skill;*
> *Redeeming time when men think least I will.*
> **Henry IV Part 1**, Act 1 Scene 2 lines 207–14

This is the heir to the throne of England speaking, explaining face to face with an audience why his first appearance on the stage is in such low company and why the first action he is involved in is planning a spoof robbery near Canterbury. He is deliberately engaged in loose behaviour, so that when he has his 'reformation' and becomes king and redeems himself at a time when men least expect it, then he will appear better and attract more 'eyes' than somebody who has been princelike all along. As early as this first speech he is warning that, for the next two plays, before he becomes king he will be spending a lot of time with lowlifes.

In terms of drama Shakespeare does an odd thing here. One might think it would be useful for maintaining suspense to leave the audience anxious about how Hal tussles with his two worlds. If this suspense were sustained over the next two plays, then the audience would be left not knowing whether Hal is really going to end up primarily as a lowlife who likes a good time or as a great king of England. Dramatically such suspense would give the playwright a powerful device. Will he want to become king? Shakespeare could have had his audience swinging wildly between different answers as he had Hal doing different things. But no, at the very beginning Shakespeare throws away this dramatic tool and lets the audience know that Hal intends to be a great king. What he calls his 'reformation' is not really a reform since he is not bad at all. It is an appearance. He knows what he is doing and tells the audience. In these three plays the struggle between the good, kingly side and the 'bad lad' side of Hal is over for the audience before it has begun.

For two whole plays, the next seven hours of drama, Hal spends more time in the tavern than in his father's court. Why does Shakespeare write it this way, since from the very beginning he makes sure that there is no dramatic suspense about where Hal will end up? Both *Henry IV* plays are preparing his audience for the way in which Henry V, when Hal becomes king, can successfully switch in mid-scene from appearing to be 'one of the lads' to being a great national leader. So for two plays Shakespeare has him moving between these worlds, not because there is any doubt about where he will end up, but because he is demonstrating the way in which Hal can use that movement between worlds for the time when he becomes king.

Shakespeare is making the point that to be a great leader it is very important to know the people you are going to lead. This goes beyond the idea of simply being 'popular'. Knowing your staff and their culture is not a matter you and your 'spin doctors' can address from the moment you begin to lead. No, the point Shakespeare makes is that you need to work at the relationship between yourself and your staff, not just from the moment that you become a leader but from the moment you acknowledge that this is where you are going to end up. If you know that one day you want to lead then you have to start getting to know your staff and their world immediately. Prince Hal explains to the audience from the beginning that he wants to be a great king, and we judge his actions against that aim from that moment on. He is saying that preparing to be a king from the moment that you actually are a king is much too late.

He is talking all the time about preparing both your staff and yourself for the time when you have to manage them. In making this point he is going beyond the important point about developing staff to emphasize self-development – as you develop staff it is vital to recognize that you are developing yourself. Shakespeare is pointing out that by spending time with people who will be subordinates you are learning how to lead. As Drucker put it nearly 50 years ago:

> This (development) applies, as cannot be emphasised too strongly, not only to the man who is being managed, but also to the manager. Whether he develops his subordinates in the right direction, helps them to grow and become bigger and richer persons, will directly determine whether he himself will develop, will grow or wither, become richer or become impoverished, improve or deteriorate.
>
> (Drucker, 1954: 342)

Drucker outlines the intensely dialectical relationship between how a manager develops his or her staff and how that development can in turn develop the manager. The more time managers spend really understanding their staff, the better the managers will understand themselves.

If you want to be a good manager it's best to have thought about it for some time before you take up your post. You have to prepare yourself for it from the moment you decide that that is where you want to end up. This means that it is best to have thought about it when you are doing other things with people who are similar to the ones you will be managing. You need to know what makes people happy and sad, what motivates them and what they are afraid of. How can you learn to use that knowledge? How can you judge what will be useful and what will motivate them later on?

From the moment in that first scene that Hal confides in us Shakespeare is telling us that we need to understand his actions in terms of that destiny as king. We need to see everything he does from that moment as leading to that outcome. The time he spends in the tavern, or out with the lads playing the fool, are all moments to learn from in preparation for leadership.

What Hal is spending all this time doing is learning language and culture. He realizes that there will be difficult times in his leadership, when it will be crucial to have the ability to move all of his people in the direction of the goals he needs them to take on. At those times too authority needs to be expressed in such a way as to fully unlock everyone's behaviour. This can only be achieved if there is some cultural understanding.

Philip Sadler outlines the importance of this process in his book *Managing Change*:

> Making gifted people productive for their organisations is not, in most instances, a matter of getting them to work harder or smarter. They are usually so involved in their work and so bright that such interventions are irrelevant. The managerial task is much more to do with dismantling barriers to performance and productivity and channelling efforts into avenues that will directly contribute to the achievement of the organisation's goals. Thus performance management in the case of highly talented people is best looked upon as a process of influence. The outcome should be for them to understand and identify with the organisation's objectives and see how their own contribution can be enhanced.
>
> (Sadler, 1995: 79)

Management is dismantling the barriers that exist inside staff that stop them achieving great performance. They will only be able to identify with the organisation's objectives and enhance their contribution if they can understand what their leader is doing and saying. Henry's great speeches before his two main battles are superb examples of such management. But as Shakespeare makes clear, to achieve this he makes sure Hal spends time learning ordinary people's language and becoming proficient in it. Again he lets us know why. In *Henry IV Part 1*, having outlined his knowledge of bar room slang, Hal says: 'to conclude, I am so good a proficient in one quarter of an hour, that I can drink with any tinker in his own language during my life' (Act 2 Scene 4 lines 16–19).

Leaders who do not know the language of their staff cannot communicate with them effectively, and without effective communication they cannot motivate them. When Hal talks to his troops he will use their own language to communicate with them. A language and a culture that he has learnt for life has been learnt by drinking 'with any tinker'. Learning language is a crucial part of understanding culture. As he says above, he is now so proficient in working people's language that he will be able to use it at any time during his life. Again this is a very telling way of letting the audience know that he is preparing for later uses of this 'tinker' language.

Later on, in *Henry IV Part 2*, his father's friend Warwick is reassuring the king about the time Hal spends with his lowlife friends. Shakespeare has Warwick explain the learning strategy with even greater clarity:

> *The prince but studies his companions*
> *Like a strange tongue, wherein, to gain the language,*
> *'Tis needful that the most immodest word*
> *Be look'd upon and learn'd*
> **Henry IV Part 2**, Act 4 Scene 4 lines 68–72

Learning the language, paying attention to the culture and studying for the future – it happens all the time. But from the original quote, at the very beginning of *Henry IV Part 1*, nearly three plays before Agincourt, Hal signals that future by talking about how his mates think of him and saying:

> *They take it already upon their salvation, that though I be but Prince of Wales, yet I am the king of courtesy; … a lad of mettle, a good boy, by the Lord, so they call me!, and when I am King of England, I shall command all the good lads in Eastcheap.*
> **Henry IV Part 1**, Act 2 Scene 4 lines 9–11 and 12–15

This is a clear demonstration of the way in which he has worked to earn the affection of the common people. He has learnt their language and their culture and in response, as far as Hal is concerned, better than being the Prince of Wales they call him a 'good boy'. As a consequence of knowing their language and culture, when he is king he will be able to command them. Again this is very future oriented. Shakespeare's Hal has spent time making sure that they think him a good boy, rather than Prince of Wales, because then he will be able to command them in the future.

We can see in Shakespeare's language echoes of the way in which staff describe good managers. Staff might say of managers, 'that manager is good because she talks our own language', or 'they talk like they are one of us', or in different parts of the world 'he is one of the boys, one of the good old boys'. Contrast this with those managers who have never spent time with people like their staff and so do not know what makes their staff tick. They cannot at crucial moments communicate with their staff, who say 'it's like they're speaking a different language'. As we can see from Henry's hanging of Bardolph, he is more than being a leader who is 'one of the lads'. It does not mean that you curry favour all the time; it does mean that you have to spend a lot more time than managers normally do learning about your staff.

Shakespeare's point for modern managers is that the best way of doing this is through lived experience. Prince Hal could have employed a 'good boy' to come to the court and talk to him about how ordinary people lived. He could have employed a language teacher to teach him the language. He doesn't. He spends time, lots of time, with ordinary people. He shares his experience of life with them. There is no substitute for learnt experience here. The separation caused by class, ethnicity or locality that takes place between many modern managers and most of their staff is ruinous of good management relationships.

Most contemporary societies contain, as they did in Shakespeare's time, considerable inequalities. It is often the case that managers have led very different lives from their staff. Different cultures have different languages that make communication difficult or impossible. If your life has so totally separated you from the lives of your staff you will lose some of the main methods of motivation. Look to your experience and also look to other ways of learning.

One of the most influential management theorists of the 1990s, Peter Senge, after reviewing the lives of some great leaders comments upon the restlessness that forces such people to go on learning throughout their lives: 'The ability of such people to be natural leaders, as near as I can tell, is the by-product of a life time of effort – effort to develop conceptual and communication skills, to reflect on personal values and to align personal behaviour with values, to learn how to listen and to appreciate others and others' ideas' (Senge, 1992: 259).

Senge is almost literally describing what Shakespeare has Prince Hal do. He spends years before he is leader learning how to communicate, how to develop behaviour in line with values and above all how to listen. Let's not forget that Shakespeare, throughout *Henry IV Parts 1* and *2* could have had Henry spending his time in court, simply waiting for his father to die. After all, short of a fatal illness himself, he was bound to be king some day. Instead of being complacent about his future he is continually restless, looking for ways to improve his abilities, looking for new ways to learn, above all improving his ability to communicate.

LEARNING THROUGH PLAYING

Since most of this learning goes on before you start the management job, it is important to spend your time from the moment you have decided to become a manager learning how you will do the job. For those who have not shared life experiences with those of their staff Shakespeare's Hal gives us another lesson in how to learn about different cultures. Throughout the three plays Shakespeare has Prince Hal playing at being someone different. On many occasions he becomes someone else. He plays these very different roles to see what it is like being that other person. In modern language he uses every opportunity for role play, and he learns from that role playing activity.

In *Henry IV Part 1* the parts Hal plays include a thief, his father, Hotspur, Hotspur's wife and in small scenes in the tavern he plays himself as a prodigal son and as a penitent. In the second act in the tavern in Eastcheap he plays his father to Falstaff's Hal. He appears to be joking with Falstaff about the king, giving his father's view of the fat knight Falstaff as a wastrel; but Hal is being a king in order to learn how to be a king – he is 'putting himself' in the king's place. As we shall see in Part 5 of this book, when a play and half later he becomes a real king and the play acting stops, he dismisses Falstaff in real life as he does in this earlier, pretend drama. By playing the king Hal learns what it is like to be king. Falstaff thinks he is play acting and will always be his friend, even when he ascends the throne. Hal is learning that this will not be the case. He is warning his friend of the future and learning, preparing himself how to dismiss Falstaff from his presence. He is also preparing Falstaff for being dismissed.

Most of us, before we become managers, don't have the opportunity to play parts in little plays, but we do have the opportunity, all the time, to think ourselves into other people's roles. This gives us the opportunity to feel what it is like 'living in their shoes' and to prepare for managing power and authority. Shakespeare is pointing out the advantages of carrying this out. If you genuinely enter a part, as Hal does his father, then you can 'learn what it is like' to be that part. This is not the same as direct experience of the lives of others, but it is much much better than reading about it. You try, in role play, to get into the other's soul.

In *Henry IV Part 2* there is more playing of parts. Hal's father is very ill and Hal goes to his bedroom and tries on his crown: literally trying on the role for size. What would it feel like to have that power? How would *we* feel about it? Again Shakespeare is showing us the detail of how a great leader prepares.

As we shall see at Agincourt, all this role playing is good practice for spending time with his troops at the moment before the battle. Throughout the play he shows us that he learns how to learn about other people, high and low, and while learning about others he also learns about himself.

The modern manager is being given both a direct warning and a way to prepare. Put yourselves in the shoes of people such as your staff. What really makes them tick? Play the role, check out the role and think it through. Above all recognize your ignorance and commit yourself to doing something about it.

Shakespeare puts Henry through all of these experiences for a very good reason: so that he can learn how to be a better leader. Despite the fact that he could have simply obtained the throne by the passage of time, Henry is forced again and again to learn how to lead better. Peter

Drucker (1990: 174) puts this process in very straightforward advice to people who would be good managers: 'Developing yourself begins by service, by striving towards an idea outside of yourself – not by leading. Leaders are not born, nor are they made – they are self-made.'

Management development, then, takes place through striving for an idea beyond you, by serving others and learning about yourself through that serving. Drucker is strongly suggesting that you really must begin this process of development before you take up the post – you need to make yourself a leader through the service of an idea. Think what this means for today. A manager may sit around waiting for promotion. For some that promotion may come, but they won't be great managers because they have not spent the time developing their capacity to manage. With Shakespeare's Prince Hal, from the first scene he appears in, there is no time to waste in this process. Place yourself in situations where you will be able to learn about your staff and learn about yourself.

SUBTERFUGE, PLAY ACTING AND BETRAYAL

Play acting has another lesson for managers and leaders. There are times when staff are 'playing a part', pretending to be a part of the wider team but actually working for themselves outside of the organization. It is important for managers to be able to recognize that difference. I would suggest that the best way of gaining that skill is to have spent some time playing a part yourself, and recognizing how your staff are actually playing a part.

There is a crucial moment in the final preparation for the invasion of France when this recognition of how his staff are really behaving beyond their appearances becomes a matter of life or death for Henry V. No modern civilian manager will ever have to organize an invasion. It is a complex logistical task involving a very broad range of skills. Being responsible for the organization of a very large merger of two companies may come close to it, but with an invasion the price of failure for everyone involved is much, much higher.

The point for us here is that whilst Henry was consumed with this, three of his closest commanders, Cambridge, Grey and Scroop, betray him to the French. They agree to kill him, for money, just before the invasion sets sail for France. One of the three, Scroop, is his closest friend, of whom Henry says:

> *Thou that didst bear the key of all my counsels,*
> *That knew'st the very bottom of my soul,*
> **Henry V**, Act 2 Scene 2 line 96

Scroop was so close to Henry that he knew the very bottom of his soul and is therefore certain to have known every element of the invasion plan. At the most vulnerable moment of the enterprise, when his mind was on something else, his closest associates will betray him. However, the plot is uncovered. In a powerful speech of condemnation Henry talks about seeing through such falseness:

> *All other devils that suggest by treasons*
> *Do botch and bungle up damnation*
> *With patches, colours, and with forms being fetch'd*
> *From glistering semblances of piety;*
> **Henry V**, Act 2 Scene 2 lines 115–18

Shakespeare's Henry beautifully describes the core basis of betrayal. All betrayal must consist of an individual pretending to be something they are not. People pretend to support you when in fact they do not. In this case for a while Scroop, who was a close friend, continues to pretend to be a close friend, but in fact is betraying Henry and will kill him. The appearance of the friend is masking the reality of the enemy.

If betrayal is happening to a manager then it is vital for that manager to be able to uncover the difference between the appearance of support in staff and the reality of various kinds of betrayal. The ability of the leader to understand the fact that all is often not what it seems is obviously very useful. Henry has that ability because, for much of his own life, he has not really been as he seems. He has not only been playing a part, but has been role playing to learn how he might play a part in the future. This provides Henry with the ability to spot subterfuge.

In this scene, there is a further twist to the play acting. Henry knows the three are traitors, but is unsure whether he should be merciful towards what are, after all, old friends. So earlier in the scene he pretends to them that the day before a man had had an 'excess of wine' (line 42) and rail'd against our person' (line 41). Henry suggests that he should pardon him, since the offence was not great. There is no such person as the pretend drunk but he is testing the traitors to discover what they will suggest about being merciful to the drunk. He is also meeting subterfuge with subterfuge. Scroop suggests the drunk must be punished and that a king who failed to punish such a person would 'Breed, by his sufferance, more of such a kind' (line 46).

Through this play acting Henry encourages the three traitors, in order that they may demonstrate how much they love the king, to suggest a harsh punishment for a drunk who insults the king with words. As Henry goes on to say:

If little faults, proceeding on distemper,
Shall not be wink'd at, how shall we stretch our eye
When capital crimes, chew'd, swallow'd and digested,
Appear before us?
Henry V, Act 2 Scene 2 lines 54–58

Henry is asking the traitors how, if he severely punishes a man who carries out such small crimes when the man has lost his temper, will he punish people who have carried out premeditated capital crimes? Through this complex play acting Henry gets the traitors to say that he should have no mercy on miscreants. In a few moments Henry springs the surprise on the traitors, unmasks them and condemns them to death. Once they have been found out, once their subterfuge has been uncovered by someone who is better at it than they are, it is inevitable that the traitors will ask the king to be merciful. However, they have already shown their views on mercy on the smaller matter of the drunk, and Henry condemns them to death.

This scene has Shakespeare showing us how useful it is for leaders to understand fully about drama and role playing. First, the traitors play a part pretending to be loyal when in reality they are betraying Henry. As such they are immediately vulnerable to a leader who understands that people can and do play roles, and one who can see through play acting. Second, Henry makes up a story involving a drunkard and uses it to uncover what the traitors really think about justice and mercy. Through drama he therefore has evidence that they are traitors and evidence from their own mouths that they are against mercy. He gets them to condemn themselves to death, the most complete application of justice to betrayal that you can think of.

All of these skills come from having learnt to play parts himself. Shakespeare demonstrates to the modern manager the usefulness of learning how to develop and play drama. In doing so, as we outline above, you not only learn what it is like to be another person, but you can tell when other people are doing it and you can write small scenes that make dramatic points. Above all playing other people and doing it well allows you throughout your management experience to 'put yourself in others' shoes'.

Role playing is an important part of most modern management courses. It provides managers with a chance to experience other people's roles, cultures and actions. On too many occasions managers dismiss these role playing experiences as having little to teach them about 'the real world'. Shakespeare's Henry shows how a good appreciation of how others play out their roles provides the senior manager with insights that could save their organization.

SHAKESPEARE'S HENRY'S LONG ROAD TO AGINCOURT

Most of the examples I have used to date are from the period leading up to the Battle of Agincourt. This battle is not only the climax of *Henry V* but is the climax of all three plays, including the two named after Henry's father. Shakespeare's Henry portrays real leadership in this victory against the odds. What are the lessons to be learnt for modern managers?

The first is to spend considerable time preparing yourself for such battles. This is not just a matter of logistics, keeping your troops fresh and replenished, but is also a matter of preparing yourself for testing management times. Throughout all three plays Henry recognizes that at some stage he will be king and must behave as a great leader in difficult circumstances. Prepare for such moments throughout your life, so that you and your staff recognize what you can achieve with confidence. Many critics comment on the difference between Henry and

Shakespeare's other kings, Leggatt (1988: 126) among them: 'The myth Henry hopes to create concerns not his office, but himself. Richard II was concerned with being a king; Henry is concerned with winning or losing a war. He will according to the outcomes of his own efforts, be a hero or a forgotten man'.

If this is the case a lot depends not on the title that the manager has, but on the person who is filling the office and managing the process. Henry is proud of being king, but the office on its own solves nothing. It is the human being in the office that wins or loses the battle and therefore it is important for that individual to prepare for that situation. This is once more Shakespeare's greatest lesson: pay attention only to the title on your letterhead, the size of your desk or your salary and you will not be able to manage any of them. Pay attention to the person you are and the learning you do about both the person you are and your staff, and you will pull off victories against the odds.

Peter Drucker (1990: 7) underlines the development of managers by recognizing that, however good leadership may seem, at some stage in their organizations there will be difficult times ahead and it is vital that they prepare themselves for leadership at those times: 'The most important task of an organisation's leader is to anticipate crisis. Perhaps not to divert it, but to anticipate it. To wait until the crisis hits, is already abdication.'

From the beginning of *Henry IV Part 1* Prince Hal prepared himself, not for an easy time as king but for some difficult battles ahead. The crisis would come when he had to lead his men out of a really difficult situation. When it comes at Agincourt Henry has failed to divert it, but he does anticipate the leadership skills he will need in that crisis and is therefore prepared.

Drucker (1990: 15) goes on to underline the sorts of activities that leaders must prepare for. Above all they need to develop their competencies, the prime one of which could have been abstracted from Shakespeare's Henry: 'What matters in developing a leader is that he or she works on the basic competencies. As the first such competence, I would put the willingness, ability and self-discipline to listen. Listening is not a skill, its a discipline.' As we shall see, at the crucial moment of crisis, after all the discipline of listening, his ability to listen and learn is the competence that saves Henry and his army.

Shakespeare's Henry's battle at Agincourt

At Agincourt Henry was facing an enormous problem. His army was at the end of a campaign, was ill equipped and unfit. A vastly superior and fresh army of French troops bars his way. As Henry says to the French messenger:

We would not seek a battle, as we are;
Nor, as we are, we say we will not shun it:
Henry V, Act 3 Scene 6 lines 162–63

Henry is weak, in the wrong place and outnumbered – all he has is his troops; to stand any chance at all he must maximize his resources. He must get the very best out of them. He and they agree that in all likelihood they will be defeated, lose the battle and die. This is not a good frame of mind in which to enter a conflict. Henry needs to raise his troops' morale to put them in the best mood for a fight. But if he does so by lying to them about their chances they won't believe him. He can only raise their morale by knowing exactly what they are feeling. So the night before the battle he leaves his council of war and goes to talk to his troops. He uses the subterfuge of role play, borrows a cloak so his troops, in the dark, cannot recognize him. Throughout the night, until dawn, he talks with ordinary soldiers about the battle and about the king.

All three plays have prepared Shakespeare's Henry V for this moment. Unlike any other of Shakespeare's leaders he has the ability to talk and to listen as a king but without appearing to be a king. He has spent his entire adult life preparing for this moment. He can talk in the language of ordinary people. He can think and act within their culture. He has learnt how to play a part and how to pretend. Through these mechanisms he can learn, not what people want him to learn, but what his troops really think and feel.

Imagine, as a senior manager, how invaluable this information would be. Of course you have your normal channels of communication, but when things are bad, really bad, how much truth do you ever get from them? You need to know what is going on, but the likelihood is that you will never know what is happening if you depend upon normal channels of information flow.

By now you should have a very good idea of how long and hard Henry has prepared, not just for the battle, but for precisely this inter-action with his troops. This is the moment that Shakespeare has prepared him for. By this stage of his career Henry is such a strong leader that he can start the interaction with his troops with a clear appreciation of how dire their position is.

It is worth going through how he carries out this work in some detail. He meets with three common soldiers, Williams, Bates and Court. But, of course, they don't recognize the man they meet as their king because he has disguised himself as a soldier – as far as they are concerned they are talking with a soldier.

> Williams *Under what captain serve you?*
> King Henry *Under Sir Thomas Erpingham.*
> Williams *A good old commander and a most kind gentleman: I pray you, what thinks he of our estate?*
> King Henry *Even as men wrecked upon a sand, that look to be washed off the next tide.*
> **Henry V**, Act 4 Scene 1 lines 91–96

For a leader to admit that their situation is as hopeless as if they were shipwrecked and just waiting for the tide to come in and sweep them away is unusual. This is a bleak picture for a senior manager to relay the night before a battle. The image Henry gives to his troops is one of just waiting for the tide of the French army to come along in the morning and wash them away. Such a helpless attitude would leave his troops with a belief that resistance is useless. So what is he doing? Is this how a leader raises morale? Isn't the work of a leader to raise morale, espe-cially if the situation is getting difficult? Don't his staff need a morale boost, and could he not raise morale by lying? For example, when he was asked how bad things are he could have said, 'It's all right because the king has a secret plan' – anything rather than admit the truth.

Shakespeare's Henry doesn't lie. Of course he is in disguise so is not seen to be the king, just another soldier. He is asked for an opinion of how things are and he tells his troops the truth. He does this because he knows his troops well enough to know that it is useless to lie to them. This is a difficult hole for leaders to find themselves in. If they really know and respect their staff then they will know that lying is useless; but, equally, they don't want to depress their staff by admitting that things are hopeless. The troops know that things are bad, and a lie will only make them despise the person who lies. So Henry starts with a true appreciation of their very difficult situation, and chooses not to lie.

The troops go on to discuss what they think about the king's valour:

> Bates *He [the king] may show what outward courage he will; but I believe, as cold a night as 'tis, he could wish himself in Thames up to the neck; and so I would he were, and I by him, at all adventures, so we were quit here.*
>
> King Henry *By my troth, I will speak my conscience of the king: I think he would not wish himself anywhere but where he is.*
>
> Bates *Then I would he were here alone; so should he be sure to be ransomed, and a many poor men's lives saved.*
>
> **Henry V**, Act 4 Scene 1 lines 110–19

These are difficult revelations for a leader to hear – that the troops believe the king would rather be anywhere than with them in their danger. They believe that despite the signs of 'outward courage' in reality the king would rather be up to his neck in the waters of the Thames than fight. Deep down they believe he is a coward. Henry, disguised as a common soldier who speaks their language and understands their fears, contradicts them and says the king will stay and fight. They then say that, if the king is mad enough to want to fight, then let him do it on his own. In fact, if Henry *was* on his own, he could be ransomed and the troops' lives saved.

In this brief discussion with his troops Henry finds out three things:

1. His troops think there is no chance that they will win the coming battle and they will all be killed.
2. His troops believe that, despite the outward appearance of courage, the king is a coward and would rather not be with them.
3. If the king does want to fight, he should do it on his own and allow his troops to live.

What does Henry do when faced with this fairly reasonable view of himself by his troops? Is this a moment for a dramatic disclosure? It would be excellent theatre for the king to throw off his cloak and reveal himself. The disclosure would be devastating but very dramatic. Revealed as the king, he would be able to argue with his troops and prove his courage – good theatre, but bad management.

It would be harsh, but it would *appear* to show show strong leadership to punish the troops who called the king a coward and spread such bleak thoughts. However, Shakespeare's Henry does not reveal himself. Neither does he simply accept the criticism and live with it. As a leader Henry takes their views so seriously that he pays them the compliment of arguing with them, not as a king but as a common soldier, their equal. Since the audience knows it is the king having this argument, but the troops do not, this makes good humorous drama. But at this time before this dangerous battle no one laughs. The humorous aspect of this scene, common soldiers arguing with someone who is in fact the king about whether the king is a coward or not, is saved for after the battle. For the moment, the battle is ahead; what Henry is engaged in is high quality leadership – of finding out what people think and then arguing with them. He stays in role as a common soldier and argues for the king against their view that the king would rather be absent from the battle. He directly argues with the soldier's view that the king would like to be ransomed:

King Henry *I myself heard the king say he would not be ransomed.*
Williams *Ay, he said so, to make us fight cheerfully: but when our throats are cut, he may be ransomed, and we ne'er the wiser.*
King Henry *If I live to see it, I will never trust his word after.*
Henry V, Act 4 Scene 1 lines 206–11

This is wonderful theatre, since the audience knows that the king is present and actively involved in the argument. We know that it is the king saying that he himself would never trust the king again if he is ransomed after the deaths of his soldiers. In terms of leadership, though, it is more straightforward – a leader trying to challenge his men's view about him and argue with them. The men are going into a fight thinking they are being conned by the king. The only reason he isn't being ransomed before the battle is to make them fight cheerfully. But when their throats are cut (note that for this soldier it is not *if* our throats are cut but *when* – a pretty pessimistic view of the near future for a soldier) and they won't be able to check up on it, well then the king will look after himself. Again the king argues back by saying that he would never trust the king again if this were to happen. Whilst the audience and the king know that he is actually talking about himself, it appears pretty absurd to the soldiers to find one of their fellow soldiers claiming that they have the capacity to trust or mistrust their monarch.

This argument is too much for Williams, who doesn't leave it there. He reminds the king (still thinking he is a fellow soldier) of the social distance between his standing and that of the king. It is absurd for a soldier to pretend to hold the king to account:

> Williams *You pay him then. That's a perilous shot out of an elder-gun, that a poor and private displeasure can do against a monarch!*
> **Henry V**, Act 4 Scene 1 lines 212–14

Williams claims it is absurd for a common soldier to pretend to be able hold his king to account, and yet *we* know that this common soldier is in fact the king. Henry continues to argue with him and in the end they exchange gloves as a mark of the fact that after the battle they will have a fight to prove who is right. The king as a common soldier is prepared to fight another common soldier for the honour of the king. Throughout this interaction Henry is picking up brilliant intelligence: his troops don't trust the distance that exists between himself and them; they, as common soldiers, can never be ransomed; death is their future; and when they are dead the king will be ransomed.

(After the battle is safely won the king and Williams meet each other without subterfuge. Williams finds not only that he has pledged to fight the king, but that he has called the king a coward to his face. The outcome of the subterfuge is a joke, and Williams is paid for being a part of the joke.)

There are some very important universal lessons for managers to learn from this interaction. Senior managers usually think that they and their staff are in the same situation, for example if the organization fails then they will both be in equal trouble. Indeed many senior managers use this argument as a way of joining with their staff and underlining their common position. In fact they are always in very different positions. There are better safety nets and more protection for senior managers than for junior staff, and a claim that we are all the same in the face of adverse circumstances will be met with the cynicism that Williams and his fellow troops met Henry's protestations that they were all in the same boat. Senior managers who forget this social gulf and believe they are exactly the same as their staff will misunderstand their situation and crucially fail to gain the intelligence about differences that they must address. In his speech before the battle Henry will address this.

The men are not only worried about dying but are unsure of the justice of their cause and the damage to their souls if they died in anger.

> Williams *But if the cause be not good, the king himself hath a heavy reckoning to make, when all those legs and arms and heads, chopped off in a battle, shall join together at the latter day and cry all 'We died at such a place'; some swearing, some crying for a surgeon, some upon their wives left poor behind them, some upon the debts they owe, some upon their children rawly left. I am afeared there are few die well that die in a battle, for how can they charitably dispose of any thing, when blood is their argument? Now, if these men do not die well, it will be a black matter for the king that led them to it; whom to disobey were against all proportion of subjection.*
> **Henry V**, Act 4 Scene 1 lines 141–55

These are a series of heavy messages for a leader to take. First, Williams does not spare Henry with a rosy glow of what happens in battles. In case anyone had forgotten, legs, arms and heads get chopped off. In addition, people will die because of the battle the king has led them into. Many will have bad consciences, and young children. Their wives will be poor because of their deaths. And, being killed in haste, they will not have time to commit their souls to God. They will not die well. Not only will these graphically dreadful things happen to the very people who are having the discussion, but the pain and the deaths are all the responsibility of the king. Whilst they don't know this, they are telling the king that all of this is his fault.

Imagine being a leader and hearing this from the very people who in all likelihood *will* lose arms, legs and life. Not only do his troops think they are going to die, but they feel they will die in a bad argument, and it will be the king's fault. Williams really thinks the king doesn't care. This is a common view of staff of senior management. They believe they have been led into difficulties by the incompetence and failure of their managers and that it is all the managers' fault: 'If our managers had been better we would never have got into this mess'. Such a view relieves the staff of any responsibility. Senior managers can feed into this view. One of the ways in which staff can sometimes follow a leader is by giving up all free will. They have to carry this out because they are told to. Therefore all ill effects fall upon the head of the leader. It may appear that this is really useful for a senior manager, since when the staff have no free will they are 'simply following orders'. Surely under those circumstances it is useful for people to be without a sense of will, which would mean that they will just do what they are told?

There is a down side, however. In this situation staff without a notion of free will have no opportunity to be innovative. They will do something only because they are told to, and if it goes wrong (in this case if they die) it is not their fault. In some ways this makes it a lot easier for staff to blame their managers; but, whilst it may be easier for staff, it is much more important for their managers that staff are able to think and innovate. Therefore Henry argues against Williams that his troops do have free will. In this argument Henry identifies the relationship between duty and individual responsibility. He argues that his troops do have to take some responsibility for their position and therefore it is within their power to improve their situation. We owe a duty to a king but we also owe a duty to ourselves. He argues that soldiers have a responsibility for their own sin that goes beyond their duty to their king. Individuals are responsible for their own actions and their own souls, not the king. He offers this ringing statement: 'Every subject's duty is the king's; but every subject's soul is his own' (*Henry V*, Act 4 Scene 1 lines 189–90).

Individual soldiers may owe him a duty, but their souls are their own to answer for. The soldiers' answer to this argument is of vital importance to the whole future of the battle. If they believe that everything is the king's fault and they have no possibility of action, then the army is in trouble:

> Williams *'Tis certain, every man that dies ill, the ill upon his own head, the king is not to answer it.*
> Bates *I do not desire he should answer for me; and yet I determine to fight lustily for him.*
> **Henry V**, Act 4 Scene 1 lines 200–04

In this way, just before a battle in which the soldiers (and almost certainly the king) expect to die, the king convinces two soldiers that they are in charge of their own destiny. One of them is so convinced that he will use that free will to fight lustily for the king. The argument is won by the manager in such a way as to increase the motivation of his staff. They are free agents and they will work much better because of that.

This whole scene contains many lessons for managers who want to be strong and effective. It starts with a recognition that if you don't know what your staff think and you don't know what is going on in your organization then potentially anything can happen. Under these circumstances you cannot be 'in charge'. Management texts point out time and again that managers are only as good as the information they have. It is also the case that there are continual structural problems with information flows. As we have seen with Richard III and Antony, leaders can easily create an impression that they do not really want to know the truth and they can therefore lose touch with reality.

Tom Peters comes back to this point on several occasions:

> Management enemy number one, perhaps for all time, but today for certain, is information distortion, especially when the information comes professionally packaged… The world today is uniquely messy with a host of new variables surfacing at lightening speed. The manager… must have an undistorted feel for the uncertainties out there on the line… the variety of your information sources must match the complexity of the real problems or you will be led to erroneous conclusions.
>
> (Peters, 1989: 425)

The not so modern world of Shakespeare's Henry also had uncertainties and complexities, for example the information flow through official channels would be pretty untrustworthy. For various reasons those with different levels of responsibility are loath to pass upwards difficult or contentious information. Managers who let their own bosses know that their staff believe that the boss is useless may be making a career-limiting move – they are more likely to keep quiet or at least limit the bad news. It is almost certain that the ordinary soldier 'on the front line' would not say what he really thought about the king and their chances in the battle to come for fear of punishment. Misinformation would therefore reach the king as sanitized truth, and would lead to erroneous conclusions.

Peters (1989: 425) recommends ways round this: 'To get that information and to "feel" what is keeping people from acting on it, you must visit and chat with these knowledgeable people and be where and when this action is at 3 am on the loading dock'. Peters' injunction to go and chat with the workers on the line at 3 in the morning is exactly what Shakespeare's Henry's does. After all that is where the information is.

Peters insists that managers cannot act correctly without information. The information they need, the information that will give them the difficult messages they need to know, is exactly what can be found from unofficial sources. He recommends that in getting that information managers should 'amble aimlessly' to ensure that there are numerous sources and perspectives. Again, exactly what Shakespeare's Henry succeeds in doing.

Up until this point in the play Shakespeare's Henry is gathering information with spectacular imagination. He now knows the very difficult things that his troops think about him and what they think will happen in the coming battle. In the next scene, when he makes his speech before the battle, he disseminates this information.

Overall there are six important lessons from this process of gathering and disseminating information:

1. Managers have to *want* to know what their staff really think. They need the courage to face what may be difficult messages.
2. Managers need the skills to find out these messages.
3. Without pulling rank, they need the strength to argue with their staff about the situation.
4. When staff tell managers that they will do what managers want, but only because they have to, managers need to argue them into free will and wanting to act the way in which they, the managers, want them to.
5. Even when faced with really hard conflict managers have to be persuasive enough to leave their staff feeling that there is a possibility of survival.
6. When managers have this intelligence, it is vital for them to use it well. If they don't listen to what their staff are saying, if they don't act upon this intelligence with their staff, they are in danger.

It is with that last point that I want to finish this part of the book, a point that every major management guru stresses again and again: your staff will make or break your enterprise and your capability as a manager. As Drucker (1954: 342) put it in one of his earliest books: '"Working" the human being always means developing him [sic]. And the direction this development takes decides whether the human being – both as a man and as a resource – will become more productive or cease ultimately to be productive'.

For some time Shakespeare's Henry has been 'working' his human beings, to make them productive at this crucial moment of the climactic battle. If at the moment of battle your troops don't really feel productive to the very pinnacle of their skill then both you and they are in for a tough time in the conflict. So spending every spare moment and skill getting them there for the right moment is vital.

At Agincourt, the dawn rises on a wet and weary set of British troops who all know this is going to be tough. The French are gearing up to attack. There are few minutes left for Henry to address his troops and raise them to a level of preparedness for battle. He knows that not only do his troops think they are going to die, but they feel that if they die he, the king, will somehow get out of trouble. They do not trust the social distance between ruler and ruled. To make matters worse, in front of the men one of the commanders (Henry's cousin, Westmoreland) wishes that they had more men in the army drawn from those who were idle across the channel in England:

> *O that we now had here*
> *But one ten thousand of those men in England*
> *That do no work to-day!*
> **Henry V**, Act 4 Scene 3 lines 15–17

It is worth analysing the whole of Henry's speech in sections. He addresses his troops, but starts by answering Westmoreland:

> *What's he that wishes so?*
> *My cousin Westmoreland? No, my fair cousin:.*
> *If we are mark'd to die, we are enow [enough]*
> *To do our country loss; and if to live,*
> *The fewer men, the greater share of honour.*
> *God's will! I pray thee, wish not one man more…*
> *No, faith, my coz, wish not a man from England:*
> *God's peace! I would not lose so great an honour*
> *As one man more methinks would share from me*
> *For the best hope I have.*
> **Henry V**, Act 4 Scene 3 lines 18–23 and 30–33

First, in front of his troops, he admonishes one of his highest commanders, who is also a close relative. He doesn't say to Westmoreland that it is an interesting thought to wish for a few more troops, and what a good idea if we could in some way magic them across the English Channel. He simply says no, you are wrong. He then begins to make the case that having so few men is in fact a good idea. Just imagine, if we do win, the honour that will be spread amongst the very few of us. He is appealing to his troops, the very troops whom he knows believe they are about to die. Here, at Agincourt, we are engaged in a battle. As soldiers, that is our trade. What do we get out of it, even if we win and even if we die? What we take with us after this battle, if we win or die, is honour. Honour is the currency of soldiers – not just winning but fighting well. The fewer of us there are, and the more French, the better will be our honour in the battle, since the currency of honour in this battle is devalued by being spread amongst too many of us.

Before returning to this point he makes a dramatic gesture:

> *O, do not wish one more!*
> *Rather proclaim it, Westmoreland, through my host,*
> *That he which hath no stomach to this fight,*
> *Let him depart; his passport shall be made*
> *And crowns for convoy put into his purse:*
> *We would not die in that man's company*
> *That fears his fellowship to die with us.*
> **Henry V**, Act 4 Scene 3 lines 33–39

John Ford's film of the Battle of the Alamo was some 350 years after Shakespeare wrote this scene. In the courtyard of the Texan mission, Ford had a line drawn in the sand and those who wanted to fight had to cross it. All the others could leave. Everyone crossed the line to fight. The offer and challenge, fight or leave, was made.

At Agincourt Shakespeare's Henry is prepared to give all his troops who want to go a passport and money for the journey. Above all he is challenging his men to go if they want to. This challenge is based upon the knowledge that many of his troops are very frightened, and at least one of them had wished that he was up to his neck in the cold water of the Thames rather than on the battlefield. This man and all the others are offered their way out – but they must leave in public, in front of everyone.

This challenge also provides his men with the 'way out' that Henry knows they think he himself will take. His troops believe that because of his position as monarch he can escape death through ransom, that he has a way of walking away from this battle in one piece. Given this knowledge, Henry makes the same offer to all of his troops: walk away if you want to; but know that I am staying. Remember that his troops think he will escape with his life even if they all die. Henry challenges this by saying that he will not die in the company of any man who will not die with him. This is a sharp and brilliant point. He is at one and the same time taking on the fact that there is a fellowship of death here. We are in this together and look, I am here as a part of that fellowship. At the moment here on this battlefield I offer you equality with me, the king. If you don't want to die with me then you can remove yourself from the fellowship.

How do you turn the fear of death that we know he knows is in his troops' mind into an advantage? How do you turn the enormous social differentiation between king and subject into a fellowship? You use what there is to hand in this argument, and what is directly at hand is the prospect of death. Look, I am here. We may be going to die (I know that is what you are all frightened of because you have told me), but I will die with you, if you will die with me.

Death is of course a great equalizer and Henry offers that equality in his own relationship as leader to his troops. If we die together it will not only be an equal death, but also you will die in the company of a king – a death that none of you thought likely.

The day of the battle is the feast of St Crispian (25 October). His speech continues with him pointing out that for as long as they live the soldiers will celebrate that day:

> *This day is call'd the feast of Crispian:*
> *He that outlives this day, and comes safe home,*
> *Will stand a tip-toe when this day is named, …*
> *Old men forget; yet all shall be forgot,*
> *But he'll remember with advantages,*
> *What feats he did that day:*
> **Henry V**, Act 4 Scene 3 lines 40–42 and 49–51

He stops talking about death, the honour of death and sharing death, and directly addresses what life might be like for the soldiers who survive. He doesn't claim that everyone will survive, but realistically starts by saying: 'He that outlives this day', and paints a real vision of how an old trooper will survive, a picture he is bound to have seen in the taverns of east London: an old soldier proudly remembering the battles that he fought. The lesson from his old drinking friend Falstaff appears here, in that he learnt from Falstaff that such old soldiers do tend to remember, with advantage, the feats they once performed. Throughout the ages old soldiers have made up stories about their valour and the battles they have fought; once they have stopped fighting they always talk about it with embellishment. There is a beautiful scene in *Henry IV Part 1* where Falstaff tells huge lies about fighting off dozens of people when there were in fact only two – so Henry has learnt this language. Every soldier in Henry's army who hears this part of the speech will smile and think: 'Henry really knows us. He knows who we are and how we will behave.' He is in Henry's own language being 'a good boy'. This is a clear example of the use to which Henry put his knowledge of common people's language, and thus he joins with his troops.

It is very significant that in this entire speech Shakespeare's Henry does not say they will win the battle and all end up rich with plunder. Given his circumstances this is not very believable, and would alienate his troops by promising them something that looks unattainable. He does, however, say that it is possible that many will survive.

He concludes the speech by stressing the brotherhood, and once more mentions their small numbers:

We few, we happy few, we band of brothers;
For he to-day that sheds his blood with me
Shall be my brother; be he ne'er so vile,
This day shall gentle his condition:
And gentlemen in England now a-bed
Shall think themselves accursed they were not here,
And hold their manhoods cheap, whiles any speaks
That fought with us
Henry V, Act 4 Scene 3 lines 60–67

We are few but we are happy, and we will shed our blood, you and I – but we will shed it together as brothers. In fact the act of being here with me, the king, should make everyone a gentleman. Here once more Henry addresses the way in which his troops are worried about his kingship separating him off into safety, and points out that he has blood to shed and that he is their brother. He is also saying, once more, imagine telling your mates about this. You and the king outnumbered 10 to 1 against the French. What a story we will have to tell!

His men know this is not rhetoric. His down to earth language and metaphor has proved it time and again and he has proved his commitment to them by staying on to face the battle. They know he has lived much of his life amongst them. For no moment in his life has he pretended to be other than a future king or king itself, yet the years of spending time with 'the lads' pays brilliant dividends. When he appeals to his troops as their blood brother he does so having learnt their language and their culture. He is sure that he has become a 'good boy'.

The important point of this speech as an example of Shakespeare's Henry V's management is how persuasive it is. His troops recognize that this king treats them as blood brothers and the play's audience believes it. If he had just put on a working-class accent and appealed to their patriotism without all the detailed cultural references they would have seen through him. He succeeds too by appealing to their pride, not just in their country but in their work as soldiers. They have come to France to fight. People come to work to work, and it is here that people can be motivated best by having pride in what they do.

The possibility of pride of workmanship means more to the production worker than gymnasiums, tennis courts and recreation areas. Give the workforce a chance to work with pride, and the 3 per cent who apparently don't care will erode itself by peer pressure. If people know what they are doing at work and are proud of it they will work well. The whole thrust of good management is to give staff an opportunity to prove this.

At the end of his speech and in the next moment Henry is warned that the French are ready to attack, and the British army must prepare itself. He is warned to get ready – the enemy is charging. After such a speech, aimed totally at motivating his troops, he concludes by saying: 'All things are ready, if our mind be so' (line 71).

This is the explanation of his previous few hours' work. He has few troops, they are tired and outnumbered. What he can do is prepare his troops' minds for the battle ahead to make sure they fight at the peak of their capacity. To do that he has had to find out what they think and then use that intelligence to focus them on the work in hand.

This is a clear example of human resource management at its highest. The way in which the staff enter a very difficult part of their work, their frame of mind, is all. Modern managers will say that it is the human resources of a company that sets the organization apart. A world-class company is only world class if its staff are fully involved and if the senior management manage them as such. But too few of those managers who claim this involvement as all important spend any time at all learning from their staff. They accentuate the distance between them and their staff, not their relationship. As a consequence when they need to prepare their staff's minds for difficult work, when they need to stretch their staff, they are useless.

Modern management theorists have made it clear that management only works when it succeeds in motivating people. John Harvey-Jones (1988: 260) puts it very clearly in terms that Shakespeare's Henry himself would have understood: 'People are self-motivated. They do their best work when they have come to believe, through their own processes, that what they are going to do is worthwhile. The free man is always better than the slave.'

Henry's troops are dramatically given the opportunity to leave the battle. If they choose to stay they are truly 'free men' and stay because they want to be there. Indeed in the battle they do 'do their best work', and do so because they are motivated.

If we look at Shakespeare's Henry's work at Agincourt we can see how, in a clear and imaginative fashion, he successfully motivates his troops to achieve more than anyone could expect. He does this by artic-ulating a vision that stresses the values of the audience he is addressing. Indeed in his major speeches, before Harfleur and Agincourt, he achieves this with some of the finest words in the English language. The speeches join him with his troops, both in the fight and in the nation, beautifully.

He involves people in the construction of that vision by listening to what they are worried about: that their king will leave them in the lurch to protect his own skin. He then deals with it effectively by demonstrating that not only is he still there, but allowing them to leave if they want to. He is enthusiastic about fighting not just with them but amongst them, all the time demonstrating how proud he is to be a part of them and their affiliations. He provides a clear role model by his visibility and his actions. And, last, he provides public recognition of their actions through speeches in front of not just the common troops but their leaders. He demonstrates his concern for the lowliest part of the organization by being so angry when the baggage boys are killed.

The lessons to be learnt are greater than this, however. Tom Peters argues strongly that leaders cannot motivate without a clear relationship between themselves and their followers. Visions are not enough, they must be shared, and sharing needs leaders to listen:

> Studies of effective leaders demonstrate that they do not induce narrow obedience to a precise objective amongst followers. To the contrary, powerful leaders make followers more powerful in pursuit of a commonly held dream, jointly defined. Furthermore, the listening leader inspires leaders (managers at all levels) to be listeners too. The listening organization is in turn the one most likely to pick up quickly on changes in its environment.
>
> (Peters, 1989: 469)

Shakespeare's Henry uses a great deal of expertise to build this commonly held dream, and makes sure that he defines it in ways that demonstrate its jointness. That jointness can *only* come from his years of listening; and because he listens he can pick up the changes in the environment of his army when his troops think he is about to desert them.

Shakespeare's Henry has three plays of listening and finding out about language and culture to enable him to do this. All of this work leads him to be able to demonstrate, not just the importance of motivation but also the jointness of the enterprise, with the ringing phrase that ends his speech and starts the battle: 'All things be ready if our mind be so.'

Part 5

Paying attention to the sub-plot

Paul Scofield as King Lear (source: Kobal Collection)

Chapter 10

ℒISTENING TO FOOLS AND KNAVES

It is a truism to stress the importance of the ordinary members of staff to a successful organization. Failing to appreciate their importance is a failure of management that may impact on the very future of the senior manager. As Tom Peters puts it when referring to the 'little people':

> The little people will get even, which is one of a thousand reasons why they are not little people at all. If you're a jerk as leader, you will be torpedoed. And usually it won't be by your vice-presidents; it will be on the loading dock at 3 am when no supervisors are around.
>
> (Peters, 1994: 35)

We saw in Part 4 that one of the main lessons managers can learn from the life of Shakespeare's Henry V is to make sure that they are in a position to learn from the staff in their organizations. This is an injunction not just to listen, but more importantly to make sure you understand the culture and the language of what people say. Over the last 40 years management books have emphasized how senior managers can only really lead their organizations if they know what is going on inside them. It always seems obvious, but it is surprising, in the real world of management, how little time and effort are given to the activity.

The quote from Tom Peters goes beyond this. It contains a powerful warning to senior managers, arguing that if you fail to pay attention to the little people, if you are a 'jerk', you will fail because, sooner or later, at that witching hour (for Peters) of 3 o'clock in the morning on the loading bay, they will get you. They have the power to stop the biggest leader – ignore them at your peril. This argument for clean recognition of the rights of the little people goes beyond the fact that it is a good, moral thing as a leader to find out what they think. It says that if you don't they can ruin you, and in claiming this moves beyond a moral argument for including people to a recognition of the material power that the little people have over their bosses.

I believe Shakespeare recognizes this, not only through the way in which he has Henry listen to people, but also in the way he develops very strong characters for some of his little people. He also passionately develops the sub-plots in his plays. Shakespeare, as a dramatist dealing with the great affairs of state, always finds time to have sections of his plays provide other voices – voices from the smaller people. In most of his plays the little people don't simply work around the lives of the bigger people in a parasitic way. They not only have a part to play in the larger plot, they also have strong and individual characters within the plots and the sub-plots. They are not mere ciphers – Shakespeare gives them their own lives. In dramatists' terms, the story that they live in is called a sub-plot – not as important as the main story, but integral to the meaning of the play. Shakespeare's plays are full of sub-plots, and sometimes they are the best remembered part of the play.

The reason that both Shakespeare and Tom Peters give for listening to the little people is not simply that it is a good, moral thing but that it is necessary – running a nation or an organization can leave individuals personally isolated. These leaders also tend to believe that what they think about the organization and its direction is the only really important knowledge around. I have emphasized throughout that a leader who fails to appreciate the ambiguities and contradictions of power will fail badly. All organizations have ambiguities and contradictions within them and it is vital for leaders to be able to find and pay attention to these messages. This does not necessarily make you a better person, but it may mean that you can manage a great deal better. In this part of the book I argue that Shakespeare develops sub-plots and strong difficult characters to demonstrate to leaders that they cannot lead without understanding ambiguities of organizations. He does this, not in the margins of his plays, but in their core.

In *A Midsummer-Night's Dream*, for example, for many audiences the main story about kings and queens is usually forgotten because the ordinary men and women of the city making a play led by the character Bottom are more interesting. In fact if you asked most people who had just seen this play what they thought about it their first comment would probably be about this part of the play, with its raw humour and developed working-class characters.

Whilst the character of Hamlet dominates the play named after him, one of the best modern plays of the last 30 years, Tom Stoppard's *Rosencrantz and Guildenstern are Dead*, is a play full of meaning, based on the nature of life, that has been developed out of a very small but crucial sub-plot in Hamlet. Two bit players, who are not really differentiated from each other, but are student friends of Hamlet, are given instructions to take Hamlet to England. Stoppard makes these two the leading players in their own play. In their sub-plot in Hamlet they are a part of a story that is aiming to get Hamlet killed – something that, if they had succeeded, would have really changed the plot!

Many people who go to see Shakespeare today love these sub-plots because they can recognize themselves and their lives, as could audiences 400 years ago. Few of us think we will be kings and queens, but many of us can just about see ourselves as being part of a sub-plot where our lives and theirs interact. We can fantasize about what it would be like if we were their close advisers, and how we might crack a few jokes with the king and queen to lighten the atmosphere, perhaps even become a court humorist.

The interconnectedness between Shakespeare's main plots and his sub-plots is one of the main dramatic forms differentiating him from some of his contemporaries. His vision of leadership and his portrayal of that vision were different from his contemporary playwright Marlowe, for example. Marlowe wrote a brilliant play about leadership called *Tamburlaine the Great*. Marlowe's Tamburlaine, having started life as a shepherd boy, conquers most of the known world. The plot places this great man on a high historical pedestal and we learn from Marlowe what it is like to be a great conquering emperor. However, Marlowe's Tamburlaine, once he has left his humble roots behind, simply uses ordinary people as his troops or as his enemies. His relationship with them is simple – he slaughters them or uses them for slaughter. In Marlowe's play ordinary people don't appear as real people, as an important part of the story; for Marlowe lessons about leadership are abstracted away from the common people.

The theatre before Shakespeare started to write was undergoing a new lease of life, both as a form of art and as an entertainment. Marlowe was for a few years the greatest dramatist the English nation had ever seen. Marlowe's inventiveness drew the crowds before Shakespeare did. It was his murder in 1593 that gave Shakespeare his chance to emerge from behind his shadow.

Shakespeare did not invent the new theatre however; his plays were the second wave in the new theatrical tide. As an economic proposition, which at one level it had to be, filling a theatre at this time was a big task – 2,000 people was a capacity crowd for the Globe Theatre in London's Southwark (fire regulations being a bit lax at the time), and a trip to the Globe could last all day, with food and transportation. Whilst a theatre trip today can be expensive, 400 years ago it cost the equivalent of a great deal more, and for most people there was a lot less disposable income then than there is now. It was therefore vital to give people something they thought was worth the cost and the effort.

The audience for Shakespeare's plays was varied, from those standing nearest the stage, the poorest, called the groundlings, to the boxes for the lords. The play had to leave them, with their different backgrounds, all wanting to come back for more. I am not claiming that Shakespeare only wrote plays as an advertising agency now writes slogans, but the 'market' of an audience was an integral part of this process. The plays must have been written with that communication to that audience in mind.

This is not an arcane point. In the very process of writing a play there is a recognition that the play can only be completed by the existence of an audience. As you write you think of the performances and you think of the audience. How will this character work with them? How will that scene work? If you write a joke, will people complete it with a laugh? If they don't the joke doesn't work. This was true for a play performed in the 1600s and is true of one performed 400 years later. The text written by Shakespeare is only completed by an audience of people, giving the opportunity for a play to be refreshed and completed by different audiences at different historical periods. The meaning of a play therefore changes over time, as the audience of the 20th century completes it in different ways from the audience of the 17th.

A play contains some 'hooks' on which an audience can hang their personal experiences. The play as it is written needs the interaction with the audience to complete its full meaning. The audience that carries out this task does so in different ways at different times. I am suggesting here that Shakespeare, partly because of the dangerous and changing times he lived in, partly because of his skill and partly because of the need to leave people wanting more, wrote plays that had important ambiguities within the characters and the plots. The work is incomplete and needs an audience with concrete experience to complete it.

There are times in his plays when he makes this relationship crystal clear. He makes a direct appeal to the audience to carry out their work of completing the play with their imagination. In the first few lines of the prologue to *Henry V* he reminds the audience that this is a play being performed on a stage, and it must not be confused with reality:

> *But pardon, gentles all,*
> *The flat unraised spirits that have dared*
> *On this unworthy scaffold to bring forth*
> *So great an object: can this cockpit hold*
> *The vasty fields of France? …*
> *And let us, ciphers to this great accompt,*
> *On your imaginary forces work…*
> *For 'tis your thoughts that now must deck our kings,*
> *Carry them here and there; jumping o'er times,*
> **Henry V**, Prologue lines 8–12, 17–18 and 28–29

Shakespeare is saying that this is a play about the fields of France. It will take place on a small wooden stage in south London, England. At the very start of the play the audience is reminded that no one from the time of Henry V will really come on to this stage, no one will really travel to France and no real king will appear. The only way these things will happen is if the audience works with the play to make them happen. But your 'thoughts must deck our kings', the audience's imagination can create the 'vasty fields of France' and can 'jump o'er times'. So, dear audience, get to work. It is the audience's 'imaginary forces', their 'thoughts' that will have to work hard to turn the stage into the fields of France.

The nature of this 'completion' by the audience is a major issue in Shakespearean drama. For a number of critics, such as Brecht, it is the extent of this completion by the audience, and the expectation that he has of his audience, that makes him a great playwright:

> With Shakespeare the spectator does the constructing. Shakespeare never bends the course of human destiny in the second act to make a fifth possible. With him everything takes its natural course. In the lack of connection between his acts, we see the lack of connection in a human destiny, when it is recounted by someone with no interest in tidying it up so as to provide someone with an idea that is not taken from life. There's nothing more stupid than to perform Shakespeare so that he's clear. He is by his very nature unclear. He's pure material.
>
> (Brecht, 1967: 119)

This is counter-intuitive to most people's views of a great playwright. People say they love Shakespeare because he seems so clear. Brecht's point is that the very thing that makes him great is the way he represents life as full of contradictions – because he is complex we recognize our 'selves' in his characters, and then together he and the audience make something clear. It is that aspect that we listen to and complete with our own sense of contradiction in our lives.

This is an important point about the work that Shakespeare expects his audience to carry out in order to complete his plays. He appears clear in different ways to different members of his audience because his plays are 'completed' in different ways by each of them. Take the example of Shakespeare's injunction to the audience in the Prologue to *Henry V*. He tells the audience that they must use their 'imaginary force' to create battles in France, as a consequence, for each member of the audience, *their* France is clear to them.

If Shakespeare presented his 'good guys' and 'bad guys' as one-dimensional we would never see ourselves as having anything to do with them. At base we all know that we are each a complex jumble of emotions, and we work with Shakespeare because we realize that our own jumble of ambiguities is, in Brecht's phrase '[taking] its natural course' in his plays.

In our own century different productions of Shakespeare can stress the dark or the light side of each play and each character. At an historical time of hope the light side is stressed, and people feel that Shakespeare is writing for those times. At other times the reverse is true. For example Shakespearean director Peter Hall, greatly affected by the horrors of the Second World War, produced from these emotions his versions of Shakespeare's plays covering the War of the Roses:

> I realised that the mechanism of power had not changed in centuries. We also were in the middle of a blood-soaked century. I was convinced that a presentation of one of the bloodiest and most hypocritical periods in history would teach many lessons about the present.
>
> (Hall, 1970: xi)

Hall is a great, historically rooted Shakespearean director. Other directors put this seeming capacity of Shakespeare to mean different things at different times in another way. This ability to direct the play in one course or another without doing violence to the text demonstrates the way in which Shakespeare writes about human interaction, representing its many dimensions. We at the turn of the new millennium use the room that he provides to complete these dimensions with our own world. We can find modern betrayal, love and leadership in a text written all those years ago.

Over the centuries critics have fought about which is the 'correct' rendering of each play. How can you laugh at what is happening in a tragedy? How can you cry in the comedy? You can because Shakespeare wrote the plays with so much movement in them and, given that amount of movement, we find our turn of the century concerns there too.

It must be stressed, however, that the Elizabethan and Jacobean theatre was not a matter of concern to the vast majority of the population, nearly all of whom worked on smallholdings in the countryside. Nearly all the population lived in villages that they very rarely left except to go to market. There they might see some travelling players, but nothing as grand as the Globe Theatre in London. This rural population looked backwards to continuity between the past, the present and the future; most were anxious about the changes that were taking place, and were generally against them. A very small proportion of the population lived in the world that included Shakespeare's theatre.

Whilst Shakespeare's audience were not all well off, they were nearly all from the urban environment and from the more advanced and progressive part of society. Shakespeare's plays may have had plots that were drawn from the past, but their meaning was about the present and the future. He wrote for those who were looking at the newly changing and fractured society and from that into the future. They were not looking backwards.

Why is this an important point? Earlier in the book I argued that there was an historical bridge between the modernity of Shakespeare's times and our own new millennial modernity. It is important to recognize that the same was true of the audiences that completed his plays originally. Now as then the vast majority of the population do not see Shakespeare live on the stage, it is an urban population and those with a high level of education that are most likely to see Shakespeare. Whilst most people who love the theatre would find this disappointing – both then and now – it is true. It follows that the stage productions of Shakespeare's plays today are nearly always aimed at a particular section of the population. Such productions are constantly trying to move the plays forward to new meanings, in new costumes, with new scenery and new special effects. Just as the 'modern' audience completed the plays in his own times so it happens now. The modernity of the plays moves forward to a modern audience.

This returns me to the main theme of this part of the book. As a playwright, Shakespeare wrote for an audience in such a way that they could 'complete' his work. He knew that his audience would consist of a wide variety of people, and indeed the economics of the theatre depended upon his attracting very different groups of people. Since his plays were written to be seen by many classes and different trades and professions he made sure that there was a real relationship between the stage and the lives of everybody who came – not just the kings and queens. That is why the little people matter so much in the main plots of Shakespeare's plays – he is making a point that connects to his audience. You matter, too. You matter on the stage, you matter in life.

However, Shakespeare recognized that most of the ordinary people would never get anywhere near seeing themselves in plays because they lived in a very different world. He could have tried to achieve that by writing a few jokes and common people into the main story. One way of giving the little people in the audience some recognition of themselves would be to have their characters representing the common people moving in and out of the main story, literally, bit players. Shakespeare rejects this approach and instead integrates them fully into the play's main plot.

Great plays ensure that the meaning of the sub-plot blends into the main plot, especially in the conclusion. So the characters, their personal stories, their part in the sub-plot and what they say all add to the characters and the story of the main plot. This is the first important lesson that Shakespeare tells us about the importance of sub-plots: they are an integral part of the main story. If you cut out the sub-plot, and just pay attention to the main plot, you don't understand the main story. The plays he writes ensure that the different plots are completely interdependent, and if you want to understand the big picture, you must understand the little ones. If, as you sometimes do in a novel, you skip the bits with people like Falstaff and King Lear's Fool to enable you to get on with the main narrative, then you will find aspects of the main narrative incomprehensible.

At one level this may appear obvious: that the big picture is after all made up of lots of little ones and they add together to make the large plot. Usually plays are not talked about in this way. The main plot is the story of the play and it has a meaning on its own – the sub-plots are less relevant. Rather than being interdependent, the plots are separate and unequal.

This is similar to the apparently different levels of importance contained in the different stories that take place within organizations. In the life of an organization the importance of what happens in the post room or kitchen is usually seen as a lot less important than, or as being unequal to, what happens in the board room. The plot that covers life and work in the board room is always treated as much more significant that the life and work of the post room. Indeed the people who live and work in the board room do so with very little reference to the post room. The plots, and here I mean the term to be about intrigue and subterfuge, that take place in the board room are the ones that appear to determine the life and death of the organization or at least its direction. Whereas, however interesting life in the post room gets, nobody of 'importance' usually pays it any attention. All of the stories are in a hierarchy, whether they are in a play, in history or in the management of the organization.

The point that this chapter makes is that both Tom Peters and William Shakespeare agree that if you are a leader or a senior manager who fails to pay attention to the sub-plot, in the end you will not understand the big picture. A failure to understand the nature and relevance of the sub-plot, in Tom Peters' example of the loading bay at 3 o'clock in the morning, could lead to the destruction of the boss. This is a significant lesson that reflects the modern democratic style of management, as clearly as it reflected Shakespeare's demonstration of the integral nature of the lives of the little people.

One US business icon who did understand the importance of involving the 'little people' was the late Sam Walton, the folksy founder and boss of the Wal-Mart discount chain. In Wal-Mart employees at the lowest level receive complete financial reports about the company, sending the message that they are important partners in the business. In another hugely successful US retailer, Nordstrom, the humblest salespeople are given smart business cards to reinforce their image of professionalism. At Nordstrom there is only one rule in the corporate rulebook: for all employees to use their best judgement on behalf of helping the customer.

In terms of modern organizations, management guru after guru points out this interdependence. They rightly claim that if an organization is ignorant about what is going on in the post room then they will only discover its importance on the day when urgent and important post will not get dealt with. Shakespeare demonstrates this interrelatedness by making his plays interdependent. He carefully constructs the relationship between the big and little worlds to show how the whole fits together. A play about the leaders, which tells their true story, needs also to be a play about the little people connected with them who make the big story work. We learn in dramatic terms how the big depends upon the little.

This interdependence underscores the point that Tom Peters and others regularly make in order to stress why senior managers need to get wider information about their firm's activities. I quoted, in Part 4, Peter's injunction to spend time finding out what the staff in the organization who carry out the work really think. He argues this point because failure to know what is going on elsewhere can ruin a manager's capacity to manage. Specifically, since Peters now works as a consultant, he tells us how he finds out what is going on in organizations he is working for:

> When digging for intelligence (of the CIA variety) in a client company, the little people are by far the best sources. They're the ones who know where the skeletons are buried, who understand the humble origins of the grand half-truths. Your intelligence as leader… will in general be directly proportional to the number and depth of your relationships with folks six levels down who have access to the real unexpurgated data.
>
> (Peters, 1994: 35)

This is another clear injunction to listen, not to the people around you, but to the little people. Of course senior managers will be given vast amounts of information about their organization. Even in the most primitive organization management information systems provide considerable knowledge about what is and what is not working. Good senior managers will spend much of their time setting up and maintaining such systems and making sure that they are providing up-to-date information. However, alongside this, really wise senior managers will spend considerable time making sure that they have other ways of finding out what is actually going on. The manager will not be getting information directly from the 'folks six levels down' the organizational structure. Peters specifically enjoins the manager to pick up information randomly and not to depend upon management information systems. Somewhere in the organization people have the real, unexpurgated data, but you will have to seek them out. They will not simply appear next to you the moment you need the information as statistics do from your databank.

As I have said, Shakespeare makes this point through the creation of powerful, interdependent sub-plots; but he goes further than this. I have already noted that he tells big histories through the characters of the people who carry out the plot. His plays are narratives, but they are more than that; they are mainly characters playing out plots as real people. He not only does this with the main plot, but in many of his plays he creates a character who has a crucial role to play in teaching the leader how to think about his (or her) work as leader. These people come to personify the importance of the sub-plot and the way in which the little people give meaning to the bigger people.

In two of the plays I have discussed already these roles are vital to the leader. First, King Lear's court employs a fool. He is very close to Lear and has a role throughout the play. As we shall see the role of the fool is an institutional one within the courts that Shakespeare writes about. Second, Shakespeare creates in *Henry IV Parts 1* and *2* what has been called his greatest role in Falstaff. For two plays Falstaff interacts very closely with the future king, giving him great strength and knowledge. Both these parts may be smaller than the 'leading players' of Lear or Henry, but when certain actors have played them their careers have been made, and some actors would define these parts as their best acting ever. The significance of these two great roles for actors of Shakespearean plays is undeniable.

The story, the main plot, would still be a good story without them, and each character, each sub-plot, contains a risk that they may detract from the main theme of the play. I treat these strong additional characters as not only of some importance, but also as having lessons to teach us about the interrelation between leadership and lesser people – lessons that both ordinary people and leadership have to learn.

LEAR'S FOOL

Jesters do oft prove prophets.
King Lear, Act 5 Scene 3 line 71

In Part 2 we discussed the story of King Lear, who decides at the very beginning of the play to bequeath his kingdom to his three daughters.

He does this not on any rational basis, but on the base of who can flatter him the most. He gives away the land on which his power is based and as a consequence has to depend upon his daughters for the rest of his life. Much of the play circles around this move for Lear from almost total autocratic power over the world to complete dependency on others – even for his food and lodgings. This is a dramatic shift.

In giving up his power in such a whimsical way, Lear feels he is demonstrating just how much power he has; but the moment he gives his daughters his kingdom the power he had, which was purely drawn from the kingdom, disappears. Lear thought that he would still have the power, whereas, even though he has been king for so long, he has no power once he has given up his kingdom. Despite the fact that this is a capricious and stupid act, which his friends advise against, Lear, throughout the play, is supported in his powerlessness by two old friends (Kent and Gloucester) and by his faithful retainer, his Fool.

Fools and jesters have a strong role in a number of Shakespeare's plays, but in Lear the Fool (sometimes called boy) has a high role in the drama. Unlike everyone else in the play this character has no name, but is called by his role.

> Perhaps the most famous of all Shakespearean fool roles is that of the unnamed 'boy' in *King Lear*, where the double act between the Fool and the King during the early part of the play allows Shakespeare to move swiftly between different dramatic registers in his exploration of rationality and madness, language and power.
>
> (Mangan, 1996: 50)

Lear's Fool is vital to this aspect of the play. His relationship with his king, and the way in which he maintains his point of view despite the awesome power of the king over him, is important to the whole play. Somebody has to find a way of letting the king know he is doing absurd things that endanger not just his kingdom but his own health and happiness. Someone has to find a way, despite all his power and anger, of telling him the truth.

It is not easy to find a way of telling kings who are doing silly things that they are wrong; as we have seen Kent tries to do this and gets himself exiled for his pains. Telling the truth can be a dangerous business – which is one of the reasons senior managers often do not get told the truth. Their very power and position creates fear for those who want to speak out. In the medieval court a role developed for a courtier who would be physically and personally close to the monarch, part of whose work was to 'tell the truth' to the monarch. One of the central aspects of this truth-telling relationship is around the aspect of the word 'fool'. A fool is someone who makes wrong decisions and bases them on foolish preconceptions.

The contradiction in this role is that, whilst he is called Fool and has the low status that the name confers, because he is called Fool he can say things that other people with higher status cannot. He can tell the truth precisely because the truth can be dismissed as foolish and inconsequential. Nobody need pay any attention to him, because he is, after all, a fool. His words, even if they are true, can be dismissed because of where they have come from. However, had a lord, duke or blood relative of the king told the same truth they would be in serious trouble because they had contradicted the king from a position of power.

The way in which the Fool speaks to Lear after he has made the decision to give away his land and become personally dependent on his daughters is through a riddle. The Fool gives sharp and direct advice. It is part of the role of the Fool in Shakespeare's *King Lear* to point out that Lear has made a foolish decision, but the way in which the Fool does this is unusual:

> Fool *That lord that counsell'd thee*
> *To give away thy land,*
> *Come place him here by me,*
> *Do thou for him stand:*
> *The sweet and bitter fool*
> *Will presently appear;*
> *The one in motley here,*
> *The other found out there*
> Lear *Dost thou call me fool, boy?*
> Fool *All thy other titles thou hast given away; that thou wast born with.*
> **King Lear**, Act 1 Scene 4 lines 154–65

The Fool could say, 'Sir, that was a really foolish decision, to give away your land', but he doesn't. He uses the fact that he is a fool to get the message across by riddle and analogy. He does this succintly enough for Lear to understand clearly what he is talking about.

Let us not forget that this is not an example of banter between equals. Earlier on in this act Lear is by far the most powerful man on the stage, demonstrated by his capriciously giving away his kingdom. In the same scene Lear also becomes so angry with one of his highest-ranked courtiers and longest-serving friends (Kent) that he banishes him from the country. This is also a capricious act, since Kent is obviously his close friend and supporter. So when the Fool tells him he has been foolish Lear has already just ruined another man's life who has simply pointed out that he may be wrong about his daughter. Shakespeare has established that the price of contradicting Lear is very high indeed, and thus that the Fool takes a great risk. It is in this context that the Fool makes the above speech and calls his master a fool.

The whole thrust of the Fool's speech is for him to point out that whilst he, the Fool, may be wearing the fool's clothes (his 'motley'), it is Lear who is making decisions as if he were a fool. The Fool reiterates this point by replying to the king (who may already be somewhat angry at being called a fool), that the real foolishness is the way in which he has given away his kingdom: 'all thy other titles thou hast given away'. This refers back to the first scene in the play where Lear carries out his decision to give away his kingdom to his daughters. It is pretty easy for us to see his decision as foolish, and carried out in a foolish way. However, for an employee to point this out is dangerous, and some-thing that could only happen within a very special relationship, in this case a relationship that appears to encourage the Fool as a 'truth teller', able to offer ideas and advice that contradict the actions of the powerful.

There is a range of different roles that could be played out in order to create such a relationship. It is clear that the courts of kings and queens in Shakespeare's time did employ people who were very close to the monarch and who had the primary aim of making people laugh. They were clowns, comedians, as well as fools. Whilst these roles were not completely interchangeable, and there were some who went on to become professional comedians, humour, foolishness and truth telling were all interlinked in these people. They were there not to only amuse but also to make sure that the monarch knew what was going on and what they (the fools) thought about it.

They, as with Lear's Fool, were with their monarchs all the time, through which proximity to power they knew nearly as much about the way in which the nation was run as their monarchs. Personally, though, they had no power and no role in the running of the nation or the court and so were different to the dukes and earls who formed the king's official council. In terms of modern organizations we would say that whilst they were personally close to the CEO and knew everything that was going on they were marginal to the power structure.

However, from that marginal position, and *because* they were marginal, they were able to comment on what their monarchs were doing under the guise of humour. The Fool's clever rhymes in the speech above, and his use of words in the other quotations I use, demonstrate how he can communicate crucial messages to the king under the guise of wordplay. The clever wordplay doesn't hide the meaning, and the king understands immediately, but it delivers a harsh message in a different way.

The Fool is playing a complex role in giving advice to the king. He is a figure that criticizes him and yet is close to the king. He depends upon the king for his livelihood and probably his life more than any other person in the play – and yet he still plays a role of criticism and truth telling. On occasions Lear's Fool directly draws out the contra-dictions of his own position, where he can be criticized for telling the truth and criticized for lying.

Towards the end of the first act he comments on how dangerous life can be for someone who tries to find the truth in a king's court that is full of conflict:

> *I marvel what kin thou and thy daughters are: they'll have me whipped for speaking true, thou'lt have me whipped for lying; and sometimes I am whipped for holding my peace. I had rather be any kind o' thing than a fool:*
> **King Lear**, Act 1 Scene 4 lines 200–05

Lear's daughters need the Fool to lie to the king about what they are doing and let him know he will be whipped if he tells the truth to Lear.

Lear expects the Fool to tell the truth and not keep quiet, but the truth, as we can see from a few lines before, consists of telling the king that he is a fool. As the Fool says in this speech, the king expects him to tell the truth or he will be whipped for lying; equally, he can be whipped for keeping his peace and not saying a word. This demonstrates that his is a very difficult job, but one that needs to be done if the king is to hear the truth at all.

Consider for a moment how few chief executives have anyone in their organization with this kind of job description. Nearly everyone they talk to has a role to play in running the organization, all of their senior executives have a particular axe to grind, and the CEO will recognize that what they all say will be said primarily from within those roles. Staff are almost all worried about their promotion and are unlikely to tell the truth about what they really think because they are worried about the CEO's power. So when CEOs ask: 'And what do you think?' they know that the reply will come from within a role and with some fear about their power. The Fool goes further than this – he not only tells the king what he thinks, but he does so without being asked. Just prior to the above speech Lear does not ask the Fool: 'and what do you think about me giving my kingdom away?' He doesn't ask for the Fool's opinion, the Fool gives it to him because that is the core of their relationship. In modern organizations no one is employed specifically to sit with the CEO all the time and tell the truths as they see them. That would be a very difficult job to create and advertise within the modern company structure.

Lear's Fool talks from a position that is structurally uncomfortable, one where he has no material power base in terms of men and money and yet is expected to tell the truths no one else does. Yet throughout the play the Fool provides truths to the beleaguered king. Earlier in the first act he chose to teach the king a lesson based upon riddles:

Have more than thou showest,
Speak less than thou knowest,
Lend less than thou owest,
Ride more than thou goest,
Learn more than thou trowest,
Set less than thou throwest;
Leave thy drink and thy whore,

And keep in-a-door,
And thou shalt have more
Than two tens to a score.
King Lear, Act 1 Scene 4 lines 132–41

Here again in the guise of clever wordplay he is advising the king to be prudent and to conceal from the rest of the world how wealthy he is. If he pretends he has less than he has then he has more than he shows and shall accumulate more. Specifically, 'ride more than thou goest' is recommending using his horse rather than his legs; 'learn more than thou trowest' recommends listening much and believing less; 'set less than thou throwest' recommends betting less for large stakes.

The Fool recommends this strategy because the end result would be that the king would end up with more than the 20 units he started with. Let us look a little at the context for this advice recommending prudence through the riddle. It is being given to a king who has just given his entire kingdom away. In the middle of the play, the Fool reminds Lear and the audience that at the opening of the play Lear displayed absurd largesse. However for the Fool it represents very strong opinion, and he gives it to the king.

The king responds in an interesting way and once more gets advice:

Kent *This is nothing, fool.*
Fool *Then 'tis like the breath of an unfee'd lawyer; you gave me nothing for 't. Can you make no use of nothing, nuncle?*
Lear *Why, no, boy; nothing can be made out of nothing.*
Fool [to Kent] *Prithee, tell him, so much the rent of his land comes to: he will not believe a fool.*
King Lear, Act 1 Scene 4 lines 142–50

Lear believes that the poem about prudence equals nothing. He will not take the Fool's advice. The Fool points out, in a wonderful sideswipe at the legal profession, that since he has been paid nothing for his advice he challenges the king to make use of his words, even if they cost nothing. This moves Lear to one of the most ringing statements of the play: 'Nothing can be made out of nothing'. This represents the fact that it is slowly dawning on him what he has done in giving away his land. It is a phrase that reflects the slow realization that his daughters – who came from him – are going to give him nothing back – leaving him with nothing, making him realize how little he has in himself. His daughters, who he felt were everything (especially when they flattered him), were in fact nothing, and now, for the rest of his life, when he is totally dependent on them, he will get nothing back. Yet he was the person who gave them everything.

Not leaving it at this the Fool returns to his main theme in this scene. He points out that now Lear has so foolishly given all his land away the rent of his land comes to what they are talking about – nothing. Time and again the fool returns to what he sees as the truth, but he also recognizes that Lear will not believe a fool.

Later in this scene Shakespeare's Fool returns to this theme of nothing, and the absence of his king's wit. Following on from saying that he would rather be anything than a Fool, he admits that:

> and yet I would not be thee, nuncle; thou hast pared thy wit o' both sides, and left nothing i' the middle: here comes one o' the parings.
> [At this point Goneril, one of the daughters to whom Lear has given his kingdom, enters.]
> Lear *How now, daughter! what makes that frontlet on? Methinks you are too much of late i' the frown.*
> Fool *Thou wast a pretty fellow when thou hadst no need to care for her frowning; now thou art an 0 without a figure: I am better than thou art now; I am a fool, thou art nothing.*
> **King Lear**, Act 1 Scene 4 lines 205–16

Here the Fool is even sharper with his master. He describes clearly what Lear has done by giving his two daughters one half of his kingdom each: he has pared his wit on both sides, leaving a nought in the middle. This underlines that the king has nothing. When one of the daughters turns up and Lear remarks on her frowning face, the Fool chides Lear, since before Lear had given away his kingdom and become dependent upon his daughter's charity he need not have worried about the frown. When he ran his own kingdom he did not depend upon his daughter's smile. He then returns twice to the notion that Lear is now a zero, nothing, ending with the thought that he, the Fool, may be a fool, but is better than the king who is a zero – nothing.

This is painful advice. It is still delivered through a very clever plays on words, but it is giving a difficult message to his master. There is something of importance in this clever play of words. The world of leadership, the world of power, sees things in straight-forward ways, with little humour and plain language. Since they have power leaders can get their message across with direction, using their power. However, the world that management tries to 'run' is not straightforward, but full of contradiction and ambiguity. If management treats the real world as if it contained no ambiguity in either language or reality then it will fail. Peters and Waterman point this out:

> The old management theories were attractive because they were straight-forward and were not laden with ambiguity or paradox. On the other hand, the world isn't like that (interestingly one of our Japanese colleagues was highly critical of a report we had prepared for one of his clients. He said that it was too pat. He felt his clients would doubt the accuracy of anything so unambiguous).
>
> (Peters and Waterman, 1982: 90)

If a description of leadership activity, a management theory, is not laden with ambiguity, it will fail. Leadership, to work, must have ambiguity built into its understanding of the world. Lear's Fool demonstrates one way of achieving this through his use of wordplay or riddle.

This appears to be a counter-intuitive message. Peters and Waterman are criticizing approaches that are too pat – too simple. We usually like explanations that are simple and clear, but Peters and Waterman warn that if such explanations are trying to describe a complex situation then it is a false and misleading clarity. If the organization and its problems are complex and full of ambiguity, then it is important to have explanations that cover all these ambiguities and complexity.

The Fool feels that his truths are being rebuffed all the time so, given this refusal by Lear to believe him, the Fool asks Lear to help him lie: 'Prithee, nuncle, keep a schoolmaster that can teach thy fool to lie: I would fain learn to lie' (*King Lear*, Act 1 Scene 4 lines 196–97).

Given that his king won't listen to the truth then he might as well, like all the others, learn to lie. This goes to the crux of the

Fool's work as the king's adviser. He has to tell the truth to Lear – it is what he is expected to do; but the truth is having no effect at all upon the king's action, so he might as well lie. However, given his job and his relationship with Lear, he can't lie organically. Therefore he will have to be 'taught' to lie by a schoolmaster, he will have to learn how to do it, because left to his own nature and his past behaviour he will tell the truth. The Fool's relationship with the king continues in this vein throughout the play, with him constantly trying to raise the difficult issues that the king ignores. This often makes the king angry, but it never really stops the Fool from playing his role as truth teller.

Later in the act he returns to his criticism of the king as a fool and makes the king angry again. However, this pointed criticism of the king by the Fool is at least getting across, and here the interaction leads to one of the fulcra of the play.

> Fool *Yes, indeed: thou wouldst make a good fool.*
> Lear *To take't again perforce! Monster ingratitude!*
> Fool *If thou wert my fool, nuncle, I'd have thee beaten for being old before thy time.*
> Lear *How's that?*
> Fool *Thou shouldst not have been old till thou hadst been wise.*
> Lear *O let me not be mad, not mad, sweet heaven!*
> *Keep me in my temper: I would not be mad!*
> **King Lear**, Act 1 Scene 5 lines 42–52

Here again is the banter of calling Lear a fool, but backed up this time by the Fool arguing that the king has not been wise in his actions, even though he may be old ('Thou shouldst not have been old till thou hadst been wise'). This observation triggers a deep insight by Lear into himself. Suddenly he realizes that his actions may not at all be those of a wise man – a powerful king giving away all his land and yet still believing he would be powerful. This painful contradiction is dawning on the king, and his dramatic response in this speech is to realize that he has started to go mad. This is recognition of the painful consequences of his own actions and indeed a different state of mind. This is one of the main aspects of the play and later Lear loses his senses completely. The situation in which he has placed himself, where he is dependent on people who do not love him and will give him nothing, drives him mad. This madness comes about not only because of his dependence and his daughters' lack of love, but the realization that it was his own activity that did this to him. Through his capricious use of his own power he has succeeded in creating his powerlessness – a juxtaposition that would push anyone to the edge of sanity.

Here, in this speech prompted by the Fool, Lear comes to realize that all this might drive him mad, and he is very afraid. This is the first time he has any realization of where his mind will go, and is a result of the Fool pushing and pushing him to appreciate the meaning of his actions. This is not the outcome that the Fool wants. He does not want to drive his king mad, and in fact it is not he who drives him mad but the results of the king's own actions. Later in the play the Fool returns to the truth of his view of these actions.

The themes and accusation by the Fool that the king has driven himself mad come later on when the king realizes that, in fact, he is going mad. The Fool again approaches it through a riddle:

> Fool *Prithee, nuncle, tell me whether a madman be a gentleman or a yeoman?*
> Lear *A king a king!*
> Fool *No!, he's a yeoman that has a gentleman to his son; for he's a mad yeoman that sees his son a gentleman before him.*
> **King Lear**, Act 3 Scene 6 lines 9–14

We need to unpack the medieval class system before we can make sense of this. A yeoman was a man who owned property and a gentleman was his better, since he also had a coat of arms. Therefore the fool is pointing out that a yeoman who gives his son the money to become a gentleman and move up the social ladder before he, the father, has moved up the social scale, is mad. This is a clear reference by the Fool to Lear's giving away his land to his daughters in the first act.

The Fool now goes one stage further than simply describing this action as foolish. He now calls it the action of a madman. This hits the king hard and he now knows he is going mad. He is impatient with the riddles. Lear knows that, behind the allusions to the yeoman or the gentleman being mad, is the reality that he, the king, is the person being talked about. The message that the Fool has been trying to get across has been communicated.

Why does Shakespeare have this Fool so determinedly giving this advice to the king? Above all it portrays the Fool not only as a simple truth sayer, but also as someone who persistently brings the truth to his master. The Fool is rejected and abused by Lear for giving such a message, but this does not stop the Fool from telling his master the truth. No other character has this persistence when it comes to giving a monarch advice. I cannot think of another character in the whole of Shakespeare who is so persistent in getting a difficult message across to someone who is so much more powerful than him. It is this picture of persistence in telling the truth to power that Shakespeare provides us with in Lear's Fool. Indeed later in the play when one of Lear's powerful daughters, Regan, begins to recognize that her world may fall apart she underlines the power of fools, clowns and jesters with the statement that: 'Jesters do oft prove prophets' (*King Lear*, Act 5 Scene 3 line 71). This is a recognition of the role that the Fool has been playing. He has not actually been predicting the future. He has however been showing how the king's actions in giving away his own lands and making himself dependent will in fact create the king's madness in the future.

This is a difficult lesson for managers. Obviously Shakespeare shows that it is wise for them to listen to the truth about what is really happening. If leaders do a stupid thing they need to listen to what their colleagues say about it. Shakespeare is much more prescriptive than this. He demonstrates that, for leaders to be told difficult messages, they need staff who are close to them, who have the telling of truth in their job descriptions. Such staff need to be outside the orthodox power structure and have a clear relationship with the leader with considerable opportunity for access. They may have to find unusual ways of getting the truth across to their leaders but they must always recognize, even under powerful pressure to lie, that this is their prime task. A wise leader will ensure that they have some sort of protection to encourage the truth telling – despite the power imbalance and despite the difficult experiences of truth telling, leaders will always need to hear the truth and devise a staffing organization that will ensure this happens.

FALSTAFF: A FOOL AND A ROGUE TO LEARN FROM

Falstaff is one of Shakespeare's greatest characters. His part in two plays (*Henry IV Parts 1* and *2*) and his posthumous part in a third (*Henry V* – a play where Falstaff is never on stage but looms large over the action throughout) make him one of the characters that most actors long to play. As we saw in Part 4 of this book, Falstaff plays a crucial role in providing Prince Hal with a close knowledge of the culture and language of ordinary people that sets Hal apart from other Shakespearean leaders. Throughout the three plays Falstaff's character develops alongside that of Prince Hal (later Henry V).

The relationship between them is one of the richest between two men in all Shakespeare's plays. The Prince Hal that Shakespeare creates over three plays listens to and learns from Falstaff even though he recognizes the considerable social distance between them. I have argued that the way in which Prince Hal learns about the language and culture of ordinary people is one of the main hallmarks of his leadership, but Shakespeare could have demonstrated Hal's learning from a wide range of very different characters. Falstaff already has a cast of friends and acquaintances from whom Hal also learns, so his necessity to learn from common people could have been supplemented by other lowlife characters without there having to be a single dominant character such as Falstaff.

With Falstaff, Shakespeare chooses to build an important character who has a strong relationship with the man who becomes Shakespeare's greatest leader. This relationship is as important to understand as the way in which Shakespeare developed his leaders themselves. We have seen that Shakespeare's fools were included in his plays to provide people of much lower status from whom leaders learn difficult lessons. They provided knowledge that cannot be found from senior members who have power. Falstaff represents another way of teaching this lesson: Shakespeare creates a character who provides Hal with a long-term relationship from which the Prince learns about real life.

Shakespeare's Falstaff is a very particular character. He is, in modern terms, middle class. His friends are of the lower orders but Sir John himself is a knight and has been an active soldier in the past. He has very little money. If one phrase were to represent his character it would be 'lovable rogue'; he is undoubtedly a rogue, but everyone through the ages loves him. He is always portrayed as a fat figure fond of his drink, juxtaposed against a strong, slim Hal.

What insights does a lovable rogue offer managers? How can a fat, drunken soldier provide modern leaders with anything useful at all? The beginning of our answer to this can be found in the very fact that he is an outsider and therefore has a different perspective upon the orthodox framework of the organization.

Here a quotation from the philosopher Ludwig Wittgenstein comes to mind. Since it might confuse us to add the third dimension of philosophy to those of Shakespeare and modern management, it is fortunate that Tom Peters has also used this quotation, with some glee, so I will quote it from his book of simple injunctions:

> 'If people never did silly things, nothing intelligent would ever get done'.
> Right on Ludwig.
>
> (Peters, 1994: 311)

Tom Peters' 'Right on' of agreement with Wittgenstein's recognition of the relationship between silliness and intelligence remakes Shakespeare's point about Falstaff. Throughout the two plays in which he appears Falstaff stands up for silliness, and Shakespeare, by placing him alongside the long-term intelligence of Prince Hal, demonstrates the importance of the relationship. In the above quotation Peters doesn't only like silliness for its own silly sake, but because it can often provide the boring leader with another view of how to run the organization.

Thus Shakespeare has the future king, his great leader, learning his lessons about leadership, people and life, from a rogue. Such a relationship demonstrates in great detail how leaders need very different forms of knowledge and information. Shakespeare shows how sometimes the people who provide that information may have very different moralities from those who are responsible for running the organization.

For the relationship between leader and unusual informant to flourish the leader needs to be strong and confident enough to overcome the difficulties that these different moralities can create.

There is one very clear example towards the end of *Henry IV Part 1* that shows how strong Hal's relationship with Falstaff has become. There has been a big battle between the loyal troops of Prince Hal's father, Henry IV, and his rebellious enemies. The battle at Shrewsbury was always going to be a difficult one for the king's troops – the sides were not only evenly matched but the rebels had one of the finest and most heroic soldiers of his time – the son of the leader of the rebels, Henry Hotspur.

Throughout the play it is Hotspur who has both the rhetoric and action of the real hero of the play. He is both a hero and a rebel. Remember from Part 4 the way in which King Henry IV worries that his son is spending too much time in taverns and not enough in court? Henry IV often compares his son to Henry Hotspur (who has the family name of Percy) and wishes he had a son of similar stature and bravery. In the very first scene of the play Henry IV contemplates the difference between Harry Hotspur (the son of the Earl of Northumberland) and, noting his high reputation and the low repu- tation of Prince Hal, his own son, he ends up hoping that it may be possible to prove that the two Henrys were switched at birth:

> *Yea, there thou makest me sad and makest me sin*
> *In envy that my Lord Northumberland*
> *Should be the father to so blest a son,*
> *A son who is the theme of honour's tongue;*
> *Amongst a grove, the very straightest plant;*
> *Who is sweet Fortune's minion and her pride:*
> *Whilst I, by looking on the praise of him,*
> *See riot and dishonour stain the brow*
> *Of my young Harry. O that it could be proved*
> *That some night-tripping fairy had exchanged*
> *In cradle-clothes our children where they lay,*
> *And call'd mine Percy, his Plantagenet!*
> *Then would I have his Harry, and he mine.*
> **Henry IV Part 1**, Act 1 Scene 1 lines 77–89

Henry the king pours praise upon the head of Harry Hotspur: he is 'the theme of honour's tongue', is the 'straightest plant' in the grove; but his own Harry has the stain of dishonour. For a father to wish his son exchanged with the son of another is a powerful set of emotions revealing disappointment, jealousy and anger. Imagine being a father and so ashamed of your son that you want to exchange him for another. This is a rejection of some power that would leave your son feeling deeply hurt.

Shakespeare writes this strong paternal emotion into his play at the very start. King Henry's speech takes place even before we have seen Prince Hal, who appears in the play a few moments later, not in the king's court but in the bad company of Sir John Falstaff.

In this scene, covered in detail in Part 4, Prince Hal tells the audience, not his father, of his intention of becoming a great king. Throughout most of the play, however, his father is left anxious and jealous of how good Henry Percy would be as a son. Given this background Prince Hal recognizes that for his father to believe in him he is going to have to take over the mantle of Henry Hotspur. To do that he is going to have to fight him and kill him, demonstrating greater honour and valour – greater heroism – than the man he is defeating. Fair and honourable personal combat is the only way of achieving this.

The Battle of Shrewsbury has two main themes. First, this is a crucial fight for the monarchy of England, between the rebels and the king, that will decide the fate of the nation. If the rebels win Henry IV's reign will be at an end and his son Prince Hal will no longer be heir to the throne. If this happens Henry Percy, as the son of the leader of the rebels, would take over as heir to the throne.

The battle is also a direct fight between Henry Hotspur and Prince Hal. Hal knows that this is his chance to prove dramatically to his father that he is as good as, and better than, Henry Hotspur. He has the opportunity to fight and kill him and in doing so not only beat his father's enemy but also to slay the ghost of the person his father is always saying is better than him. Prince Hal says as much to his father:

> *I will redeem all this on Percy's head*
> *And in the closing of some glorious day*
> *Be bold to tell you that I am your son;*
> *When I will wear a garment all of blood...*
> *   for the time will come,*
> *That I shall make this northern youth exchange*

> *His glorious deeds for my indignities.*
> *Percy is but my factor, good my lord,*
> *To engross up glorious deeds on my behalf;*
> **Henry IV Part 1**, Act 3 Scene 2 lines 132–35 and 145–49

Harry Hotspur comes from Northumberland, in northern England, and is therefore a 'northern youth'. Prince Hal claims to his father that all Henry Percy has been doing throughout his life through his courageous deeds has been gathering up 'glorious deeds on my behalf'. This means that when Henry Percy finally meets Prince Hal in battle, these deeds, this courage, will pass to Hal, providing he wins the fight and kills Harry Hotspur. Through this action, he tells his father, he will redeem all the slurs and anxieties about his own past behaviour on Percy's head. He has to prove himself by killing Percy. Shakespeare writes the build-up to the Battle of Shrewsbury as leading to a crescendo for Prince Hal.

In the battle Hotspur and Prince Hal meet. Prince Hal makes clear what they are fighting about:

> *I am the Prince of Wales; and think not, Percy,*
> *To share with me in glory any more:*
> *Two stars keep not their motion in one sphere;*
> *Nor can one England brook a double reign,*
> *Of Harry Percy and the Prince of Wales.*
> **Henry IV Part 1**, Act 5 Scene 4 lines 62–66

This leaves the audience in no doubt that this is really the decider for Prince Hal – one way or another there will no longer be two stars or a double reign in England. For Hal and country this is a crucial fight. If it is really going to eliminate one star in the sky, then the fight must be to the death.

The build-up to this fight has been developing from the king's first speech at the beginning of the play. The public prestige that would accrue to Prince Hal is enormous. Given this importance, what Shakespeare makes happen after their fight is all the more dramatic and demonstrates the power of Prince Hal's relationship with Falstaff.

The battle starts. Prince Hal has a clean fight with Henry Percy and kills him. As he makes his victorious and magnanimous speech over

Harry Percy's body Prince Hal notices that there is another body on the battlefield. It is that of Falstaff. He believes him dead and, standing over the fat body, provides this kind, but distant, epitaph:

> *What, old acquaintance! could not all this flesh*
> *Keep in a little life? Poor Jack, farewell!*
> *I could have better spared a better man:*
> *O, I should have a heavy miss of thee,*
> *If I were much in love with vanity!*
> *Death hath not struck so fat a deer to-day,*
> *Though many dearer, in this bloody fray.*
> *Embowell'd will I see thee by and by:*
> *Till then in blood by noble Percy lie.*
> **Henry IV Part 1**, Act 5 Scene 4 lines 101–09

Hal is genuinely sad to see a friend die, and in his grief manages to allude to Falstaff's fatness several times, questioning whether 'all this flesh' could 'keep in a little life', how he will have 'a heavy miss of thee' and how he is the fattest deer struck down today. He expresses his ambivalence towards his loss by saying that he 'could have better spared a better man'. Sadly, but not sentimentally, he leaves the body of his friend next to the body of his enemy.

Falstaff, however, is just pretending to be dead in order to get out of the rest of the battle, because he is frightened and wants to save his skin. Just before the battle Falstaff had spoken one of the clearest soliloquies that Shakespeare wrote with a message that nobody could fail to understand, wherein he argues strongly against the established morality of the day. Even though his argument is subversive morality it is still compelling. He and Hal are talking just before battle commences and Falstaff starts by wishing that the day was over and he was tucked up in bed.

> Falstaff *I would 'twere bed-time, Hal, and all well.*
> Prince Hal. *Why, thou owest God a death.* [He leaves and Falstaff talks to the audience alone.]
> Falstaff *'Tis not due yet: I would be loath to pay him before his day. What need I be so forward with him that calls not on me? Well, 'tis no matter; honour pricks me on. Yea, but how if honour prick me off when I come on? how then? Can honour set to a leg? no: or an arm? no: or take away the grief of a wound? no. Honour hath no skill*

in surgery, then? no. What is honour? a word. What is in that word honour? what is that honour? air. A trim reckoning! Who hath it? he that died o' Wednesday. Doth he feel it? no. Doth he hear it? no. 'Tis insensible, then? Yea, to the dead. But will it not live with the living? no. Why? detraction will not suffer it. Therefore I'll none of it. Honour is a mere scutcheon: and so ends my catechism.
Henry IV Part 1, Act 5 Scene 1 lines 127–40

What is Shakespeare doing in writing such a speech just before a battle and at precisely the time when honour looks to be so important? Falstaff is plainly scared, but starts off thinking that 'honour pricks him' on the battlefield. He says that he has no choice, as a soldier and as a knight, but to fight in the battle. He is bound by honour. But then, in an extraordinary set of didactic questions to the audience (which he answers himself), he, from the point of view of a real soldier going into a real battle, destroys the whole notion of honour. Quite rightly he points out that honour cannot give back an arm or a leg that is lost in fighting, nor can it stop the pain of a wound, nor has it skill in surgery. For a soldier facing battle each of these is a powerful, unanswerable question.

Before a battle all soldiers worry about losing limbs and are frightened of the pain of wounds and the possibility of death. In Falstaff's time most soldiers who suffered wounds died horribly, so his is a real fear. Falstaff goes on to point out that someone who died last Wednesday may have honour, but what does that mean to him since he cannot hear and feel? He ends up saying honour is a mere scutcheon (a grave-shaped attachment for coffins), and Falstaff will have no more of this honour. Honour will not 'prick him on' to a dangerous battle.

I find these arguments very powerful, and I suspect that Shakespeare intends them to be so for every audience. I have never been in battle, but can imagine that this is what I would be thinking before it took place. Why am I doing this? How painful will it be? All the rhetoric spoken by my distant commanders will mean nothing if I am to die in pain. At this point, if I could walk away, I think I might. Falstaff's lines are delivered straight to the audience and meant to collude them into strong empathy with him and root his world-view into the audience's consciousness in a favourable way. This speech always works, and I have seen this play performed a number of times. Audiences do empathize with Falstaff and recognize that he is simply looking after his skin – most of us would do the same thing.

As the battle starts Falstaff, keeping out of the way of the dangerous fighting, comes across the body of a famous knight who had fought – with honour – on the king's side. Sir Walter Blunt had been dressed as the king to attract the opposition away from the real king and had in that disguise been killed by Harry Hotspur – a brave and honourable death. Falstaff stumbles across his corpse and immediately takes it as the final evidence of his catechism about honour. Look, he says to the audience, if you want proof about how stupid honour is, look at the dead body of Sir Walter here – 'there's honour for you!' (*Henry IV Part 1*, Act 5 Scene 3 lines 33–34).

The audience is confronted, in the middle of a battle for the monarchy of England, with two very different and indeed opposite moral codes – one of honour and one of artifice. On the one hand, most of the play underscores the importance of honour. The audience is invited to admire both Hotspur and Prince Hal and, when they fight, is thrilled by the honourable way in which they both behave. Yet just a few moments before this demonstration of honour Shakespeare invites the audience to agree with the opposite view. At this time, Falstaff persuades most into loving his dishonour. Shakespeare wants the audience to hold these two opposing views at the same time and constructs plot, character and narrative to achieve this.

To get out of danger Falstaff feigns death and, having heard Prince Hal's kind words over what Hal believes is his corpse, he rises from this pretence and comments on death and the battlefield. He expands upon this pretence of being dead and rejects it as a mere pretence because in fact it has saved his life:

> *Counterfeit? I lie, I am no counterfeit: to die, is to be a counterfeit; for he is but the counterfeit of a man who hath not the life of a man: but to counterfeit dying, when a man thereby liveth, is to be no counterfeit, but the true and perfect image of life indeed. The better part of valour is discretion; in the which better part I saved my life.*
> **Henry IV Part 1**, Act 5 Scene 4 lines 113–19

His morality is opposite to that of his friend Prince Hal, who has just met and killed his nemesis in the bravest of ways. In contrast, Falstaff gets out of danger by pretending to be dead and has a completely coherent philosophy for his actions. He cannot be accused of pretence, of counterfeiting, because real counterfeiting only happens when a man is killed. As long as someone is alive that person is a true and perfect image of life indeed. Just a few moments before there had been a classic display of heroism between the two great Henrys, Percy and Prince Hal. The reverse of this is portrayed by Falstaff but in a way that is just as understandable to the audience.

Having survived the battle by pretending to be dead, Falstaff realizes that he is next to the body of the warrior Hotspur, and that one further pretence would have a dramatic impact. Having successfully pretended to be dead, why not pretend to have killed Hotspur? 'I'll swear I killed him' (*Henry IV Part 1*, Act 5 Scene 4 lines 122–23). He carries Percy's body away, and the first people he comes across are Prince Hal and his younger brother. He presents Percy's body to the princes and claims to have fought with the dead warrior for an hour. Of course Prince Hal is surprised, since he knows he killed Percy himself, and he says as much to Falstaff and his younger brother.

Falstaff responds to this claim with vigour:

> *Didst thou? Lord, Lord, how this world is given to lying! I grant you I was down and out of breath; and so was he: but we rose both at an instant and fought a long hour by Shrewsbury clock. If I may be believed, so; if not, let them that should reward valour bear the sin upon their own heads.*
> **Henry IV Part 1**, Act 5 Scene 4 lines 148–54

Falstaff backs his claim by turning attention away from his own lie about Percy. He claims that the reality that both Hal and the audience know is true is in fact false.

Let's stop for a moment and see what is happening here. Throughout the play Hal has been unfavourably compared by many important people, including his father, to the bravest man in the kingdom, Hotspur. Hal meets him in mortal combat and, after a fight, kills him. By fighting and winning he has demonstrated to himself that what everyone said about him was wrong, he is brave and heroic. At this moment nobody else knows that this has happened, but a few minutes later his friend Falstaff claims that he, Falstaff, has killed Percy and, even more powerfully, accuses Hal of lying about who killed Percy for his own advantage – 'how the world is given to lying'. What would most people do in Hal's situation, having faced the demons and won, and then to be accused of lying about it? What Hal does is extraordinary. Instead of getting angry and claiming his rights over his own actions, he colludes with Falstaff's lie:

> *Come, bring your luggage nobly on your back:*
> *For my part, if a lie may do thee grace,*
> *I'll gild it with the happiest terms I have.*
> **Henry IV Part 1**, Act 5 Scene 4 lines 159–61

In public he asks Falstaff to carry Percy's body with nobility, but in private he colludes with Falstaff's lie and agrees to provide it with as much cover as he can in the happiest terms. He does this because, in Falstaff's world, a lie may do him good. Within minutes the play ends.

The fight between Prince Hal and Harry Percy is, for Hal, his real moment of truth. His personal victory over Percy is the way in which he proves himself. It is therefore startling that Shakespeare writes a scene for him where he so easily gives up something for which he has longed for most of the play. He has the proof of his own bravery and transformation in his hand. He could take Percy's body to his father, remind his father of how he always felt that Percy was better than him and say, 'Look at this body. You always felt Percy was better than me, but I killed him and I can prove that all his glory is now mine.'

Such a claim would not only be true and confirm what the audience has already seen, but would be wonderful theatre. Such an ending to a play would be very fulfilling drama, with a wonderful climax completing both the plot about who will run England and the sub-plot of the king's relationship with his son. Father could recognize how good his son was; son could become reconciled with his father. They have both defeated their enemies and can be safe in the kingdom – a great end to a great play – father and son and country united.

But Shakespeare's Prince Hal was never written to give this simple and straightforward lesson. Despite all that has gone before Shakespeare's Hal gives all of that glory and honour up to Falstaff, a man who lies and cheats. Falstaff believes that honour is a complete waste of time, and would rather duck out of battles, but he gets the honour of apparently killing the warrior – when the audience knows he is a coward who hid from the battle. Instead of there being a simple and unifying message at the end of the play something much more complex is written into it.

Why does Shakespeare do something that is so counter-productive to the main plot? Why does he throw away such a simple and wonderful ending? What lesson does this provide?

Shakespeare, as he nearly always does, chooses to tell a much more complex story. Hal, as the main character in the play, lives in two worlds, and he can switch between them in seconds. In one world, the world of court and of kings and dukes, morality is clear and of a mainstream historical nature. For that morality courage is clear and obvious. A man has to do what a man has to do, and if he does it he is admired and rises. For Prince Hal this means the necessity of a fair fight with Hotspur, the best man winning and in doing so gaining all the honour he can. Over the play Prince Hal develops great skill at this process and his honour grows. Shakespeare provides the audience with a clear picture of Hal doing this. On several occasions Hal talks straight to the audience about what he is doing and why he is doing it. The audience is meant to, and usually do, love him for it – as their hero prince.

Falstaff lives not just in a different moral world, but in an opposite world. In Falstaff's world a man pretends in order to survive, and then lies to gain advantage. As we saw from his catechism before the battle, for him honour is a dangerous joke. Shakespeare's Falstaff is good at this opposite morality and gains in competence at it as the plot of the play grows. Shakespeare has him, like Hal, talking to the audience and arguing for his morality with wit and force. These words of Shakespeare's are meant to persuade the audience that Falstaff is right. It would have been very easy for Shakespeare to have done otherwise, to have painted Falstaff as an unsympathetic character – but he didn't, because Shakespeare wants the audience to agree with him.

Therefore sometimes in the same scene, within minutes of each other, he portrays with great sympathy two very different and opposite moralities – one from Prince Hal and one from Falstaff. Even though they are opposites they exist side by side in the organization. Not only that, but Shakespeare makes sure that he and the audience give them both – even though they have opposite morality – credibility within the whole morality of the play.

In the complex conclusion over Harry Percy's body it is clear that Prince Hal has come to recognize that these two different moral worlds do live side by side and that their coexistence is a normal and necessary part of everyday life. If Hal wants to run his kingdom he needs to know that both moralities coexist in the one world; and if he wants to be a good leader he needs to be able to move between these two worlds with ease. The only way in which Prince Hal can gain this important knowledge about the organization that he is to run, the only way he can be constantly reminded of how to do it, is through the complex character that is Falstaff.

Shakespeare's Falstaff is one of the most famous comic characters ever created. He has attracted great actors and scholarship. Critics have tried to understand which real-life character he was based upon. His speed of mind and his pleasure in life are attractive characteristics, but above all it is his relationship with Prince Hal and the way that the narrative is worked out within that relationship that makes both characters so compelling. Shakespeare's Falstaff matters both in the drama and within the plot of the play because he is so closely linked to a future king. But their link makes good drama precisely because they are so very different. Time and again, as we have seen from the example above, Falstaff is not just different from the king that Prince Hal wants to be but is in contradiction to it.

For modern senior managers wanting to understand how to run their organization this is very powerful material. Shakespeare teaches them that they have to find out what is going on within their organization through unorthodox means – a lesson outlined in Part 4 of this book. He also insists that they need to recognize the strengths of certain individuals in their organizations who appear to be completely 'out of the loop' of both mainstream values and information. Many of their other senior managers, as Prince Hal's father and most of his court do, advise you to have nothing to do with these people. You will be warned that they will only teach you garbage about the organization, they will lead you astray from the crucial corporate paths that you need to tread. They will subvert those paths and will ruin your career. So stay away from them.

In fact Shakespeare shows the opposite message. If you listen to these larger than life figures in the organization, if you really get to know them as people and find out what makes them tick, even if they are against the organization, then you will gain a very great deal for your leadership. Crucially for the senior manager, Shakespeare's Hal demonstrates that you don't have to behave like Falstaff to learn from him. You can still have your own morality, one that is much more in the mainstream of the organization. You can demonstrate that you are still aiming for the cultural goals of the enterprise in the way that Hal does in his slaughter of Harry Percy. However, if you really need to know what is going on, find the awkward characters, get to know them well and listen to what they say.

In the scene over Percy's body Shakespeare's Hal leaves two more very difficult lessons for senior executives. First, the pinnacle of Hal's public success in the play, the fight and victory against Percy, is given to someone else to gain the glory and public relations success. He has killed the man, he stands over the body and could have taken it to his father or his younger brother and proved it. He could have had public plaudits – all the headlines – been paid a bigger bonus than he has ever achieved before. But he gives it up. Having achieved the reality, which both he and the audience know he has achieved, he is less interested in the PR. The goals that he set himself looked throughout the play as if they were goals being set by the court or by his father. Once they are achieved – for himself – it matters little what his father or others think.

In organizational terms the difficult lesson for the senior executive is that on some occasions, even on some crucial occasions, the success of your actions is much more important for your own personal development as a leader than for PR purposes. This can add more to you and to the organization as private knowledge than as a part of a large fanfare. For you to achieve this it must be clear both that the goal is achieved without argument and that you know you have achieved it. If you are clear on these two issues then the organization grows both because something important has been achieved and because one of its senior executives grows with it – even if no one else knows it.

The second lesson Hal leaves us with is that when the task has been clearly achieved, when you know that you have achieved it, you can on occasion give the PR to someone else, perhaps even an ally in the organization, so that this confirms the overall goals of the organization.

This is a harder lesson. Occasionally you can even give the PR success to someone who espouses a set of organizational goals that are in opposition to its mainstream goals.

Why do this? Hal, by the end of this play, knows so much about the nation that he will one day run that he understands, for example, that soldiers, real soldiers, are frightened before battle. Under these circumstances appeals to abstractions such as honour are rubbish. He knows this important fact not through his own heart but because of his relationship with this strange man. Falstaff has over the years made sure that Hal knows these difficult lessons. It is no use wanting all soldiers in the nation to be honourable. It just won't happen. You will need to appeal to real experiences of kin, of relationship, or just appeal to the nature of their work as soldiers. To become a great leader Hal needs to recognize that reality. Falstaff is the person who has made sure he understands it.

This may seem paradoxical. Why should senior managers reward a morality that goes against that of the mainstream? Shouldn't they always be bolstering the message of the mainstream corporate goals? Shakespeare's lesson shows that organizations materially are much more complex than this. If leaders want to lead them properly they not only need to know this, but must also listen to the odd people who have that different morality. This results in a real knowledge of the organization, one that you will only get by knowing someone in the organization who is your Falstaff

In this example the organizational leader is prepared to sacrifice all the good PR of his crowning success in return for the continued relationship with the subversive person who will continue to keep him in touch with the darker morality of the organization. This is a complex message for leaders and will only be understood by those who recognize that their organizations will always be full of contradictions. This works in these plays through the characters of these two very different characters who are both, in their own contradictory way, essentially English. Pay attention to only one and you fail to understand the nation. Again Peters puts this in simple language:

> Maintain one good friend who revels in telling you that you are full of hooey. When you get to the top of the heap, nothing you hear is true (or at least the whole truth). Keeping things in perspective is very very difficult.

The difficulty is directly proportional to the size of the heap you are sitting atop... Quite simply no matter how hard you try, no matter how open you are, you'll end up being surrounded by 'yes people'. It's hard not to believe people who are repeating your own ideas. Resist the temptation.

(Peters, 1994: 47)

Whilst, in rejecting a 'yes-man', Peters does not go so far as to suggest that you should always make your friend a 'no-man', he does recognize that without such a figure you will inevitably end up being surrounded by 'yes-people'. It is hard to resist believing you are right.

The differences and contradictions between Prince Hal and Falstaff run through many different parts of the play. Time and again Hal has to learn some significant lessons form his fat and odd friend. As with many parts of Shakespeare these lessons are sometimes played out within a plot but they are often played out through the individual characters themselves.

TIME: THE FUTURE AND THE IMPORTANCE OF THE PRESENT

Consistently, through both parts of *Henry IV*, Falstaff has a very different attitude to time and planning. As we saw in Part 4 Prince Hal, at the very beginning of *Henry IV Part 1*, tells the audience that the reason he is spending all his time learning about the culture of ordinary people is that he wants to be a great king one day. He spends two whole plays underlining the importance of the king he will become rather than the man he is at the moment. Such a relationship with the future is obviously a vitally important part of senior management. The future needs to be in leaders' minds all the time. If they are to successfully lead their organization they need to know where they are going and they need to know how to get there from where they are. Indeed it is this capacity for an eye to forward-looking strategy that sets them apart from their staff.

It is clear from Hal's planning throughout the two plays that he thinks very clearly about his road from the present to being a king. For example, he knows that the battle with Hotspur is not just a battle for that moment and for his life. If he wins, the fight will give him the strength and knowledge of his capacity to beat his rivals that will see him to his throne. Falstaff is different – he lives for the moment and enjoys that moment all the time. His memory for recent events is at best vague and often completely absent – especially when it comes to enjoying himself.

This difference with Hal about the importance of time is shown at their very first meeting in the play. Falstaff asks Hal the time, and Hal replies:

> *Thou art so fat-witted, with drinking of old sack and unbuttoning thee after supper and sleeping upon benches after noon, that thou hast forgotten to demand that truly which thou wouldst truly know. What a devil hast thou to do with the time of the day?*
> **Henry IV Part 1**, Act 1 Scene 2 lines 1–6

This is the first clue that Shakespeare gives to the audience about their relationship and it centres upon the fact that, obviously, Falstaff doesn't know the time of day. Hal explains to him and the audience that given his lifestyle it is indeed unlikely that he would know the time. He is obviously drunk much of the time through drinking 'old sack'. Sack was probably a sweet wine from Spain or the Canary Islands that, because it was a fortified wine (like modern sherry), would have been able to 'travel' in a way that most unfortified wines of the day could not. However, because it was fortified it was strong, and because it was strong it was a good way of getting drunk. Falstaff obviously also enjoyed 'unbuttoning [himself] after supper', a phrase that both portrays a loosening of clothes from eating too much and a loosening of morals from the wine. All of this leads to Falstaff sleeping 'upon benches after noon' and generally becoming confused about the time of day.

It is at the end of this scene that Hal explains how he is planning carefully for the time he will become king – a long time in the future – so the relationship between the two starts with a dramatically different attitude to time. Falstaff does not know what time of day it is, but Hal is living in a very complex chronological relationship between the fun of the tavern and his real life in the future as king. The present really only matters because of its capacity to teach him things that he will need to know in the future.

This different approach to time continues throughout the plays and often involves drink or disorder. In one scene where Falstaff has already drunk a great deal he cries out to Hal for another glass of wine – although, as we will see, he claims he has not had a drink all day:

> Falstaff *Give me a cup of sack: I am a rogue, if I drunk to-day.*
> Prince Hal *O villain! thy lips are scarce wiped since thou drunkest last.*
> Falstaff *All's one for that.* (He drinks.)
> **Henry IV Part 1**, Act 2 Scene 4 lines 170–75

For Falstaff the immediacy of life and pleasure means that his wine has barely passed his throat before it is forgotten. It is all the same if he has had a drink before this one, because it is this one that matters to him. Hal on this occasion (rather more gently) points out that, just a few minutes ago, he had had a drink. For Falstaff this makes no difference at all. It's all the same to him – 'All's one for that.' It is the present that matters, never the past, however immediate that past is.

In Act 1 Scene 2 Falstaff has described to Hal what he hopes will be the activities and duties of a squire or knight such as Falstaff when Hal is king:

> Falstaff *when thou art king, let not us that are squires of the night's body be called thieves of the day's beauty: let us be Diana's foresters, gentlemen of the shade, minions of the moon; and let men say we be men of good government, being governed, as the sea is, by our noble and chaste mistress the moon, under whose countenance we steal.*
> Prince *Thou sayest well, and it holds well too; for the fortune of us that are the moon's men doth ebb and flow like the sea, being governed, as the sea is, by the moon. As, for proof, now: a purse of gold most resolutely snatched on Monday night and most dissolutely spent on Tuesday morning; got with swearing 'Lay by' and spent with crying 'Bring in;' now in as low an ebb as the foot of the ladder and by and by in as high a flow as the ridge of the gallows.*
> **Henry IV Part 1**, Act 1 Scene 2 lines 26–43

These are two very different views of how life will be for Falstaff under Prince Hal when he reaches the throne. Falstaff's whole speech is a plea, when Hal is King, for them to be 'gentlemen of the shade, minions of the moon', that is, people who are only active at night. He draws the analogy of the moon that governs the sea as if he would have it as his own mistress.

Hal replies in kind, and interestingly in the first line includes himself as someone who spends a lot of time in the night at present ('the fortune of us that are the moon's men'). Whilst he also talks about the moon, the ebbing and flowing that he draws from the analogy of the tidal pull of the moon is one of morality. For not only do the moon's men work at night but their work involves stealing, snatching a purse of gold by shouting 'Lay by' (an early translation of 'Stand and Deliver'). For the moon's men when it comes to daytime the money is spent in a tavern shouting for more food and wine from the waiter – 'Bring in'. Crucially, in Prince Hal's view, this ebb and flow of morality leads in the end to walking from the foot of a ladder up to the top of a gallows to be hanged.

Prince Hal gives a clear moral lesson for those who confuse the daytime and night-time as their time of work. The moral concludes that getting the times of the day wrong is not just a matter of getting time confused in itself, but raises crucial questions about a person's morality and could lead to a very ignoble death.

Why does this disagreement about time matter? What is Hal learning from it? And if there are lessons for a man who will be a king, what lessons can a modern manager learn from it? Surely both Hal and the modern manager are right to concentrate upon looking to the future, keeping their eye on the plan and not being diverted? Isn't the story that they must concentrate on the big picture, and that any diversion from Hal's strategy is a mistake? That is true – a diversion from the strategy of concentrating on the future would be a mistake, but on the other hand the strategy contains the important aspect of learning from people who are different from him. In this case the learning involves time.

Falstaff says throughout the play that the immediate matters as well. This is a lesson that strategic managers must remember. Of course the future is important, but a failure to fully experience the immediate, the present in all its richness, will mean that the decisions taken about the future will be incomplete or wrong. All the management information systems about the future may provide interesting pictures and visions, but the only real data that plans can be based upon is the data about the present. So listening to the present, indeed as Falstaff does, luxuriating in the moment, is a really useful skill. It provides the leader with the capacity to really know what is happening today. Today is always the starting place for any movement to the future. However good your strategy is you cannot live entirely in the future.

Whilst most management theory underlines the importance of a long-term vision Peters, in his own style and in a very personal way, argues that we must also seize the day:

> Goals are (mostly) stupid; seize the day. Having a vision. Not a bad idea. In fact a pretty good idea – it motivates you and inspires those around you... Fact is I am sugar-coating this. I've long felt goals are rather stupid. The notion, in the midst of life's turbulent flow and fabulous cacophony, of following one currently shining star (to the exclusion of the rest of the galaxy) makes little sense to me. Instead, look at each day as a new canvas on which to paint. Hey what works for me may not work for you. But at least think about it my way.
>
> (Peters, 1994: 50–51)

This is a provocative and dangerous statement, very like the character of Falstaff himself. But both the statement and Falstaff have their purpose. The statement is meant to shout in the face of the received wisdom about the importance of long-term goals to an organization (incidentally it flies in the face of a lot of Tom Peters' work too!). The message from today, treating each day as its own motivational tool, also needs to be heard. Without this a whole organization may only see its work as making sense in the future, and it gives no attention to what is going on today. The paradox is, of course, that to get to that future goal it is vital to work hard today. If we are ever going to get to the goal of the strategy it is vital to recognize the importance of this day, live in it and work in it – and, if you are Falstaff, luxuriate in it.

There is even an important lesson from the banter about daytimes and night-times. As for the importance of the night-time rather than the daytime, we have already seen in Part 4 the importance of night-time to both Tom Peters and to Henry V when it comes to obtaining information from their troops. The fact that Prince Hal learnt to operate in the night as a minion of the moon proved very useful for him when he became king. Then the night-time provided a cloak, not for snatching a purse of gold but for finding out the morale of the troops before the Battle of Agincourt. If he had spent his youth with people who went to bed at 10 o'clock he would not have had the capacity to recognize the importance of the night-time and the ability to use the cloak of darkness to appear to become somebody else.

From the first discussion between Prince Hal and Falstaff about time the scene is set throughout the plays. Shakespeare's characters are not only different but often show how they are in contradiction to each other. Given such differences and arguments, why does Shakespeare make their relationship so important to the development of the play? We are used to thinking about relationships as between people who are similar, not between people who are contradictory, yet the success of Shakespeare's Falstaff is the fact that he is created to be in opposition to the high morality of his Prince Hal.

The whole point of the relationship is that they are in contradiction, and that Hal all the time is learning about difference. If Falstaff is to represent a different set of ideas and a different morality then, given that he does that against the morality of all the powerful people in the play, his character must be powerful. If it was not so strong it could not sustain this difference from the main character of the play. Hal would dwarf a small contradictory character and we would lose the measure of difference. Hal keeps Falstaff near him not only to learn about different ways of thinking but about opposites.

The essence of Shakespeare's Falstaff as a character is that he is strong and he is different. If he were weak he could not sustain the criticism that he continually gets from Hal. On issues of time, on issues of honour, he knows he is right – just as Hal knows *he* is right. The audience is left feeling that they are probably both right – even though logically they can't be.

The immediate lesson for the modern manager is a difficult one. There will be people in your organization, strong people, who represent a very different view of how the organization works and where it is going. Sometimes these strong characters will not only represent different views from yours but will believe that the organization should be going in a contrary direction. Such strong characters do not whisper their differences in corners, but present them boldly in a way that makes them difficult to ignore. Yet because they are both different and strong, many managers are frightened of them and do not feel they should be allowed to contribute to the organization.

Peters demonstrates the importance of the leader receiving messages that are not within the main purpose of the organization:

> The very purpose of the vision is to provide the bedrock upon which constant evolutionary opportunistic change can take place. However, it is all too easy for even the most compelling vision to become static, impeding the very change it is meant to induce.
>
> (Peters, 1989: 407)

This argues that all leadership, management or vision will be useless if it becomes static. To survive and thrive organizations need very different information and viewpoints to stop this happening. This means that senior managers must find ways of listening to these different currents, and reject the simple strategy of crushing all opposition. In many organizations the moment there is any challenge senior managers use their power and the organization's power to destroy opposition. Such a strategy of crushing opposition will certainly deal with it.

Shakespeare's lesson is very different. His Hal, as a successful leader, rejects simple authoritarianism. Shakespeare is suggesting that a really strong leader can learn from a contradictory view even when that point of view is provided by a really strong character. In fact it is precisely because they are strong characters that they need to be listened to. A weak contradictory position may not be saying very much.

A strong senior manager will find within that opposition at least two things. First, these different views will certainly not be the view of one strong character alone. It will almost certainly represent a current of opinion or morality in the organization. That current may at the moment be weak, but it could under different circumstances become a lot stronger. If the senior manager takes any opportunity to destroy the current, this would not lead to any understanding of the ideas.

Shakespeare argues that strong leaders should keep strong characters close to them. This does not mean that the strong oppositional characters are involved in the creation of the overall strategy of the organization, that is left to senior managers, but from their opposition they do provide a great deal of knowledge. Senior managers must, as Hal does with Falstaff all the time, argue with them and not simply listen to them, since it is through the testing of their ideas in argument that those ideas, that philosophy, will be best understood.

Second, Shakespeare demonstrates that as roles in the organization develop there may come a time when it is necessary to change the relationship. This is a potentially ruthless moment for a manager and will usually contain some personal difficulty. It will always have a sharp effect upon the organization. Let us look at how this appears to the rest of the organization.

Moving Shakespeare to the modern day, let us imagine a case where a chief executive has been spending a lot of time in both informal and formal settings with a strong character in the organization. Everybody knows that this person has very different values and would argue for a very different direction for the organization. Indeed through their life style they demonstrate that they are the very opposite of where everyone knows the CEO wants the organization to go. In addition, because they are a strong character they do not go about this process lightly – they cheat, get drunk and rarely show up on time. Of course everyone can recognize that the CEO is ambivalent about this person and their values, but still the CEO spends time with them and listens to them. This is curious, especially for the nine-to-fivers in the organization who do their job, keep their noses clean and follow the corporate policy all the way down the line. Such people may never even get as much as a nod from the CEO and may feel let down that a very different character gets so close.

One day the CEO decides that she has had enough of this relationship and it turns from one of ambivalence to clear rejection. The previously close person is rejected. He may have felt that he had a secure relationship with the CEO but suddenly he is sacked and banished from her presence.

What are the various reactions to this? To the previously favoured person it is a painful puzzle. To the rest of the organization it is a joy. To the CEO it may give a little pain but it is neither a surprise nor a joy, it is an essential part of running the organization.

In one of the most dramatic scenes in any of Shakespeare's plays, Henry rejects Falstaff at the very end of *Henry IV Part 2*. Henry's father has died whilst Falstaff is away from London in the country. He rushes to London in high expectation of great advancement, believing he is now a friend of the most powerful person in the country, the king. He arrives in London at the end of the coronation that creates Henry V the new king of England. He approaches Henry as he returns from his coronation and is rejected completely:

> *I know thee not, old man: fall to thy prayers;*
> *How ill white hairs become a fool and jester!*
> *I have long dream'd of such a kind of man,*
> *So surfeit-swell'd, so old and so profane;*
> *But, being awaked, I do despise my dream.*
> *Make less thy body hence, and more thy grace;*
> *Leave gormandizing; know the grave doth gape*
> *For thee thrice wider than for other men.*
> *Reply not to me with a fool-born jest:*
> *Presume not that I am the thing I was;*
> *For God doth know, so shall the world perceive,*
> *That I have turn'd away my former self;*
> *So will I those that kept me company.*
> *When thou dost hear I am as I have been,*
> *Approach me, and thou shalt be as thou wast,*
> *The tutor and the feeder of my riots:*
> *Till then, I banish thee, on pain of death,*
> *As I have done the rest of my misleaders,*
> *Not to come near our person by ten mile.*
> **Henry IV Part 2**, Act 5 Scene 5 lines 50–68

It is difficult to imagine a more powerful rejection. Let us not forget that these two men have been together for a considerable amount of time. Hal has spent time in Falstaff's company, drinking and playing, and has learnt a great deal from him. It is true that on several occasions Hal has reminded Falstaff that things will be different when he is king, but Falstaff has never really got the message. In this speech he is left in no doubt.

Henry reviles him for his age and white hair; his fatness and appetite 'surfeit-swell'd'; his gormandizing, so that when he died he would need a grave three times bigger than other men. Falstaff is now someone to be dismissed as a fool, a jester with 'a fool-born jest'; someone who had led the king astray, was profane, and 'the tutor and the feeder of my riots'. Worse, Henry dismisses the whole relationship not only as a dream from which he has now awoken, but as a despised dream.

This is breathtaking stuff for the audience. For two plays they have seen Prince Hal and Falstaff as close, and presumed the relationship would last forever. They have even seen Hal give Falstaff the opportunity to take his greatest glory – the killing of Hotspur – away from him. But for Falstaff the surprise nearly finishes him off.

The new King Henry drives the point home with a brilliant phrase: 'Presume not that I am the thing I was'. In saying this he uses language about his previous existence with Falstaff that dehumanizes himself as a thing. He claims that God knows he has changed and that the rest of the world will perceive this in the future; and having turned away from his former self, he will also turn away from those who kept him company. He goes further and banishes Falstaff on pain of death to stay 10 miles away from him.

What sense can we make of this? In some ways the lesson is crystal clear. Henry has become king and will now realize the promise of reformation that he made to the audience two plays ago in his first scene on stage. The moment has come, he must make good his promise and must change his attitude in order to become a good king. The most dramatic way he can do this is to demonstrate to everyone that he is a changed person . The whole world must no longer presume that he is the 'thing' he was.

More is happening here than a general change following his coronation as king, however, and it contains a very specific lesson – the rejection of Falstaff. Why is this done so completely? Why does Shakespeare leave Falstaff so little? As a demonstration of power and clarity this part of the book, building on its predecessors, argues strongly for the importance of building ambiguity into organizations. It also argues for the existence, close to the leadership of organizations, of strong characters who canvass for these ambiguous messages. Yet here is one clear, unambiguous act, in which Shakespeare dramatically moves the play forward, and in which he rejects the strong and difficult character completely. How can this be reconciled?

First, the point of ambiguity is that the tension between different moralities and opinions that it builds into an organization will ensure that there is change and movement. If there is no recognized ambiguity, if the leadership of the organization only ever hears one message, then the lack of tension in the organization means that there are real problems of movement and development. However, at the risk of sounding semantic, ambiguity itself is ambiguous. There are times when it will move into a very different model and in doing so will be changed completely.

In this example, Falstaff has come to represent the way in which ambiguity can be opposed to the mainstream. Over that time Prince Hal learns a great deal about the other side of England, and he does so through the power of a strong character – Falstaff. However, times change, sometimes dramatically, and a new form of ambiguity needs to be built in. When Hal becomes King Henry, in law and in history, he becomes a very different person, and he needs to change his relationship with everything. Throughout the rest of his life a different method of incorporating ambiguity needs to be found – some of which we discussed in Part 4. So in rejecting Falstaff he does not reject ambiguity so much as reject the ambiguity of the past. We have seen how in the climax of *Henry V* he spends hours listening to his troops to ensure that their fears and emotions are incorporated into his final speech, his vision for the army.

Second, the main point about this rejection is the way in which it clearly draws a line. It recognizes that from this day Henry has become a different person and whilst this appears to be a rejection of Falstaff, it is in effect a rejection of his past. He points this out by letting Falstaff know that if he hears that Henry has become as he was in the past then Falstaff too can behave that way and come back to him. Why is this so important? Obviously within the world of kings and queens the moment of coronation does create a different person with different powers. When a king dies, the shouting out of 'The King is dead! Long live the King!' demonstrates how death has no dominion over the continuity of the institution of the monarchy. It also demonstrates how strong the change would be for an individual who suddenly becomes that institution.

Of course this happens to modern leaders. There are times, usually through promotion, when a radical change needs to be signified. That signification needs to go beyond the size of the salary or bonus, or the size of a new desk, to demonstrate *real* change.

Sometimes this can be done directly by the behaviour of those involved, but more often they need to demonstrate it clearly by some change in their environment. This is important for organizations. There is an expectation that individuals are continuous, with the same ideas and activities they always had – Jo is always the same; Jane says the same things now as she did when she was several rungs down the ladder from her present position. That's what individuals want of other individuals.

Organizations know that structures are different, but don't people stay the same when they inhabit different bits of the structure? Of course this can never be true. People have to change when they are in different parts of the structure – not completely, but significantly. King Henry V is similar to Prince Hal, but everyone must recognize that he is different, too. Modern organizations usually have less ritual than the medieval state, but they need to find ways of signifying this change and development where individuals are different when they have secured promotion.

Third, the rejection demonstrates a new ruthlessness. Heads of organizations will always have to make some hard decisions that will cause them and others pain. Organizations need to have confidence that this will happen and that somebody will bite that bullet. Henry decides to demonstrate that ruthlessness at the very beginning of his reign. We saw in Part 4 that, when necessary, ruthlessness would characterize his leadership – not all the time, but especially when necessary in battle. The French army would learn that, despite the time he spent as a young man carousing, he could be ruthless. It would have been wise if they had paid attention to this rejection of Falstaff and understood the measure of the man. There are times when modern managers have to be just as ruthless in pursuit of the goals of the organization – a symbolic act, which demonstrates change, could teach the whole organization and its competition the measure of the leader.

CONCLUSIONS

Shakespeare wrote plays that were full of contradiction and ambiguity. These were no simple, linear, morality plays. His plays contained ambiguity in order to reflect the real nature of the world. He chose many different dramatic ways of building ambiguity into his plays, and in this chapter we have looked at one of the clearest – the use of strong characters, fools or rogues to give his leaders alternative messages.

The world of management power also has its ambiguities, and when it fails to recognize this it fails. Here I have suggested that one of the ways in which managers can be constantly confronted with this ambiguity is to ensure that there are strong individuals around them who will demonstrate different ideas and moralities. These relationships will never be easy. They will cause considerable friction for the other senior staff in the organization, but whether they are fools or rogues they must be listened to.

REFERENCES

Adair, J (1984) *The Skills of Leadership*, Wildwood House, London

Brecht, B (1967) From a talk introducing his radio version of *Macbeth* in 1927, in *Brecht Gesammellt*, Frankfurt, vol 15

Deming, W (1982) *Out of the Crisis*, Cambridge University Press, Cambridge

Drucker, P (1954) *The Practice of Management*, Heinemann, Oxford

Drucker, P (1990) *Managing the Non-profit Organisation*, Butterworth-Heinemann, Oxford

Hall, P (1970) *War of the Roses*, BBC Books, London

Handy, C (1996) The new language of organizing and its implications for leaders, in *The Leader of the Future*, F Hesselbien *et al*, Jossey-Bass, San Francisco, CA

Harvey-Jones, J (1988) *Making it Happen*, HarperCollins, London

Helgein, S (1996) Leading from the grass-roots, in *The Leader of the Future*, F Hesselbien *et al*, Jossey-Bass, San Francisco, CA

Leggatt, A (1988) *Shakespeare's Political Drama*, Routledge, London

McAlpine, A (1997) *The New Machiavelli*, Aurum Press, London

McEachern, C (1995) Henry V and the paradox of the body politic, in *Materialist Shakespeare*, ed I V Kamps, Verso, London

McGregor, D (1966) *Leadership and Motivation*, MIT Press, Cambridge, MA

Mack, M (1965) Introduction to the Signet Classic edition of *Henry IV Part 1*, American Library, New York

Mangan, M (1996), *Shakespeare's Comedies*, Longman, Harlow

Moss Kanter, R (1983) *Change Masters*, Allen & Unwin, London

Moss Kanter, R (1988) *When Giants Learn to Dance*, Simon and Schuster, New York

Peters, T (1989) *Thriving on Chaos*, Pan, London

Peters, T (1994) *The Pursuit of Wow*, Macmillan, New York

Peters, T and Waterman, R (1982) *In Search of Excellence*, HarperCollins, London

Sadler, P (1995) *Managing Change*, Kogan Page, London

Selznick, P (1957) *Leadership in Administration: A sociological interpretation*, Harper & Row, London

Senge, P (1995) *The Fifth Discipline*, Currency/Doubleday, New York

Tennenhouse, L (1994) Strategies of state and political plays, in *Political Shakespeare*, ed J Dollimore and A Sinfield, Manchester University Press, Manchester

Wells, S (1994) *Shakespeare: The poet and his plays*, Methuen, London

All Shakespeare quotations are taken from *The New Penguin Shakespeare* (1977), general editor T J B Spencer, Penguin, London

INDEX

References in *italic* indicate illustrations

FURTHER READING

New and Bestselling Titles from Kogan Page

Renaissance Management
The Rebirth of Learning Through People and Organizations
Stephen Carter
£18.99   Hardback   0 7494 2374 9   224 pages   1999

The War Lords
Measuring Strategy and Tactics for Competitive Advantage in Business
Jorge Alberto Vasconcellos e Sá
£16.99   Paperback   0 7494 2824 4   256 pages   1998

Managing in the New Local Government
Paul Joyce, Paul Corrigan and Mike Hayes
£14.99   Paperback   0 7494 2915 1   160 pages   1999

The 21ˢᵗ Century Manager
Future-focused Skills for the Next Millennium
Di Kamp
£14.99   Paperback   0 7494 2950 X   224 pages   1999

Persuading Aristotle
A Masterclass in the Timeless Art of Strategic Persuasion in Business
Peter Thompson
£14.99   Paperback   0 7494 3011 7   224 pages   1999

12 Ladders to World Class Performance
How You Can Compete With the Best in the World
David Drennan
£16.99   Paperback   0 7494 3000 1   256 pages   1999

In the Company of Heroes
Release Your Entrepreneurial Spirit – And Your Organization's
David Hall
£14.99   0 7494 3060 5   256 pages   1999

Driving Change
How the Best Companies are Preparing for the 21st century
Jerry Yoram Wind and Jeremy Main
£11.99   Paperback   0 7494 3017 6   368 pages   1999

Releasing Creativity
How Leaders Can Develop Creative Potential in Their Teams
John Whatmore
£16.99   Paperback   0 7494 3010 9   224 pages   1999

Running Board Meetings
Tips and Techniques for Getting the Best From Them
Second Edition
Patrick Dunne
Published in association with 3i
£19.95   Hardback   0 7494 3015 X
£12.99   Paperback   0 7494 3014 1   192 pages   1999

Accountability
Practical Tools for Focusing on Clarity, Commitment and Results
Bruce Klatt, Shaun Murphy and David Irvine
£12.99   Paperback   0 7494 2993 3   136 pages   1999

The Adventure Capitalists
The Success Secrets of 12 High-Achieving Entrepreneurs
Jeff Grout and Lynne Curry
£16.99   Hardback   0 7494 2638 1   192 pages   1998

Great Myths of Business
Revised Edition
William Davis
£9.99   Paperback   0 7494 2685 3   256 pages   1998

The Making of a Manager
How to Launch Your Career on the Fast Track
Donald A Wellman
£12.99   Paperback   0 7494 1794 3   288 pages   1997

Managing People is Like Herding Cats
Warren Bennis
£12.99   Paperback   0 7494 2849 X   180 pages   1998

The 12 Pillars of Business Success
How to Achieve Extraordinary Results from Ordinary People
Ron Sewell
Foreword by Sir John Harvey-Jones
£14.99   Paperback   0 7494 2476 1   192 pages   1997

The New Leaders
Achieving Corporate Transformation Through Dynamic Leadership
Paul Taffinder
£14.99   Paperback   0 7494 2229 7   192 pages   1997

Not Bosses But Leaders
Revised Edition
John Adair
£10.99   Paperback   0 7494 0270 9   192 pages   1997

Jungle Rules
How to Be a Tiger in Business
John P Imlay Jr. with Dennis Hamilton
£11.99   Paperback   0 7494 2181 9   256 pages   1997

Professional Paperbacks Series
Published in association with the Institute of Directors

The Handbook of Project Management
Revised Edition
Trevor Young
£19.99   Paperback   0 7494 2843 0   224 pages   1998

Profitable Customers
How to Identify, Develop and Keep Them
Charles Wilson
£15.99   Paperback   0 7494 2825 2   224 pages   1998

International Management
The Essential Guide to Cross-Cultural Business
Second Edition
Edited by John Mattock
£16.99   Paperback   0 7494 2827 9   176 pages   1999

Creating A World Class Organization
10 Essentials for Business Success
Second Edition
Bryan Prescott
£16.99   Paperback   0 7494 2583 0   192 pages   1998

Designing Organizations
The Foundation for Excellence
Third Edition
Philip Sadler
£18.99   Paperback   0 7494 2580 6   192 pages   1998

Goal Directed Project Management
Second Edition
E S Andersen, K V Grude, T Haug and J R Turner
Published in association with PricewaterhouseCoopers
£19.95   Paperback   0 7494 2615 2   224 pages   1998

Total Leadership
How to Inspire and Motivate for Personal and Team Effectiveness
Jim Barrett
£16.99   Paperback   0 7494 2577 6   302 pages   1998

Transform Your Management Style!
Hilary Walmsley
£16.99   Paperback   0 7494 2581 4   192 pages   1998

Visit Kogan Page on-line

Comprehensive information on
Kogan Page titles

Features include

■ complete catalogue listings,
  including book reviews and
  descriptions

■ special monthly promotions

■ information on NEW titles and
  BESTSELLING titles

■ a secure shopping basket facility
for on-line ordering

PLUS everything you need to know about
KOGAN PAGE

http://www.kogan-page.co.uk